When GOD was KING

Rebels & Radicals of the CIVIL WAR & Mayflower GENERATION

"The Christian Church – particularly the Protestant bit of it – is particularly adept at bifurcation. This was never more evident than in the seventeenth-century. Whittock leads us through the luxuriant undergrowth of politico-religious fragmentation and rival sincerities. His book well deserves to be set alongside Christopher Hill's classic The World Turned Upside Down.*"*

Derek Wilson, historian and author

Also by Martyn Whittock
A Brief History of Life in the Middle Ages
A Brief History of the Third Reich
The Viking Blitzkrieg (with Hannah Whittock)
A Brief Guide to Celtic Myths and Legends
Christ: The First 2000 years (with Esther Whittock)
1016 & 1066 (with Hannah Whittock)
Norse Myths and Legends (with Hannah Whittock)

When GOD was KING

Rebels & Radicals of the CIVIL WAR & Mayflower GENERATION

MARTYN WHITTOCK

LION

Published by
Lion Hudson Limited
Wilkinson House, Jordan Hill Business Park,
Banbury Road, Oxford OX2 8DR, England
www.lionhudson.com/lion

Hardback ISBN 978 0 7459 8041 6
Paperback ISBN 978 0 7459 8042 3
e-ISBN 978 0 7459 8040 9

First edition 2018

Acknowledgements
Every effort has been made to trace the copyright holders and obtain
permission to reproduce this material.

Scripture quotations taken from the Geneva Bible, 1599 Edition. Published by Tolle Lege
Press. All rights reserved.

Extracts from The Book of Common Prayer, the rights in which are vested in the Crown,
are reproduced by permission of the Crown's patentee, Cambridge University Press.

Cover images: Mayflower © nicoolay/iStockPhoto.com;
map © bauhaus1000/iStockPhoto.com

A catalogue record for this book is available from the British Library

Dedication

In memory of John Whittock of Rode (Somerset) and Thomas Whittock of Frome (Somerset); accused in the Constables' Presentments of being for "rebellion" and "riot" during the Monmouth Rebellion of 1685; perhaps the last uprising of the godly in England.

In memory of Gustaphus Adolphus Whittock, baptized at Hemington (Somerset) in May 1693; named after one who was greatly admired among the saints.

And to David Bowater and Chris Scorer, who share my interests in theology, politics, and history. With thanks for their friendship.

Martyn Whittock

Contents

Acknowledgements	ix
Timeline of key events	x
Introduction	xv
1. Roots of Radicalization	1
2. "The World Turned Upside Down!"	17
3. North of the Border: A Very Scottish Godly Rule	32
4. A Godly War?	49
5. Hunting Down the Enemies of God	65
6. The "Rule of the Saints" in Ireland	79
7. Social and Political Justice for the Common Man? The Levellers	95
8. A Very English Kind of Communism: The Diggers	111
9. "God's People Must Be a Bloody People!" The Fifth Monarchy Men	123
10. Not Very Quiet Quakers!	139
11. Cromwell and the Rule of God	155
12. The End of the "Good Old Cause"	170
13. A New Jerusalem in the New World?	185
14. The Legacy of the Godly in Britain	202
15. The Legacy of the Godly in North America	215
Notes	227
About the author	243
Glossary	245

Acknowledgements

I am grateful to Tom Morgan, David Bowater, and Chris Scorer for reading and commenting on sections of the book. I am also grateful to my alma mater, Bristol University, and also the British Library, for use of their excellent collection of books relating to seventeenth-century history and, in the case of the latter, copies of the original pamphlets. I also wish to thank Robert Dudley, my agent, and Ali Hull, Jenny Muscat, and Jessica Tinker at Lion Hudson for all of their encouragement and support. It goes without saying that all errors are my own.

Timeline of key events

1603: Death of Queen Elizabeth I; accession of King James VI and I

1604: Hampton Court Conference: monarch to continue to rule the church through bishops

1611: *Authorized* – or *King James* – *Version* of the Bible published

1616: First English Baptist church founded at Southwark

1618: Five Articles of Perth forced on Scottish kirk by King James

1620: *Mayflower* sails to North America with the Pilgrim Fathers

1625: Death of King James VI and I, accession of King Charles I

1629: Start of "Eleven Years Tyranny" (to 1640): Charles I rules without Parliament

1630: Winthrop Fleet: 700 godly colonists sail to North America

1636: Start of Pequot War in New England: massacre of Native Americans by Puritan settlers

1637: Riot in St Giles' Cathedral, Edinburgh, against royal imposition of *Book of Common Prayer*

1638: Signing of the Scottish National Covenant
Bishops abolished in Scotland; Presbyterianism established as national church system

1639–1640: Bishops' Wars in Scotland

1640: Start of the "Long Parliament" (lasts until 1660)

1641: Abolition of royal Court of Star Chamber
Abolition of royal right to raise Ship Money
Start of Irish Uprising

1642: Start of British Civil Wars

1643: Parliament forms alliance with Scottish Covenanters
Parliament promises to reform the Church of England
along Presbyterian lines in exchange for Scottish military
assistance

1644: Scots Army of the Covenant marches into England to fight
King Charles I
Publication of Calvinist Baptist *London Confession of Faith*
Start of witch hunts in East Anglia, led by Matthew
Hopkins (lasts until 1646)
Start of laws banning Christmas festivities

1645: Execution of Archbishop Laud
Formation of New Model Army

1646: Abolition of episcopacy (bishops) in England and Wales
Parliament agrees to set up a *limited* Presbyterian system in
England (eventually fails)
Charles surrenders to Scots (who eventually sell him to
English Parliament in 1647)

1647: Publication of *Westminster Confession of Faith*
George Fox begins Quaker movement
Putney Debates between Levellers and Parliamentary army
commanders, led by Cromwell
Charles signs secret treaty to get Scottish support and
promises to establish Presbyterianism in England, initially
for three years

1648: "Pride's Purge" of the "Long Parliament"; replacement with "Rump Parliament"
Cromwell defeats the Scots at the Battle of Preston
Cambridge Platform establishes Puritan forms of church government in New England

1649: Execution of Charles I; House of Lords abolished; republic declared
Start of the Commonwealth (lasts until 1653)
Diggers occupy St George's Hill, Surrey
Irish rebels place their armies under royal control
Leveller mutineers executed at Burford church
Start of Parliamentary campaigns in Ireland, led by Cromwell
Start of Ranter movement
A new Witchcraft Act becomes law in Scotland
Sieges of Drogheda and Wexford, many Irish civilians slaughtered

1650: Treaty of Breda, Charles II accepts the Solemn League and Covenant, to get Scots support
Cromwell defeats Scots at Battle of Dunbar
Last Digger community broken up by force

1651: Defeat of the Royalist-Scots alliance at the Battle of Worcester
Start of Fifth Monarchy movement

1652: Act for the Settlement of Ireland transplants huge numbers of Irish to Connacht

1653: End of British Civil Wars
John Lilburne, Leveller leader, imprisoned for life
Cromwell ends sitting of "Rump Parliament"
"Barebone's (or "Nominated") Parliament"

Start of the Protectorate (lasts until 1659)
End of Parliamentary campaigns in Ireland; huge numbers of Irish dead

1654: Widespread Quaker preaching campaign across southern England

1655: Rule of the major-generals (lasts until 1657)

1656: Quaker, James Nayler, arrested for blasphemy in Bristol

1657: Cromwell turns down offer of the crown
Failure of Fifth Monarchist plot against Protectorate (another plot crushed in 1659)

1658: Death of Oliver Cromwell, succeeded by his son Richard as Lord Protector

1659: End of the Protectorate

1660: Restoration of King Charles II
Execution of regicides

1661: Fifth Monarchist uprising in London (Venner's Revolt)
Restoration of episcopacy (bishops) to Church of England
Corporation Act bans Separatists from holding public office

1662: Act of Uniformity: all ordained clergy must accept the doctrines and liturgy of the Church of England

1665: Five-Mile Act prohibits Nonconformist ministers from living within five miles of any church they had held before the act

1673: Test Act bans Catholics from holding public office

1675: King Philip's War in New England, deaths of many Native Americans

1676: Gerard Winstanley, Digger leader, dies as a Quaker

1680: Last Covenanter revolt crushed: the "Killing Time"

1685: Monmouth Rebellion

1691: New England Puritan colonies finally brought under royal control

1692: Start of Salem witch hunts in New England

Introduction

This book was inspired by two particular experiences. The first occurred when I was writing my third-year dissertation at the University of Bristol over thirty years ago. Entitled "'The Sword Drawne': Christian Dissent and Politics 1649–1666, Particularly in the Fields of Millenarianism and Antinomianism",[1] it examined the ideas of some of the groups of Christian radicals during the period of the Civil Wars in seventeenth-century England and Wales. Ever since then I have been fascinated by these radicals who tried to impose "godliness", as they saw it, and "the rule of the saints" on a society dislocated by the upheaval of civil war and regicide. The second formative experience was co-writing *Christ: The First 2000 Years* with my youngest daughter, Esther.[2] In the chapter entitled, "King Jesus and the heads upon the gates!" I once more made the acquaintance of these radicals (both on the Continent and in Britain). Indeed, the chapter title was taken from a battle cry of the Fifth Monarchy Men in London, during Venner's Revolt in 1661. I realized, once more, how intrigued I was by the ideas and actions of these political radicals and the kind of society and life experiences that produced them. This book is the result.

In many ways the people examined in this book were driven by two overriding concerns: that Christian beliefs should dominate government and society; and a widespread belief that they were living in the "End-Time" and that the return of Christ was at hand. For some of them this latter belief meant that the Last Judgment would soon occur; while others among them held that it was their task to establish "godly" government on earth and only then would Christ return and they would rule with him. Either way, if correct, they held the key to interpreting the chaotic events of their own generation and the tools with which the immediate future could be predicted. Like Marxists of a later age they were convinced that they had the means by which the course of history could be understood and the ability to plan for a certain future. In contrast with Marxist

Dialectic, they had biblical (especially prophetic) revelation and a belief in Providence, which can be compared with the later belief in "Manifest Destiny" among nineteenth-century politicians and westward-bound settlers in the US.[3] This gave them great personal confidence. Not only that, but in the Bible they believed that they had the blueprint for creating a contemporary "godly society" through law and government. Since the New Testament was geared toward personal salvation and transformation, and building a faith community (a minority one at odds with the world) that was based on love and, consequently, did not offer the detailed programme necessary to establishing a theocracy, they looked instead to the detailed legal system that they found in the Old Testament. Although there was no agreed programme among the varied radical groups, many were generally inclined that way. As a result, they often appeared more enthusiastic about enforcing a strict legal system in the style of Moses or conquering the Promised Land like Joshua, than putting into practice the humility and mercy found in Jesus' Sermon on the Mount. There was often more of "smiting the Amalekites"[4] than "Blessed are the merciful"[5] about their radicalism! But in this they were very much people of their time and, it must be remembered, not all of these groups subscribed to such an outlook. Some were more pacifist in attitude and gentler in their relationships; but not many.

What is clear is that they were people living at a time of great upheaval. The previous century had seen medieval Christendom violently fractured by the Reformation. In this process many Catholics and Protestants denounced their opponents as agents of the Devil and as anti-Christian. In Britain this upheaval – that started under Henry VIII (ruled 1509–47) – had resulted in a compromise Protestantism emerging under Queen Elizabeth I (ruled 1558–1603) that increasingly left more-determined members of the Church of England – from the 1560s termed "Puritans", though they preferred the term "the godly" or "the saints" – increasingly dissatisfied. This dissatisfaction only increased during the reign of Charles I (ruled 1625–49) when the development of High Anglicanism signalled an increase in ritual that Puritans saw as backsliding into Catholicism.

A more "reformed" (as they would have termed it) Calvinistic and Presbyterian version of Protestantism had developed in Scotland after 1560. However, there was tension there too, with James VI (ruled Scotland 1567–1625 and England 1603–25, as King James I) and most violently with Charles I after 1639, when he attempted to impose his English form of the church on the kirk of the Scots. It did not go down well.

Many in Scotland saw themselves as a new Israel and in the seventeenth century many English Protestants held similar views concerning their own country's unique significance within God's Providence. In contrast, the remaining Catholics were regarded as disloyal "others" and in Ireland this was compounded by ethnic tensions caused by Protestant settlers being granted land at the expense of the majority population of native Catholic Irish. Hundreds of thousands were to die when these tensions exploded into violence between 1641 and 1653.

As if all this was not enough, Europe was torn apart by the Wars of Religion, most notably the Thirty Years' War (1618–48) which pitted Catholics against Protestants in a conflict that caused the deaths of perhaps 20 per cent of the civilian population in the German states, often as a result of atrocities committed by armies of mercenaries. People living in the British Isles were keenly aware of these European wars. Many who would later fight in the 1640s as officers in the New Model Army, studied the tactics of Protestant heroes such as King Gustavus Adolphus of Sweden (ruled 1611–32). In my own family, in Somerset, religious loyalties led to two little boys being baptized Adolphus Whittock and Gustaphus Adolphus Whittock as late as 1686 and 1693! In an ironic twist, it seems that Sarah Whittock, their mother, was not married and, therefore, both were apparently illegitimate ("base born"), which is not what one would have expected. Clearly, even in the late seventeenth century, not all was necessarily straightforward among the saints.

In the context of such turbulence it is little wonder that many of the godly, who already felt that God had appointed them to cleanse their nations of "false religion" and vice, increasingly interpreted the mid-seventeenth-century upheavals as the fulfilment of the

Four Horsemen of the Apocalypse (representing Conquest, War, Famine and Death) referred to in Revelation 6:1–8, as part of End Time prophecy.

Echoes of these ideas would continue to reverberate in the British Isles and North America long after the end of the attempts to establish the rule of the saints which had occurred in the 1640s and 1650s. All did not end at the Restoration of Charles II in 1660, although that was a terrible shock of disappointment and confusion to those who had previously predicted the course of future history so confidently. Consequently, we will look at both the "after-shocks" as well as the "early tremors", and not only the "seismic events" of the 1640s and 1650s.

The people who held these views were inspired by an access to English translations of the Bible that had been unthinkable before the middle of the sixteenth century. It was then that versions of the Bible, translated from the Hebrew and Greek texts, first became freely available in English; although an earlier unauthorized translation had cost William Tyndale his life in 1536. These, for English Protestants, were (there had been earlier versions that met various degrees of official opposition): the *Great Bible* (1539); the *Geneva Bible* (1560); the *Bishop's Bible* (1568) which was an early attempt to create an authorized version for use by all Protestant English speakers; and the *Authorized* – or *King James* – *Version* of 1611. Of these, the *Geneva Bible* was the version used among the godly until it eventually gave way to the *Authorized King James Version* from the 1650s onwards. The *Geneva Bible* had been produced without official sanction since it was the work of Protestants exiled under Queen Mary in the 1550s. It was famous for being the first English Bible with chapters divided into verses. It also contained many marginal notes to assist with study. These marginal notes revealed the reforming and Calvinist outlook of its Protestant authors and were to inform and inspire the godly in England and irritate royal authorities; mostly notably King James after 1603 (who objected to anti-monarchical marginal comments) and English church authorities (who objected to its perceived Calvinism). Nevertheless, it was commonly used among those of a godly outlook for several generations, both in Britain and in

North America (to where it travelled on the *Mayflower* in 1620). It actually informed a lot of the *Authorized King James Version* (which in 1611 was shorn of those controversial marginal notes) and in a number of places its style is arguably more direct and a little more modern in tone. Consequently, it was the *Geneva Bible* that was the version most commonly to be found among the saints in their godly congregations and in their private study.[6] What is striking is how biblically literate so many were and this, and its (often controversial) interpretation and application, underpinned their outlook and led to the dramatic events that we will explore shortly.

This book is about the kind of society that gave rise to such people and such events: the ideas, the values, the actions, the triumphs and the tragedies. A time, especially after the overthrow of Charles I and Britain becoming a republic, but even before that momentous event, *When God Was King*.

Roots of Radicalization

In 1649, following the beheading of King Charles I in January of that year, the radical Welsh preacher Vavasor Powell published a poem which summed up his view of the political and religious turmoil of that momentous year in British history. It contained these arresting lines,

> *"Of all kings I am for Christ alone,*
> *For he is King to us though Charles be gone."*[1]

Shortly before that, an anonymous Scottish pamphlet-writer had urged the English Parliament to overthrow King Charles because, in his view, there was a stark choice that lay before the people of the British Isles: "The quarrel is whether Jesus shal be King or no?" And, as if that question was not enough to shock his readers out of any support for earthly monarchy, the pamphleteer rammed the message home further: "O that England may never seek the death of crowned King Jesus! May never comply with dying Antichrist..."[2] The choice was simple: King Jesus or Antichrist (Charles I)? God as King or the agent of the Devil?

This book explores a dramatic period in British history, which reverberated in North America too. At its heart lies the period of the British Civil Wars (1642–53),[3] and the Commonwealth and Protectorate that followed and which lasted until the Restoration of King Charles II in 1660. Its subject matter, however, spills out of this time period since the upheavals in Scotland dated from the signing of the Scottish National Covenant of 1638 and the activities of some of the radical actors in this political and religious drama continued well after 1660, as we shall see. This book explores the ideas and actions of these seventeenth-century Christian radicals along with the legacy that they left in the United Kingdom and in North America.

"SAINTS" AND "SINNERS"

It was a period in which large numbers of influential Christians came to believe that they had to choose between having God as King or, at best, a poor human substitute or, at worst, Antichrist himself![4] Even many men and women who would draw the line at the killing of the king still saw themselves in a unique position in history in which they had the opportunity to use law and government to build the kingdom of God on earth in a way that had never before been possible. Technically, most did not intend a "theocracy" (government in which priests, or their equivalent, rule in the name of God or a god),[5] since they were content to work this righteous revolution through existing institutions, such as a godly Parliament or civil magistrates. But it *was* semi-theocratic, since it aimed to make the nation more accountable to God than ever before and this would not be achieved through an earthly monarch but through the "rule of the saints". Plus there were those whose aim was theocracy, however narrowly defined.

For those who were dissatisfied with what they saw as the lack of biblical holiness and order in both the established church and their society, it was a revolution that was about to break out and transform the nation. With regard to terms: from the 1560s onwards the description "Puritan" was used to identify those who were demanding a stricter, more "reformed" Protestantism in the Church of England, although they themselves preferred the labels "the godly" or "the saints". The same process of puritanical dissatisfaction and radicalization was going on in Scotland too. Since then, the term Puritan has so entered popular use that it is negatively *and* inaccurately used of a wide range of groups but it will be used here when describing those who stayed *within* the national church – and the trend they represented – in a more neutral sense than was used at the time by their enemies. In contrast, the terms "the godly" and "the saints" will be more frequently used of groups both *within* and *outside* the national church, and especially when referring to the way they regarded themselves, their values, and the kinds of outlook they espoused. This is particularly important to remember as many among the godly were, as we shall see, Separatists who decided to leave any national church system. When the word "puritanical" is used it will be in a general sense that describes attitudes across these groups.

When these groups used the term "saints" they meant people like themselves of a radical puritanical outlook who had come to believe that their view of God, their interpretation of the Bible, their understanding of what form the church should take, and their vision of how society should function, was superior to all other outlooks and, indeed, was the only one that was truly in line with God's will and purpose. All alternative views were at the least mistaken and more likely to be the work of the Devil and Antichrist. Clearly, if there were "saints" who should rule, then there were also "sinners" who required disciplining. For the saints, though, it truly was a time *When God Was King*. And since the period saw the breakdown of the established Anglican church, with its system of bishops, and the expansion of semi-independent congregations of believers (alongside breakaway groups), this opportunity for influencing the running of the country drew in people who would never previously have been included in the religious leadership of the nations involved.

As Cromwell himself told the "Barebone's Parliament" in 1653,

You are as like the forming of God as ever people were…
You are at the edge of promises and prophecies.[6]

That this parliament – which only sat for just over five months – is also remembered as the "Nominated Parliament" or "Parliament of Saints" only adds to the sense of special calling, apocalyptic hope and expectation that is clear in Cromwell's words. It is an illustration of how history can seem stranger than fiction to recall that it was named after one of its members, Praise-God Barebone, who represented the City of London, and that he had a brother named Fear-God Barebone.[7] Their given names are signposts to the age in which they lived; an age of the saints. For the 1640s and 1650s were a time in which old certainties and conformities had collapsed and anything seemed possible. And for some at the time, the boundaries of "anything" stretched very far indeed; heaven did not seem beyond reach. Either God would come down or his elect would build a society so godly that it would, as it were, be raised up to him.

Many of those who held these views were well educated and sophisticated; while others were self taught and, made confident by their beliefs, had overcome the kinds of social controls and stigma that had hitherto been used to keep them in their place. The key point is that this was not just the outlook of one isolated social group of discontented people. Rather, it was a widespread movement. It cut across class, gender, wealth and educational experience. It united fenland gentlemen-farmers like Oliver Cromwell and Scottish Presbyterian ministers; a violent Fifth Monarchist prophetess such as Mary Cary and soldiers of the Parliamentary New Model Army of the Civil Wars; MPs and street preachers; London apprentices and emigrants to the New World of North America; women and men. In a short period of time this disparate group would find enough things to fall out over among themselves. Then they would be willing enough to redefine Antichrist so that he took the form of those who were in opposing camps of the godly movement itself; earlier they would have united behind identifying him with the papacy and/or Charles I. But between them, at key points in the seventeenth century, these hugely confident and driven men and women were influential (if at times mutually antagonistic) participants in the chaotic kaleidoscope of winning the British Civil Wars, overcoming monarchy, killing the king, setting up a republic, attempting to implement a theocracy, enforcing the rule of the saints on the rest of society, establishing rural communism, and founding godly colonies in North America.

A MIXED MESSAGE

At times some of the views of these radical Christians echo surprisingly modern concepts of individual worth, participation in government and social equality. At other times their attempts to impose the rule of the saints (and even Old Testament law) is reminiscent of issues relating to Islamic Sharia Law and society in the twenty-first century. While some of them were precursors to modern parliamentarians and, in the case of Oliver Cromwell, merit a statue to that effect outside the House of Commons,[8] some others possessed a mindset more reminiscent of ISIS/Daesh or Boko Haram. And if the latter parallel seems extreme, the shocked reader might be referred to what happened to Irish Catholics (the Infidel-equivalent) at Drogheda and Wexford in 1649 at the hands of an army of saints. Furthermore, as we shall see in Chapter 6, largely as a result of the 1649–53 campaigns of Parliamentary forces in Ireland, it has been calculated that perhaps as many as 500,000 (overwhelmingly Catholic) Irish died, out of a total Irish population of 1.5 million. The vast majority had died as a result of the actions of the Parliamentary army.[9] The rule of the saints could lead to something that today would be described as ethnic cleansing and genocide. And there were many and varied victims of godly rule as it sought to root out sinful opposition and track it to its source. For example, as we will explore in Chapter 5, it has been calculated that 60 per cent of all those (almost always women) who were executed for alleged witchcraft in Britain between 1450 and 1751, died between 1644 and 1646.[10] The evidence suggests that almost all were innocent of the charges laid against them. Godly rule could come at a very high price for those classified as its enemies, whether they were Irish Catholics or East Anglian alleged witches.

Faced with this we are justified in asking: how had this astonishing situation developed and been made possible? We shall shortly explore the situation in the years preceding the Civil Wars that led to this tumultuous explosion of ideas. First, however, it will help to look at two very different traditions that these radicals drew on. For these contradictory back stories will help us understand both something of the competing outlooks at the time, and also the sharply contradictory cross-currents that flowed in this turbulent river of ideas.

TWO RATHER DIFFERENT BACK STORIES

Many of the godly in seventeenth-century Britain looked to the way that Protestant Christian politics had developed on the Continent in the sixteenth century. But they drew their inspiration from two different sources; sources that were not designed to work together, to put it mildly. This was because the Reformation had caused such an upheaval in church and state across Europe that it had been experienced and implemented by a wide range of different groups whose motives and objectives varied hugely.

In 1521 Martin Luther had made his decisive break from the authority of the pope, following the Diet of Worms before the leaders of the Holy Roman Empire. Luther himself had wanted no such break but was hoping to reform the Catholic Church. However, others were in favour of a more radical break with the past and were committed to challenging society as well as church. Though they were not strictly part of this process of Reformation, the peasants who rose in revolt across Germany in 1524 and 1525 took their cue from a sense of radical change being possible. Huge numbers died during the German Peasants' War and it sparked wildly different reactions among early Protestant reformers. Martin Luther condemned it. One can get a flavour of his attitude from the title of a pamphlet that he wrote, *Against the Murdering Plundering Hordes of Peasants*, in which he advised lords to crush the revolt. On the other hand, some Christian leaders, of a more revolutionary disposition, applauded it and later sought to emulate its attack on the wealth and power of the world. As a result, among many south German peasants there would be calls for a much more radical definition of "Reformation", in defiance of Luther and the established order. Later revolutionaries at Münster in Westphalia, in 1534–35, would see themselves as the heirs of this revolutionary tradition that had earlier been seen in the bloody events of the German Peasants' War. These were the Anabaptists whose exploits would later thrill or horrify different groups among the seventeenth-century British saints, depending on their predilection. Clearly, the Reformation was to have both a socially conservative and a revolutionary track.

From 1529 the term "Protestant" entered the vocabulary as some German princes backed Luther's calls for reform; they were also keen to restrict the power of the pope and the Holy Roman Emperor. By 1541 any hope of reconciliation between Catholics and Protestants broke down following the Diet of Regensburg. Years of indecisive warfare between the Catholic emperor and German Protestant princes led in 1552 to the Treaty of Passau, which recognized the continued existence of the Protestant German states; then the Peace of Augsburg (1555) ended this period of fighting. For these Protestant German states the Reformation basically meant significant changes in the church but without this threatening the status quo in state and society. Something similar happened in Sweden and Denmark, where there was little or no violence or disruption to society. Under the rule of godly princes the new German Lutheran church put great emphasis on the Bible and on preaching; rejection of Catholic devotion to the Virgin Mary and saints; the use of German (not Latin) in services; and the acceptance of married ministers in place of celibate priests. However, Lutheranism allowed ideas and practices associated with Catholicism as long as they were not banned in the New Testament. This was in contrast to more extreme Protestants who only allowed these to continue if they were explicitly commanded in the Bible. This meant that Lutheran churches had rather more of a Catholic look and feel than the more austere churches (and doctrines) that developed in harder-line communities. Luther, therefore, got off the "Reformation bus" several stops earlier than some other Protestants.

Elsewhere things were more complex. In France and the Netherlands, where rulers attempted to suppress the new ideas, there was violence and upheaval. In Switzerland a more austere Protestantism developed under Huldreich Zwingli (1484–1531). Zwingli stayed on the "bus" much longer than Luther. In fact he and Luther irretrievably broke off relations in 1529. In the Swiss churches there was a far more intense form of Protestantism: organs, pictures and statues were all removed. Switzerland was soon divided between Catholic and Protestant cantons. War flared but the division survived and Zurich and Geneva became standard-bearers of a more "reformed" kind of Protestant church than was developing in the Lutheran areas. Eventually the Catholic Counter-Reformation would roll back early Protestant advances in Bavaria, Poland, Austria, France, Belgium, and Bohemia. Here many Protestants were to die for their faith as Catholicism reclaimed these areas of the Continent.

While all this was happening, a different kind of Protestant Reformation was developing on a parallel route. The fragmentation of papal power had allowed the appearance of groups well to the left of Luther and with more challenging ideas. Those termed "Anabaptists" believed that only adult believers should be baptized, church members should elect their leaders and be involved in church decision-making, and that all beliefs should come from the Bible only. The belief in adult believers' baptism was a revolutionary statement since, if a person could choose faith (rather than it be mediated through family and church hierarchy or state power), then it was not much further to claim *political* rights too. And many did. Some were pacifists, such as the Mennonites in Germany and the Netherlands. They were founded by Menno Simmons (1496–1561) in Friesland. On the other hand, a minority were prepared to use force to enact change, such as the revolutionaries at Münster in 1534. Some were communistic, such as the pacifist self-sufficient Hutterite communities in southern Germany and Bohemia. Most were lower class or a little better off. They were feared by those who had more of a stake in society and by those who feared the disintegration of a national church into fragmented individual congregations. With their challenges to church, state, society, and economy, Anabaptists faced opposition across Europe: they were executed by other Protestants in Zurich; by Catholics for spreading their ideas in Moravia; and in semi-reformed England, where they were opposed both by Catholics seeking to defend the old ways and also by Protestants espousing the establishment of a state-led Protestant church. The way that, later in the seventeenth century, the term Anabaptist was "just a loose term of abuse like, 'Red'"[11] has been noted and there is a great deal of truth in this conclusion. As late as 1662, the English *Book of Common Prayer* found it necessary to state, "The Riches and Goods of Christians are not common, as touching the right, title, and possession of the same, as certain Anabaptists do falsely boast."[12] They had clearly made an impact on the consciousness of those in power.

So what of the Reformation in Britain? Here, two separate monarchies (until 1603) in England and Scotland traced different Reformation trajectories in the sixteenth century. In Scotland, by 1560, Protestants of the Swiss type were in the ascendant and they set up a more austere Presbyterian church under the likes of John Knox. South of the border things were more complex. Henry VIII (ruled 1509–47) wanted an end to papal interference but oscillated between an English semi-reformed Catholic church – largely Catholic but under royal control – to something more Lutheran, and back again. Ironically, the current British Protestant monarch's title of "Defender of the Faith" (*Fidei defensor*, feminine: *Fidei defensatrix*) was granted to Henry, in 1521, by Pope Leo X as a reward for Henry writing a book, *Assertio Septem Sacramentorum* (*Defence of the Seven Sacraments*), which among other things defended the supremacy of the pope and was regarded as an attack on the ideas of Martin Luther.[13] The original Catholic title still appears on British coins in the abbreviated form: *FD* or *FID DEF*. In fact, both Catholic loyalists and enthusiastic Protestants (notably Anabaptists) died for their faith under this Tudor monarch. His son, Edward VI (ruled 1547–53) was enthusiastically Protestant and, consequently, stained glass windows, statues of saints, rood screens, seasonal festivals and traditional church practices fell victim to a Protestant purge of what remained of Catholic traditions.[14] Under Mary (ruled 1553–58) things swung back to Catholicism. Then under Elizabeth I (ruled 1558–1603) a more moderate Protestantism was established as the norm within the Church of England, with the monarch as Supreme Head. Services would be in English, English Bibles would be prominent, preaching would be to the fore; but formality, use of Prayer Books (albeit in English), bowing and kneeling in worship and a strict church hierarchy under bishops would still be features of this very English compromise. In this it contained all the ingredients of its own temporary implosion in the three decades of the 1630s to 1650s, since High Church Anglicans would emphasize its formality and liturgy, while dissatisfied Puritans would draw on its Bible-based preaching and Protestant roots to call for "Reformation of Reformation" in order to achieve either a root-and-branch transformation of the national church, or even its dissolution as a national institution altogether.

CHOOSING HEROES TO EMULATE: CASE STUDY GENEVA?

Many among the godly in the first half of the seventeenth century looked to Geneva for inspiration. They even used the English-language *Geneva Bible* which had been translated there in the middle of the sixteenth century by Protestant exiles fleeing persecution under Queen Mary. Indeed, it was not until the second half of the seventeenth century that the *Authorized* – or *King James* – *Version* of 1611 would gradually overtake it in terms of popularity among the saints.

The community in Geneva had been greatly influenced by the work and ideas of John Calvin. Calvin was French and had broken with Catholicism in 1533. He first settled in the Swiss city of Basel where a large number of other French people lived. It was there that he wrote *The Institutes of the Christian Religion* in which he outlined his version of the new Protestant beliefs. Like Luther and Zwingli, Calvin believed that all Christian beliefs had to be rooted in the Bible. He also laid great stress on the sinful nature of unregenerated human beings; that is people before God's power changed them. He is also closely associated with the belief in Predestination. For many people, the words Calvinist and Predestination have become interchangeable terms so important is this idea as part of his legacy, although he certainly did not invent it or the belief.

At its simplest, Calvin taught that the heart, mind, and will of every person born is corrupted and depraved. As a result of this, all actions and intentions, regardless of whether they seem good or bad can never please God. Calvin taught that people still make choices which appear good (as any human might judge them) but they can never be accepted by God, because even the best action is fatally flawed by sin. This raises the question: how can a person be saved from being damned by God and condemned to hell? Calvin's answer was the assertion that before the creation of the world, God chose those people whom he would bring to know him and be saved. The key points being that: this was not based on any merit shown by that person (who was saved only by God's undeserved love or "grace") and neither was it based on God foreseeing that the person to be saved would come to faith. In short, it owed nothing to the person whatsoever. Calvin argued that God has "elected" to save some people but not all; for this reason such people are sometimes referred to as "the elect", this election to eternal life being based solely on God's will. As a result, some people are chosen for heaven/glory and others for hell/damnation before they are born. In the Calvinist scheme of things, Christ died for many people but he did not die for all. Furthermore, if a person is among the elect, they can never fall from grace; their salvation is assured. Indeed they cannot resist God's grace either. For this reason, when Cromwell on his deathbed had (according to some reports) last-minute doubts regarding his salvation, his – Calvinist – chaplain advised him that the elect cannot fall from grace and so Cromwell concluded, "I am safe, for I know that I was once in Grace."[15]

All of this could have a tremendous effect on the believer. In some cases it was confidence-sapping, since God's election was unknowable and was not dependent on faith or practice. Nevertheless, for others – who felt that their experience of God or their possession of a particular type of faith indicated that they *were* one of the elect – it made them feel assured of their status and salvation. In other words, "The elect were those who thought they were elect, because they had an inner faith which made them feel free."[16] Success could also be interpreted as a sign of God's favour and Cromwell, in the 1640s, was inclined to refer to what he termed "mercies" (such as battles won) as signposts of right standing with God. In these cases a dynamic energy could flow from such a sense of assurance and people recognized it in each other; they were kindred spirits. They drew together in what came to be called "gathered" congregations and separated themselves from other believers. Many of the godly in seventeenth-century Britain felt they were definitely of the elect and, consequently, they felt empowered to bring society into line with the rule of the saints.

However, Calvinism was not without its critics. Chief among these were those who subscribed to one of the various forms of Arminianism. Arminianism is based on the theology of a Dutch theologian, named Jacob Arminius (1560–1609). In essence, Arminians believe that God's grace restores free will to human beings who are therefore able to accept or reject God's offer of eternal life. People are, therefore, morally responsible beings. God saves those who he foresees will have faith in him. Christ died for all human beings and, consequently, eternal life is offered to all but conditional on them responding in faith. God does not overwhelm free will and people are capable of resisting his saving grace. Finally, Arminians believe that it is possible for a person to fall from grace, having been saved. By the seventeenth century in Britain one could find both Calvinists and Arminians among members of the Anglican Church *and* the so-called gathered congregations. Indeed, among the Baptists the descriptions "Particular Baptists" and "General Baptists" came to be used to describe whether they were Calvinist (Particular) or Arminian (General). However, Calvinism was the outlook of most of those in the more godly bloc and predominated among Presbyterians and most of the gathered congregations of the godly, in their various forms.

In 1536 Calvin had moved to Geneva. Things did not go well at first as there was a power struggle with the city council over the running of the church. In 1538 he was exiled from Geneva and moved to Strasbourg for three years. In 1541 he reluctantly returned; a shift in power in the city had led to his recall. However, it was not until 1555 that Calvin and his supporters were able to gain control over the church in the city. Anything not mentioned in the Bible was forbidden in church services, ornaments and statues were removed, preachers wore simple robes instead of ornate vestments, musical instruments were banned and congregational hymn singing was unaccompanied.

The form of church structure they established came to be known as "Presbyterian". It was a tightly controlled and efficiently run system in which pastors and a council of lay elders constituted church government. Pastors were chosen by other pastors (and approved by the church members) and a strict control was exercised over church members, their beliefs and behaviour.

Despite conflicts with some members of the city's government, the church became increasingly influential in deciding the laws of Geneva. Between 1541 and 1546, fifty-eight people were executed for infringing laws that had been promoted by the church. A further seventy-six were expelled from Geneva. Taverns were shut down and games of cards and dice forbidden in 1546; certain types of fashionable clothes were banned in 1547; dancing was made illegal in 1550. In one case, a man who left the church noisily during a sermon was imprisoned in 1547. In addition, all Catholic practices were banned. Homes were inspected by pastors in order to ensure godly conduct and spies were used to monitor behaviour. People said that they were so closely monitored in Geneva that it was like living in a city made from glass. The most famous victim of the Calvinist culture of government was Michael Servetus who in 1553 was burnt at the stake (Calvin had failed to get this commuted to execution by sword), for denying the doctrine of the Trinity and infant baptism. After 1555 the city council conceded the power of excommunication to the church leadership. This greatly increased Calvin's power and the numbers of excommunications escalated. He wrote to the young Edward VI of England, and to other leading members of the king's government, in an attempt to spread his ideas. However, Queen Elizabeth later rebuffed his advances, since she associated him with John Knox, the Scottish reformer of whom she disapproved.

However, despite these godly ordinances, Calvin did not get things all his own way. The city council in Geneva could block a pastor's appointment, and execution and exile relied on the agreement of the council. Taverns were soon reopened, despite Calvin's disapproval. In a similar way, an attempt to pass a law enforcing the giving of biblical personal names only, was vetoed by the council. In this sense even Geneva fell short of becoming the godly theocracy of the saints that Calvin desired. There was a separation of church and magistracy, which was in line with Calvin's ideology, but he could not entirely influence the latter which reduced the godly governance of the community somewhat. And he was only able to impose the ordinances that he did because key citizens were members of both the city council and the church consistory (its overall ruling group). Nevertheless, Geneva set a pattern for the trajectory that a godly community might follow (a semi-theocracy). In the seventeenth century many in the godly communities of Britain looked to Geneva for inspiration as they faced the challenge of creating the rule of the saints in church and state.

However, while many looked to Geneva, there were others in the 1640s and 1650s who looked to a very different model. They looked toward Münster.

CHOOSING HEROES TO EMULATE: CASE STUDY MÜNSTER?

As we have already seen, a version of Protestantism grew up among a group that has been described by the umbrella term of Anabaptist. The label was one used with alarm by many of their opponents, whether they were better-off believers or simply those Protestants who drew the line at adult baptism. As an insult it was thrown about with great frequency in the period of the Civil Wars. In fact, Cromwell was often accused of harbouring Anabaptists in his regiments, since this was a way of suggesting that they both came from the wrong social class *and* threatened chaos with their ideology. He usually denied that they were present in his regiments or asserted that it was irrelevant anyway, since all that counted was the quality of any particular soldier.

By Cromwell's time many Anabaptist communities had developed into the Separatist Baptist churches, whose descendants still exist today. Some were Calvinist and some were Arminian. They certainly had members in the Parliamentary army (whatever Cromwell asserted) and among the politically active groups of the time. What they all had in common was a revolutionary heritage. It was one that some embraced unashamedly and others tried to live down, despite it constantly being brought up against them. And this revolutionary heritage was one of social and religious upheaval that had grown out of the radical wing of the Continental Reformation. No example of this was more notorious than what occurred at Münster in Westphalia in the 1530s. It was an incident that reverberated over the next century and either inspired or horrified, depending on one's outlook.

In the year 1534, John Mathias or Matthys of Haarlem (in the Netherlands) and John Buckhold or Bockelson of Leiden (also in the Netherlands) led a group of extreme Anabaptists who seized control of the city of Münster. What followed went far beyond theological experiment and social change. Instead, the social order of the city was violently turned upside down. A reign of terror was soon in place and old patterns of behaviour abandoned. There were precedents for this in the so-called *Bundschuh* (peasants' clog) uprisings that had eventually escalated into the German Peasants' War. These lower-class uprisings declared nothing less than a God-sanctioned overturning of the social order, and such a revolutionary spirit soon spread to Münster.

Lutherans and Catholics were expelled from the city, the Anabaptists there being as antagonistic to one as the other. The city itself was soon besieged by the Bishop of Münster who found himself locked out of his own town. Claiming to be a prophet, Mathias and his supporters began a reign of terror against their critics. They seized all gold and silver and held it communally. All books were destroyed since they offered alternative sources of knowledge. In March 1534, Mathias was convinced that he had been ordered by God to take a small force out of the city to break the siege. He did so and was killed. He was replaced by John Buckhold – sometimes remembered as "Jan of Leiden" – who took the title "King of Justice, King of the New Jerusalem".

Buckhold proclaimed a policy of polygamy and then took fifteen wives. The policy was used to justify the sexual excesses of those in leadership. Women who refused to be given in arranged marriages were executed on Buckhold's orders. All sexual norms had soon broken down in the city; but the situation soon deteriorated even further. In August 1534, John declared that he, not Christ, was "Messiah of the Last Days", and would rule the world as a descendant of the Old Testament king, David. Buckhold's coinage proclaimed, "The Word has become Flesh and dwells in us", and it was clear that this referred to King John. While the city starved, he lived in luxury but proclaimed that since he was dead to the world there was no sin in this.

Finally, in 1535, the besiegers gained entry to the town. They slaughtered the Anabaptists and captured King John. In 1536 he was tortured to death with red-hot irons. Despite the crushing of the revolt, others took inspiration from the example. In 1567 a cobbler who was named Jan Willemsen, set up yet another "New Jerusalem". This was also in Westphalia and, as with Buckhold, he declared he was the Messiah. In time, he and his supporters were captured and executed; Willemsen himself was burnt at Cleves in 1580.

There was nothing about Anabaptist beliefs that made the horrors of Münster inevitable. But it did offer a salutary lesson in what could happen if traditional social order broke down; those who defended the social and religious order (or who wanted it to change without social and economic upheaval) explicitly referred to Münster as a warning. However, among those who dreamed of more radical changes in society, it was remembered as an event whose reality had been distorted by its detractors in order to undermine Anabaptists. Theirs was a very different version of history and a very different kind of hero, compared with those who looked to Geneva as a model of change, but change accompanied by discipline and structure. As things did unravel during the Civil Wars, and as groups competed to produce a society where God was King, the question polarized over whether the kingdom would be more like Geneva or Münster?

2

"The World Turned Upside Down!"

In 1647 a woodcut print appeared on the cover of a pamphlet that has since become strongly associated with the turmoil of the British Civil Wars. On it a man — at centre — wears gloves on his feet and spurred-boots on his hands; his bottom half is clothed in a jacket while his arms wear trousers; a fish flies above his head; a mouse chases a cat and a hare a hound; a church and a candle are upside down in the sky; while another man pushes a wheelbarrow with his feet and an upright horse drives a cart. The title above the illustration reads,

> *The World turn'd upside down: or A briefe description of the ridiculous Fashions of these dustracted Times.*

It proclaimed itself to be the work of one "T.J. a well-wisher to King, Parliament and Kingdom". Its title echoed a phrase found in the 1611 *Authorized — or King James — Version* of the Bible, referring to turmoil in the Greek city of Thessalonica caused by opposition to the preaching of the Apostle Paul, in which the apostle and his supporters were described as, "These that have turned the world upside down are come hither also."[1] The *Geneva Bible* — hitherto more popular among the godly — put it less memorably as, "These are they which have subverted the state of the world." The choice of the more memorable phrase for the 1647 pamphlet suggests that it was the 1611 version of the Bible that had inspired its title. And that pamphlet, in its turn, inspired Christopher Hill's 1972 study of the most radical and revolutionary movements of the 1640s: *The World Turned Upside*

Down;[2] and then a stage play by Keith Dewhurst, named from the title of Hill's book.

Clearly, by the middle of the 1640s, the increasingly heated clashes between Charles I and his opponents seemed to have turned the established order on its head. In no area was this more striking than in the field of religious ideas and church organization. The church in England, which had once seemed a strong pillar of the state, was in turmoil. Religious and political ideas (always closely intertwined in the seventeenth century) were up in the air and old certainties had been disrupted. Only two years after that pamphlet was published, the upheaval would hit a new height when King Charles I was executed in January 1649.

In this febrile atmosphere the most radical versions of Christian politics flourished and were both debated and (some at least) implemented. How had this occurred? In many ways the roots of this upheaval can be traced back to the nature of the Church of England as it had been decided during the reign of Queen Elizabeth I. It was a compromise arrangement that had left some significant sections of the church dissatisfied. And this dissatisfaction had only increased during the later reigns of James VI and I,[3] and especially during the reign of Charles I. It was then that it exploded into violent upheaval that splintered the church and the nation.

A RATHER ENGLISH COMPROMISE

In the years 1558–59 the newly crowned Queen Elizabeth I needed to settle exactly what character the Church of England would assume. Over the previous two reigns it had ricocheted from radical Protestantism under her half-brother, Edward VI, to Catholicism under her half-sister, Mary. And this was on top of the rather muddled mixture of old-style Catholicism and new-style Protestantism that had been bequeathed by Henry VIII.

What emerged has been called by historians "the Elizabethan Settlement". It emerged after a short period of political and religious manoeuvring, which was required in order to get a majority in the House of Lords to pass the final Settlement. This was necessary because the continued existence of Catholic-inclined bishops and peers needed some careful handling. It would be going too far to assume (as was once the case) that Elizabeth only wanted a semi-Catholic church and was pushed into a more Protestant model by reforming enthusiasts in the House of Commons. Elizabeth was certainly more conservative in matters of religion than some of her subjects but was still prepared to see a Church of England emerge that would have been recognisable to her enthusiastically Protestant half-brother, Edward VI. The foundation to this Settlement was formed by two Acts of Parliament. The first was the Act of Supremacy which became law in 1558. This reasserted the Church of England's independence from Rome, and Parliament conferred on Elizabeth the revised title "Supreme Governor" of the Church of England, which dated from the reign of her father, although he carried the title in the form "Supreme *Head*".[4] The second law was the Act of Uniformity, passed in 1559. This law basically established what form the Church of England should take. This included the re-establishment of the *Book of Common Prayer* (containing the words of liturgical – formal – services of worship). Although one should not exaggerate the reluctance of Elizabeth to set up a fully Protestant church, things were definitely complex. This is evident in the fact that her first archbishop of Canterbury (the Cambridge intellectual, Matthew Parker) was consecrated in that post in 1559 by two bishops who had gained their position under the church arrangements brought in by the Protestant Edward VI, and by two who had come to office in the 1530s under Henry VIII. Clearly, Elizabeth's Church of England was going to claim continuity from the past, even as new ideas were being enshrined in its teachings.

On one hand it was a break with the past and recognizably Protestant. Clergy could marry; the authority of the pope was gone; elaborate clergy vestments were outlawed; stone altars were removed; statues of saints were taken down; rood lofts and screens (the partition between the chancel and nave and decorated with an elaborate carved or sculptured crucifixion scene and often with attendant saints' statues) were removed after 1561. No Catholic would have found it acceptable and many Protestants were relieved that it established a church that had broken with the past.

On the other hand there were aspects that many enthusiastic Protestants would have been unhappy about. The queen herself was known to allow the occasional use of the cross and candlesticks in her private chapel; it remained the custom that many still knelt to receive communion and this could be seen to imply something of the Real Presence[5] of Christ without actually making any reference to the Catholic belief in Transubstantiation that was totally unacceptable to Protestants; the abuse of the pope, which had been included in the early forms of the litany (the wording of services), was removed from the *Book of Common Prayer*; the wording of the Communion Service was ambiguous enough for both Protestants and Catholics to read their inner thoughts into its description of the bread and wine; bishops and priests continued to wear a surplice; wafers, rather than ordinary bread, could be used at Communion.

Overall, Elizabeth's Church of England was a long way from the Catholic Church that had been the status quo at the start of her father's reign. But it was also a long way from the "Reformed" church found at Geneva and favoured by those English Protestants who had been exiled there under Queen Mary. Elizabeth had walked a difficult middle path between her Catholic lords who had wanted the re-establishment of a Catholic church (even if an adapted one) and the more Reformed church desired by those returning from exile. Queen Elizabeth and many of her closest advisors were distrustful of Calvinist ideas about a church that was independent of the monarch, and she detested the Calvinist, John Knox, who was actively working to reform Scotland in the image of the church in Geneva (see Chapter 3).[6] Ruling for forty-five years meant that Elizabeth's very English compromise bedded down and became the established norm. Those who were comfortable within this church – and there were many by the queen's death in 1603 – are often referred to as "Anglicans". The new-style Church of England, with its reduced but still distinct formality, its orderly services dictated by the *Book of Common Prayer*, its hierarchical structure of bishops under the monarch, and its acceptance of sufficient ritual and order, gave them a community that stood its ground against *both* the more enthusiastic Protestants *and* against

Catholics. But there were those who were not satisfied with this state of affairs within the English church and, as time went on, their dissatisfaction only increased.

The growth of puritanism

To the confusion of modern readers, historians use the term "Reformed Church" to describe a particular type of Protestant community. While it sounds like it should describe any church that broke away from Catholicism ("Reformation"... "Reformed"...) it does not. In fact it is deliberately *not* used to describe the churches founded by Martin Luther and those inspired by his actions. Instead, the term is used to describe those churches that were part of the Swiss Reformation in cities such as Zurich and particularly in Geneva. While Lutheran ideas were influential at first, it was the Swiss (Reformed) model that was eventually most influential among the most progressive advocates of change in the Reformation-England of Edward VI and Elizabeth I and, especially, in the Scottish church. This was where the seeds of later conflict lay, because the Swiss model – even when it failed to make as much headway as its adherents had hoped for in Switzerland – was always more radical and had more of theocracy about it than the Lutheran churches.

From the 1560s, those in England who were dissatisfied with the Elizabethan Settlement were labelled "Puritans". Almost all of them were Calvinists (although not all Calvinists were Puritan members of the Church of England as we shall see). Some of them favoured a Presbyterian form of church government, while others could live with a church overseen by bishops as part of a hierarchical church structure, as long as the teaching and lifestyle was in line with Reformed expectations. At its simplest they envisaged a church community centred around Bible preaching rather than elaborate ceremony and they actively campaigned for a society that was brought into line with strict morality that they felt embodied biblical principles. They personally became associated with simpler dress-sense and strict personal moral behaviour. They were not alone in these goals and many who opposed them also wished to see the same changes in church and society but in combination with a more hierarchical church structure and a level of ceremony that Puritans found offensive.

By the second decade of the seventeenth century the term Puritan was being used to describe anyone of this outlook, including those who had broken away from the structure of the Church of England, although we will use the term "the godly" to describe this broader community. The militancy of such people (whether within or without the Church of England) was to dominate the British Isles in the 1640s and 1650s once they had overthrown those who stood in their way.

THE RISE OF THE SEPARATISTS

At the same time as Puritans were growing restless within the Church of England of the Elizabethan Settlement, there were those who were committed to breaking away from the established church altogether. The Act of Uniformity's demand that all English subjects in the parishes of the Church of England attend Sunday service had placed those looking to break away on a collision course with the church. But who were they?

As we saw in Chapter 1 there were two great Continental inspirations for those wanting to change the church in the British Isles. On one hand, there were the related streams of Lutheranism in Germany and the Reformed churches of Switzerland. It was the latter that had rather more influence in the established church over time, although its influence became increasingly challenged by those Anglicans who had a less radical concept of the English Protestant church. On the other hand, there was another Reformation unfolding across the channel that influenced people in the British Isles.

Anabaptist ideas (as well as actual refugees from persecution) appeared in sixteenth-century England alongside the more influential Lutheran and Reformed ideas. These Anabaptist ideas inspired native versions although they were not great in number in England and even rarer in Scotland. And they met fierce persecution as their belief in adult believers' baptism set them at loggerheads with both Catholicism and emerging official Protestantism. As such they were burnt as heretics under every monarch from Henry VIII to James VI and I. Apart from a common belief in adult believers' baptism, these groups covered a wide range of sects whose members' outlook and beliefs varied from those who were fairly mainstream (apart from on baptism and church government) and politically inactive, to others who would have been classed as heretics by most other Christians and some who were politically very active indeed. Where individuals stood on this spectrum varied greatly. Some might be generally mainstream, while combining this with a political activism that was intent on promoting active godly government. What is common to all is that they alarmed their contemporaries. When in 1594 Thomas Nash wrote a story entitled *The Unfortunate Traveller*, it was a cautionary tale about a character who became entangled with fanatical Anabaptists in Germany.[7] Today, a comparable story might tell of a young Muslim who was the subject of attempted radicalization by ISIS.

One of the groups who had Continental roots but came to have English adherents was known as the Family of Love. They were also known as the *Familia Caritatis*, and the Familists. Founded by a Dutch mystic named Hendrik Niclaes, enigmatically referred to by his followers as "H.N.", members of this sect appeared in England during the reign of Edward VI (1547–53) and records refer to them as late as the 1640s. They believed in adult baptism and in freedom of religious belief. This concept of people being able to hold their own religious beliefs without the state policing them and punishing those that transgressed beyond "acceptable boundaries" was very radical indeed in the sixteenth and seventeenth centuries. They were also pacifists. Their beliefs were not only socially radical, since they also held doctrinal beliefs that would have been regarded as heretical by mainstream Christians at the time and since. For example, they rejected the doctrine of the Trinity and they held that human society was ruled directly by nature rather than by God. In this way they doubly fell out with most other Christians since most believers stood by the doctrine of the Trinity and also felt that, however difficult to understand, the affairs of men and women were directed by God. Members of the sect considered themselves made pure by God and that they were a spiritual elite who were united with God; and with no imperative to spread their beliefs or even to publicly declare them. As a result, they could be found as members of the official church and might even deny any connection to the sect. This policy of holy deception makes it hard to assess their numbers but there is some evidence to suggest that Elizabeth I tolerated some holding these views among her personal servants. In the 1580s some of the Yeomen Guards in the Tower of London were accused of being members of the sect but no action was taken against them. Indeed, Elizabeth seems to have adopted a strategy of "Don't ask, don't tell" and, furthermore, to have been unwilling to act to enforce official church beliefs on them even when they were discovered. Under James VI and I, the Keeper of Lions at the Tower of London was accused of being a member of the sect but seems to have escaped punishment. Another man accused of sympathies was Reginald Scott (1538–99) who was a Member of Parliament and the author of a book entitled, *The Discoverie of Witchcraft* (1584), which was written to challenge belief in witches and to demonstrate that witchcraft did not exist. It also set out to explain how acts of "magic" were done and it is today considered to be the first textbook on conjuring. The limited influence of this on popular and official outlook is revealed by the fact that godly government in the 1640s and beyond led to the deaths of many hundreds accused of working magic.

What evidence there is of their membership indicates that the members were better educated than the norm and often included artists and intellectuals (but in very small numbers overall it should be remembered). And they kept their beliefs quiet. As a result they did not suffer the persecution meted out to more active groups of "Anabaptists"; but neither did they grow to any perceivable influence. Since they only shared their ideas with like-minded people we are only aware of their presence when that confidence was either broken or discovered. Some of their ideas influenced some Baptists and Quakers but, while challenging the norms of the day, they were certainly not an Anabaptist sect set on forcing on others the rule of the saints. For them "God was King" in their personal lives but not in a radical agenda for political control of society.

More orthodox in core beliefs but more likely to contain members who would wish to influence government policy were the Baptists. During the lead-up to the Civil Wars they became an increasingly influential minority. Baptist ideas had influenced a number of English Separatist congregations living in exile in the Netherlands in the late sixteenth century. Their connection with earlier Anabaptists is a matter of debate as they were very keen to play this down and there is, in fact, little evidence for direct organizational connections. The matter has continued to divide historians.[8] However, there is no doubt that ideas and members certainly passed between groups, without revealing themselves in surviving faith statements and publications by leading Baptists. This informal passage of ideas and influence has been described as a "Dynamic Model" of church development, as opposed to the more systematic "Organic Model" that requires an unbroken continuity of descent through particular leaders, organizations and faith statements.[9] This is reinforced by the fact that, in the 1650s, a number of Baptists flew in the face of the denial of links with earlier politically radical German Anabaptists and both defended them and drew parallels between their own revolutionary activism and the actions of earlier radicals. As we shall see (in Chapter 9) these "Fifth Monarchy Men" were very much cast in the familiar stereotypical Anabaptist mould of violent insurrection. As Dr E. A. Payne memorably put it, "Religious life in the seventeenth century was like a tumultuous sea, blown about by winds from several directions. That one strong current of air came from the Anabaptist movement... I am convinced."[10]

By the 1640s some Baptists were Arminian – or General – Baptists. These traced their origins to a Separatist congregation which was formed at Gainsborough (Lincolnshire) in 1606. This group emigrated to Holland, where it was led by a man named John Smyth, in 1608. Another prominent member was Thomas Helwys, who financed the venture. In Holland, Smyth published a book called the *Character of the Beast* in 1609, which was consistent with a lot of contemporary emphasis on seeing their current experiences as realizations of biblical prophecy. That same year he baptized himself and other members of his congregation.

25

His administration of this rite was a significant move away from his former belief in infant baptism. Thomas Helwys and others returned to England to found a church at Spitalfields in 1611 or 1612. Helwys and his group had earlier rejected amalgamation with Anabaptists on the Continent (Dutch Mennonites). Churches at Coventry, Lincoln, Salisbury, and Tiverton arose out of the original Helwys congregation and by the 1640s there were General Baptist congregations scattered across England.

The first Calvinist – or Particular – Baptist church was established in the 1630s by John Spilsby. It had its origins in the Baptist faction of a London church, founded in 1616 at Southwark by Henry Jacob. By 1644, Spilsby's church had been instrumental in the production of the Calvinist *London Confession of Faith*. It had done so in close collaboration with seven other Particular Baptist churches. The Particular Baptist churches of the 1640s, '50s and '60s had their origins in an English Calvinistic tradition that stretched back into the sixteenth century. They arose out of the Calvinist outlook that was prevalent in large areas of the Church of England by 1600, married to the more controversial Separatist traditions inherent in some parts of the Church of England since the sixteenth century among those who felt its theology could not be sufficiently reformed and were anyway distrustful of its hierarchical system. By the 1640s more English Baptists were Calvinists than Arminians and in this they were part of a trend that could be seen across the godly spectrum from Independents to Presbyterians.

Although the General and Particular Baptists did not work together and, indeed, formed their own competing coordinating organizations in the 1650s, they were influential in the New Model Army of Parliament during the Civil Wars and many were committed to the establishment of godly government once the established political and church order broke down in the 1640s.

THE 1640s: THE WORLD *TURNING* UPSIDE DOWN

The tumultuous decade of the 1640s saw the disintegration of the status quo in British state, politics and religion and the ascendancy of the godly. As the control exercised by the king and his bishops broke down, many "Independent" congregations emerged within the Church of England. Although independent in name, these congregations usually did not want to separate from the Church of England, but instead wanted an authority that was decentralized and which gave greater autonomy to local congregations. This accompanied a desire for the demolition of the episcopal system, whereby bishops enforced conformity, and the abandonment of the Prayer Book (which dictated the form and content of church worship). This independent model was never fully realized in England but those Puritans who emigrated to the North American colony of Massachusetts Bay, and elsewhere, found that they had an opportunity to establish just such a system there (as we shall see in Chapter 13). In 1645 and 1646 the English Independents fell out with attempts by Parliament (encouraged by the Scots) to set up a Presbyterian system of church government and church services, since this seemed too close to the very formal control and a sense of "system" that they had found so irksome under the old Church of England.

The reason they wanted independence was because of the increasingly divided nature of the Church of England. It was a division that spilled out across politics and society. The Church of England in 1600 was largely Calvinist in its outlook and this applied both to those who were content with the way the church was run and those unhappy with its limited "Reformed" character. However, as early as the 1580s some university-based clergy began to argue for the revival of more ceremony in the church, and belief in the power of the sacraments, and they stressed the English church's continuity from ancient times. They are often described as "High Church", a term first employed in the seventeenth century. These people were not very influential until the reign of King James. From then onwards their rise was fairly meteoric until, by the reign of Charles I, they were represented in no less a person than the archbishop of Canterbury himself, William Laud. Just to confuse later students, these High Churchmen became labelled as "Arminians" by their Calvinist Puritan opponents although they were actually much more interested in ceremonial and church hierarchy under the Crown than in the debates over predestination.[11] It was much the same as the way that the terms "Roundhead" and "Cavalier" would be tossed about during the Civil Wars and the way that the term "Anabaptist" was loosely applied as a pejorative term to anyone thought a threat to the church and social order.[12] But if Calvinist Puritans were aghast at what they considered the rising tide of "Catholic practices" backed by royal power, their opponents were equally weary of the "prophesyings" by people they regarded as too imbued with personal spiritual authority and too independent of the control of bishops and the king. To such Arminians the formal liturgy of the Prayer Book offered a bulwark against what they considered out-of-control enthusiasm and lack of ecclesiastical discipline.

These Church of England Arminians never achieved a wide following but they had support where it counted: at court. With their enthusiasm for changing church furnishings and the ceremonial – coupled with support for royal authority over the church – they became embroiled in acrimonious debate and conflict with their Puritan opponents as the 1630s progressed. To the godly, intent on ensuring that God was King in a community where the saints could dictate to an earthly king and society over acceptable behaviour, the Arminians were like a red rag to a bull. To Charles I, on the other hand, they offered a powerful counterbalance to forces that were starting to run out of control. It was not that the Puritan agenda was republican (although it would eventually assume that character), it was more that it (and especially its Parliamentary form) ran counter to the Stuart concept of royal power. To this was added the fact that Charles I certainly favoured the more elaborate ceremonial that was being proposed and, indeed, enforced by the Arminian High Church faction. When one also adds that his wife Henrietta Maria was a French Catholic one can see how Puritan sensibilities, already highly attuned to threats from Catholicism and royal power that was not in line with godly rule, would be affronted. A perfect storm of religious, constitutional and social strife was gathering pace and the barometer continued to fall.

After William Laud became archbishop of Canterbury, in 1633, he energetically attempted to impose uniformity on the church in

England. In order to do this he used two controversial methods. One of these was the Court of Star Chamber. Meeting in a room in Westminster, where the ceiling was decorated with stars, this was the king's council sitting as a court of law. Until its abolition in 1641, the court was used to harry and punish opponents of the king and archbishop. One of its famous victims was Henry Burton, vicar of a London parish who was imprisoned in 1629 for attacking the authority of bishops. In 1636 he was tried for sedition in the Star Chamber and, in addition to a heavy fine, lost both ears and was sentenced to perpetual imprisonment (he was released in 1641 as royal authority collapsed and he became an Independent minister). Tried at the same time as Burton, William Prynne was a lawyer and an opponent of both the Arminian leadership of the church and of royal authority. He had earlier had his ears cropped in 1634 and had what was left of them cropped again in 1637. He would later show himself equally antagonistic to Catholicism, bishops, Independent church ideas and Presbyterian church authority; between 1647 and 1658 he fell out with the leadership of the Parliamentary army and every government, so much so that he was imprisoned under Cromwell between 1651 and 1653. One could describe him as fairly "catholic" in his detestations were that word not already taken in the list of what he opposed! He eventually welcomed and then criticized the royal Restoration in 1660. He survived that, though, and surprisingly ended up as royal archivist at the Tower of London until his death in 1669 – but that is to get well ahead of our story.

This period of intra-church conflict coincided with the so-called "Eleven Years Tyranny" (1629–40) when Charles I (king since 1625) ruled without calling a parliament. Relying on unpopular devices to raise cash such as Ship Money (from 1634 until it was declared illegal in 1641),[13] and Tonnage and Poundage,[14] Charles attempted to weather the gathering storm of criticism. This was indeed a time of growing political tension as Charles punished opponents, seized land for the established church in Ireland from Anglo-Irish and newly settled English landowners, and largely ignored the Scots (he was not crowned there until 1633) unless he was antagonizing them. Between 1639 and 1640 he fought the disastrous Bishops' Wars in a failed attempt to force his favoured High Church Arminian form of church and church services on Scotland.

Short of money, Charles finally recalled Parliament in April 1640. After a barrage of criticism levelled against his royal government, within a month he quickly dissolved what is now remembered as the "Short Parliament". Still short of money, he was forced to reassemble Parliament in November 1640. This – the so-called "Long Parliament" – was to technically last in one form or another until March 1660 when it was finally dissolved and new elections took place. In the first few months of the Long Parliament, Charles was in headlong retreat before those intent on purging royal government and settling political grievances. This included the arrest of Archbishop Laud, in 1641, which would lead to his eventual execution in 1645. Puritanism and Parliamentary power was in the ascendant. However, these political concessions by Charles I appeared to have defused the crisis.

It was not to be. Never a man to miss an opportunity to miss an opportunity, Charles squandered all this good will over the next two years. This was clearly because he bitterly opposed every concession that had been forced out of him. He fell out with Parliament over who would control the army being raised to suppress the Irish Rebellion of 1641; in January 1642 he attempted the arrest of leading Parliamentary opponents (the "Five Members") only to find that they had been tipped off and, in his own words, "all the birds are flown". As the situation continued to disintegrate, Charles eventually left London to rally Royalist support and, in August 1642, he set up his royal standard at Nottingham. At the same time Parliament took control over the Trained Bands of as many of the county militia regiments as it could.[15] The country had slid into civil war. Now at last it might be decided who was really king. To Charles it was himself under God. Over the next six-and-a-half years an increasingly influential number within the godly would finally come to the decision that it would be God and his representatives among the saints. Within a week of the raising of the royal standard at Nottingham, the wind blew it down. It was a portent of things to come.

The situation on the eve of the Civil Wars

As we shall see in Chapter 4, the descent of the nation into the Civil Wars after 1642 gave those who were unhappy with the state of both the church and society in England and Wales an opportunity to attempt to remake both in an acceptable image of their ideal. The first great move toward the rule of the saints and the establishment of godly government was now possible. Religious differences were only one among many causes of the conflict that would tear apart the British Isles over the next decade; but it was a major factor. And such was the nature of seventeenth-century society that disputes over religion affected society and politics generally.

The imposition of radicalized Christian ideas and the first stirrings of semi-theocracy shook the fabric of church, state and wider society as the status quo unravelled. Just what form that godly rule would take and how easy it would be in practice to implement such ideas will be further explored, but first we must shift our focus northwards because even before England and Wales were shaken by the Civil Wars, seismic shocks had already found their epicentre in King Charles I's northern kingdom of Scotland. Already, in the period 1639–40, church and state had been shaken there and the outcome of this Scottish turmoil would set a precedent for significant aspects of what would occur after 1642 south of the border. For in Scotland, God's kingship, as defined by many of his Scottish subjects, seemed more secure than that of Charles Stuart.

3

North of the Border:
A Very Scottish Godly Rule

We need to remember that Scotland in the sixteenth century was a separate country. Even in the seventeenth century, after the accession of James of Scotland to the English throne in 1603, it remained a separate kingdom. It then shared a monarch with England and Ireland,[1] rather than forming a united kingdom. Under the "Union of the Crowns" Scotland remained significantly separate with its own institutions and identity, despite James' efforts to create an imperial rule over a "Great Britain". In a sense, all the rulers after 1603 until the early eighteenth century were wearing two separate crowns at the same time. The formal union into a united kingdom did not take place until 1707 when one "Parliament of Great Britain" was established to rule both the kingdoms of England and Scotland; and this was to meet at Westminster, the established home of the existing English Parliament. The Acts of Union passed between 1706 and 1707, referred to as the "Union of the Parliaments", established the single united kingdom of "Great Britain". A similar union with Ireland (ending the existence of its separate Irish Parliament in Dublin) did not occur until 1801. All of this needs to be borne in mind when considering the events that are the focus of this book because Scotland had its own path that was not identical to that of England, and would influence events in a way that only makes sense when one remembers that it was a separate kingdom, with its own legal identity and religious character. Furthermore, it had experienced a very different kind of Reformation and had its own distinct concept of what constituted godly rule. In fact, in many ways it was Scotland which was the trailblazer for this, rather than England.

What we can call "the Scottish Reformation" saw Scotland break with the Catholic Church and then go on to develop a predominantly Calvinist national church – the *kirk* – which was strongly Presbyterian in outlook. In this there were real differences with the way that the Reformation occurred in England. Then, with the removal of the Scottish king to London in 1603, this Scottish kirk enjoyed a considerable amount of freedom to go its own way and in this it benefited from much looser royal oversight than was developing in England. This was the key reason that godly rule took on a very particular form north of the border and the seeds of future conflict with a London-based monarchy were sown under Charles I when he attempted to bring the northern kingdom into line with England.

THE REFORMATION IN SCOTLAND

From the late fifteenth century onwards the ideas of those critical of the established Catholic church began to reach Scotland. In this period there was a lively meeting of minds between Scottish and Continental thinkers who were growing dissatisfied with aspects of Catholicism. As the ideas of Martin Luther began to appear in Scotland, they influenced the writings of an influential Scottish Lutheran named Patrick Hamilton, who was executed in 1528 as a result of his radical ideas.

This difficult start for Protestant ideas mirrored the experience in England where Protestant martyrs also died for their beliefs. But in Scotland there were differences. Unlike Henry VIII in England, his nephew King James V of Scotland (ruled 1513–1542) steered clear of making major changes to the church. In contrast, he used the Scottish church both as a source of income, which boosted the royal treasury and for providing jobs for his illegitimate children and his court favourites. This meant that the church in Scotland did not initially experience the turbulent changes that occurred south of the border where the royal court became the battle ground of traditionalists and reformers. Although James V did show some interest in Protestant ideas, he did so mostly in order to alarm the papacy into granting him tax concessions.

Change came in 1542 with the death of James V. He left a child, Mary (Queen of Scots) as his heir, but dynastic weaknesses presented an opportunity for the English to interfere in Scottish politics through a series of armed invasions (1543–51), later termed "the Rough Wooing".[2] The English aimed to stop the Scots from acting in alliance with France against England to prevent a continuation of the Franco-Scottish alliance (the "*Auld Alliance*") that had lasted from 1295 to 1560 in response to the common – English – threat to both nations (the "*Auld Enemy*"). It also aimed to neutralize any threat from Scotland by forcing the marriage of Mary to Henry VIII's son, the later Edward VI – hence the "wooing". This marriage never took place. The "Nine Years' War", as it was called in Scotland, also had a religious dimension as the English forces distributed English-language Bibles and Protestant literature in the Lowlands which they invaded in 1547. They also encouraged any Scots who would collaborate with this English project.

At the same time as the English were attempting to introduce Protestant ideas in, as it were, the baggage train of their invading armies, Protestant ideas were growing independently in Scotland. In 1546 a Scottish Catholic cardinal, David Beaton, ordered the execution of the Protestant George Wishart, who was burnt at the stake. Wishart was influenced by the ideas of the Swiss reformer Zwingli, and his execution led to a backlash from his supporters, among whom were a number of landowners, or *lairds*, from Fife. In retaliation they arranged the assassination of Cardinal Beaton and went on to seize control of the castle at St Andrews. Despite opposition from forces sympathetic to Catholicism, they succeeded in holding the castle for a year, only succumbing following the involvement of French troops in a bloody demonstration of the *Auld Alliance*. Those taken prisoner, when the castle was finally captured in 1547, included their chaplain, John Knox. He and others were condemned to serve as galley slaves in the navy of Catholic France, which, not surprisingly, did nothing to reduce their opposition to Catholicism. Back home they were hailed as Protestant martyrs and this fame grew alongside growing resentment at how France was shoring up Scots Catholicism. Despite this resentment, Scots royal politics continued on a familiar course and, in 1548, the defeat (with French assistance) of the latest English invasion led to the eventual marriage of Mary[3] to the French heir to the throne (the *dauphin*), Francis (later Francis II).[4] This accompanied the setting up of a regency over Scotland which was exercised by the queen's mother, Mary of Guise.

Despite the earlier setback at St Andrew's Castle, Protestantism slowly grew in influence in Scotland. It was assisted by a lack of robust persecution by the church and state authorities and also by the influence of exiled Scots who were living in other countries. In 1557 a group of lairds declared themselves "Lords of the Congregation" and took to advancing the cause within Scottish politics. This, in turn, was assisted by a number of factors: the collapse of the French alliance, in 1560, following the death of Francis II; the death of the regent, Mary of Guise, in 1560; followed by English intervention which led to the Treaty of Edinburgh by which both the French and the English agreed to withdraw their troops from Scotland. All of this meant that a small but highly influential group of Protestants – the Lords of the Congregation– were able to impose Protestant reforms on the Scottish church. This involved an emphasis on Bible teaching and there was also a flurry of iconoclasm (breaking of Catholic images in churches) in 1558–59. Plans were prepared for local parish worship that would be in the style of the reformed Swiss churches, along with increased levels of preaching, and local congregations began to appoint ministers who were sympathetic to Protestant ideas. All of this occurred while Mary of Guise was still regent because she lacked the power to supress it at a time when she was trying to ensure Scottish support for her pro-French foreign policy. Things spiralled out of control in the last years of her life as regent. In 1559 she faced open revolt from the Lords of the Congregation, who had been encouraged by the accession of Elizabeth I to the English throne. Catholic religious houses were sacked and Mary was forced to agree to religious tolerance, which effectively meant tolerating the rising tide of Protestantism.

John Knox was at the heart of this resurgent Protestantism. In 1549 he was released from the galleys and lived in exile in England from 1549 to 1554. When the Catholic Mary Tudor came to the throne he went into exile on the Continent in 1554, where he lived in Geneva and Frankfurt, before returning to Scotland in 1555. The amount of support he received meant that he was able to preach openly despite being in opposition to the Catholicism of Mary of Guise. Nevertheless, in 1556 he returned to Geneva on the invitation of a congregation and remained there until 1559 when he again returned to Scotland. While in Geneva he wrote his famous pamphlet, *The first blast of the trumpet against the monstruous regiment of women* (1558), which was directed at Mary Tudor in England and Mary of Guise in Scotland; although it also ended up antagonizing another female ruler: Elizabeth I.[5]

The rise of the Protestant party climaxed in 1560, when the Scottish "Reformation Parliament" adopted a Protestant confession of faith, rejected the authority of the pope, and repudiated belief in the Catholic Mass. The Swiss Calvinist beliefs of the Scottish reformers, led by Knox, meant that the style of church preferred was a Swiss-inspired Presbyterian system, which rejected most of the ceremonies of the established medieval church. It did, though, take some time for this system to become the dominant one and bishops and archbishops continued to exist in a hierarchy over the Scottish church until they were finally abolished in 1638 (a state of affairs which then lasted until 1661 and the Restoration).

PRESBYTERIANISM

We have touched on this system of church government with regard to the reformed church in Geneva, but it will help to remind ourselves here of what it meant in practice because it was so important in the seventeenth century. Presbyterian theology emphasized the sovereignty of God in line with Calvin's beliefs, the authority of the Bible, and salvation through faith in Christ without dependence on good works. These features were accepted by most reformed Protestant groups.

Where Presbyterianism was distinct was in its focus on a particular method of church government. Typically this involved the rule of assemblies of "presbyters", or "elders". It envisaged that local churches would be governed by a body of elected elders who in time were usually called "the session" or "the consistory". Two classes of elders were ordained: Teaching Elders and Ruling Elders. They were responsible for the discipline, teaching, and outreach of the local congregation. The Teaching Elders (later referred to as "pastors") oversaw the biblical and moral teaching, the style of worship, and the sacraments (primarily Holy Communion).

Above the sessions were "the presbyteries", with area responsibilities, made up of Teaching Elders and Ruling Elders from each of the local congregations (the sessions). Each area-presbytery was to send representatives to a national assembly, the General Assembly. It was envisaged that local congregations would appoint their Teaching Elder(s); a decision to then be ratified by the local presbytery.

This system did not emerge overnight and, as we have seen, there were bishops in the Scottish church until 1638, but the goal and the direction of travel of the system was clear.

It rejected the simple hierarchies of bishops (called an "episcopal polity") with their hierarchy of dioceses and parishes under their authority; while, at the same time, rejecting "congregationalism", favoured by Separatists (see Chapter 2), in which each local congregation was wholly independent of any wider system. In Presbyterianism authority flowed both from the *top down* and *the bottom up*. It flowed *downwards* because the higher assemblies (the presbyteries) had authority over individual congregations, such as in the matter of ordaining ministers. On the other hand it also flowed *from the bottom up* since church officers were elected by local churches and they had the right to call ministers. It was this theory of church government that was developed in Geneva under Calvin and was then introduced to Scotland by John Knox after his experiences in Geneva.

SCOTLAND UNDER MARY AND HER SON, JAMES

When her husband, Francis II, died in 1560 the Catholic Mary returned to Scotland. It went badly. Her reign was characterized by a number of crises, caused largely by the rivalries of the leading nobles. When opposition to her third husband, Bothwell, increased, it eventually led to the creation of a coalition of nobles intent on overthrowing Mary. In 1567 they eventually succeeded in capturing Mary and forced her to abdicate in favour of her son – James VI. Mary was forced into exile in England where she would be found guilty of plotting against her Protestant cousin, Elizabeth I, and executed in 1587.

James VI was brought up a Protestant, but resented the way in which the Presbyterian system sought to reduce the authority of the monarch over church structures. As a result he resisted Presbyterianism and the independence of the Scottish kirk. His aim was to ensure the survival of episcopal rule (i.e. bishops) in Scotland, since he felt these enhanced royal authority.

When he eventually became king of England in 1603 (as James I) he found the hierarchy of the Church of England much more to his liking. So much so, that at the Hampton Court Conference of 1604 he told the leaders of the English church that his preferred model was the status quo he found there: the monarch ruling the church through bishops. This was reinforced by his assumption that English Puritans were much like Scottish Presbyterians and he was not minded to accede to the demands of either of these groups. Indeed he declared that,

> *If you aim at a Scottish Presbytery, it agreeth as well with a monarchy, as God with the Devil…. No bishop, no king… I will make them conform or will harry them out of the land.*[6]

In 1599, James had written a letter to his heir, which was entitled *Basilikon Doron* (Greek: royal gift). In it he described the Scottish Reformation as: "inordinate" and "not proceeding from the prince's order".[7] This objection went to the heart of godly rule: *who was to exercise it?* Traditionally, it had been the prerogative of monarchs to articulate it and enforce it, guided by the church. But in the seventeenth century, increasingly influential groups of the saints were demanding that *they* should be the ones who played a major role in this. This would indeed be a semi-theocracy if implemented through existing parliamentary institutions and something of a real theocracy if leaders of churches or sects ever directly took the reins of political power. In 1604 such demands were only in their infancy and no one in their wildest dreams envisaged a semi-theocratic *republic* in which the godly exercised power without an intermediary monarch. But in 1649 they would have it. And James was correct in his analysis of the relationship between bishops and kings. The abolition of kingship followed only eleven years after the abolition of bishops in Scotland (1638) and less than three years after their abolition in England (1646).

In trying to roll back the tide of Presbyterianism in Scotland, in favour of episcopacy, James ran headlong into opposition from both the kirk and from the Scottish Parliament. In 1610 his commitment to the cause of preserving the authority of bishops was seen in the fact that the boundaries of the old pre-Reformation dioceses were re-established in Scotland. Then, in 1618, James' bishops forced his "Five Articles of Perth" through a General Assembly of the Scottish kirk. These included: kneeling during communion (which many reformed church members associated with Catholicism); confirmation by a bishop being necessary for membership of the church (which entrenched episcopal authority); and promoting the traditional celebrations of Christmas and Easter (the former a target for later Puritans). It took until 1621 for the Scottish Parliament to ratify these ordinances, so great was the opposition to them, and they remained both widely resented and resisted in Scotland.

James' efforts to force the Scottish kirk to conform had very limited success. His failure was partly because his accession to the English throne had shifted the centre of political gravity hundreds of miles to the south; the Scottish court – with its power and patronage – had moved to London. This left Scotland somewhat marginalized but it also provided a remarkable opportunity for the kirk and its supporting nobles to define a new Scottish identity that was increasingly out of sync with the monarchy south of the border. Godly rule by the Scottish saints might be possible after all, with a monarch who was an absentee landlord. And this in a Scotland which was increasingly considering itself as something of "a new Israel", chosen by God to implement his rule of holiness on earth.

THE IMPACT OF GODLY RULE ON SCOTLAND

The Reformation in Scotland had profound effects on Scottish society, including plans to establish a school in every parish and plans for major reforms of the Scottish university system. These reforms flowed from two main sources. The first was the background influence of "humanism", which in a contemporary context meant something very different from its meaning in the twenty-first century. In the sixteenth century the term was certainly not one that involved concentrating on human intellect and progress to the exclusion of divinity. Then, it involved the encouragement of education and careful exploration of both the scriptures and the world in order to better understand both. It was late-fifteenth- and early-sixteenth-century humanist scholars, for example, who had emphasized the study of the Bible in the original Greek and Hebrew texts. Although this critical approach to education soon became associated with challenges levelled against the controlling hand of the Catholic Church it was certainly not anti-spiritual or anti-Christian. The second input came from the desire to better acquaint people with the Bible and disciplined thinking in order to foster godly attitudes, hard work and opposition to practices and customs that were regarded as superstitions and without biblical foundation.

The level of success achieved was mixed. Although the *First Book of Discipline* (compiled by Knox and a committee of distinguished churchmen in 1561) envisaged a school in every parish, the financial demands of this ambitious plan soon proved unmanageable. Most rural areas lacked the finances or personnel to make such a scheme work. Things were better in towns, where so-called "burgh schools" grew out of a mixture of existing schools, reformed song schools (that had once supported the musical traditions of the Catholic Church) and new foundations, which developed into grammar schools that were supported by the local kirk or borough authorities, or better-off parents. Local kirk sessions kept a check on both the educational and the doctrinal standards evident in the teaching and learning. School masters often doubled up as the clerk within the local kirk.

The progress made was more noticeable in universities, but then the scale of the job was smaller there to start with due to there being fewer universities to reform. At Glasgow University languages and the sciences were now accorded the same status as philosophy, and the theology taught was brought into line with that of Geneva, since Andrew Melville, who became principal in 1574, had studied there. Separate subjects were to have their own dedicated staff and the study of metaphysics was abandoned, to be replaced with compulsory Greek. Aramaic, Hebrew, and Syriac were also taught. Numbers of students increased to a remarkable degree in line with the rising curriculum standards. The colleges at Aberdeen and St Andrews were similarly reformed and the University of Edinburgh was established in 1582 (from a tradition of public lectures given in the city since the 1540s). As a result of these reforms, Scottish universities became the equals of any in Europe. It was a remarkable achievement for godly rule.

The impact on artistic culture was no less profound but was very restrictive. The kirk frowned on many forms of plays and poetry unless they could be seen to be encouraging Christian piety (as defined by Calvinist reformed theology). Despite this there were still significant Scottish playwrights such as George Buchanan (1506–82); although his use of Latin meant that few appreciated him below the very well educated. It is noteworthy that no Scottish equivalent to the professional players and theatres that developed in England emerged, almost certainly as a result of the kirk's disapproval; although James VI arranged for a company of English players to erect a playhouse and perform in it in 1599. Poetry too should be devotional and instructive, although it was difficult to impose this on court society as evidenced by the so-called "Castalian Band" of poets in James VI's adult reign, who modelled themselves on French Renaissance poetry (*La Pléiade*). On a less exalted social level, older behaviours proved more difficult for the kirk to excise. Citizens in Aberdeen were criticized for dancing in the street with bells at weddings and at Yuletide in 1605; there is evidence for the survival of *Robin Hood* and May plays at Kelso in 1611; and Yuletide "guising" (going about in disguise during festivities) was recorded at Perth as late as 1634.[8]

In the same way, the activities of the kirk aimed at stopping other lower-class popular activities such as well dressing, seasonal bonfire festivities, penny weddings (paid for by money collected from the guests), and community dancing. These were under tremendous pressure by the late seventeenth century, although hard to entirely stamp out.

The church art of Scotland soon also fell victim to reformist Protestant iconoclasm. There was an almost complete destruction of medieval stained glass, sculpture, and paintings. This had a dramatic impact on the visual arts that was directly attributable to godly rule and mirrored the artistic tastes of Geneva. The only significant example of Scottish stained glass to survive is at St Magdalen Chapel of Cowgate, Edinburgh, where a window of four armorial roundels, dating from 1544, survives.[9] Some medieval wood carving has survived at King's College, Aberdeen and in Dunblane Cathedral, but little else escaped the comprehensive destruction organized by the kirk. This was part of a puritanical culture of artistic restraint that came to be a striking feature of the rule of the saints; although not everyone subscribed, as can be seen in the form of painted ceilings and walls in the private homes of burgesses and lairds.[10] Clearly, the visual austerity of the local church was not always adhered to in the secular sphere. Nevertheless, a "purified" visual style was still widespread.

Church architecture was transformed by the new visual culture. Established churches were adapted for the new reformed services and this was particularly clear in the placing of the pulpit centrally in the church, as a result of the emphasis on preaching and biblical exposition.[11] Church furnishings and ornaments were destroyed and new churches were constructed with no ornamentation and with a severe and simplistic rectangular layout. This rectangular layout can clearly be seen in the church of Greyfriars in Edinburgh, built between 1602 and 1620. Some others were constructed on a T-plan which grouped the largest number of parishioners as possible close to the centre of preaching. Examples include: Anstruther Easter, in Fife (built in 1634–44) and New Cumnock, in Ayreshire (built in 1657).

The reforms by the Scottish kirk had a massive impact on church music. The song schools were shut, church choirs were disbanded, and their books of music were destroyed. As part of this musical Reformation, organs were removed from churches and church music was replaced by congregational psalm singing. The settings for these psalms were simple by their nature since they had to be suitable for a congregation of mixed musical talents, rather than a trained and talented choir. The efforts of James VI to reverse this through the refoundation of song schools and choral singing failed in the end due to the determined opposition from the reformed kirk. By 1633 (in the reign of his son, Charles I) there were at least twenty-five of these refounded song schools, with polyphony incorporated into editions of the Psalter from 1625. But this revival did not last. In 1638 the victory of the Presbyterians in the National Covenant was reflected in a purge of church music. Polyphony was banned and in 1650 a new Psalter was produced in common metre, and without tunes. Godly rule would not be accompanied by complex or elaborate church music.

The impact of godly rule on women was complex. On one hand, the traditional view of women as limited in intellect and moral capacity (compared with men) continued and may even have intensified. On the other hand, the culture of a society of saints who were actively engaged in a personal search for holiness meant that women were, at the same time, required to learn and know the reformed catechism and instil godly standards in their families. This involved an ability to read and reflect on the Bible, albeit under the ultimate authority of a husband or the ministers of the kirk. This led to increased education for girls through the – albeit limited – system of parish schools but at a length and to a standard well below that of boys. Many girls were taught to read but not to write; a division of literacy that we find puzzling but which was also common in the medieval period in both genders. If the ability to sign ones name can be taken as an indicator of literacy then as late as the late seventeenth century female written-literacy among the serving class stood at no higher than 10 per cent and overall at about 15 per cent.[12] Women could not hold office in the kirk but if they were heads of households then some kirk sessions would allow them a vote in that capacity when it came to the calling of a new minister.

At the same time as these (limited) areas of progress that can be directly attributed to godly rule, that same outlook was also responsible for the increased criminalization of women through gender-specific prosecutions for scolding, prostitution and witchcraft. In all these areas it was women who felt the weight of cultural and legal prosecution more than men. These were areas where the male-orientated kirk and society could apply sanctions designed to curtail women, hold them more responsible than men for moral problems, and, in the case of witchcraft, to scapegoat them for wider social stresses.

In Scotland, it has been estimated that 60 per cent of all cases brought before the kirk sessions were about sex. This reflected a godly concern with righteous living and upright morals. Fathers were made to recognize their illegitimate children and adultery was punished. At the same time, accusations of promiscuity were investigated. Kirk sessions used excommunication and denial of baptism as a way of enforcing godly behaviour. In more difficult cases of immoral behaviour, and in cases where a solely religious sanction was not considered severe enough, they cooperated with local magistrates. The system copied that used in Geneva.

By the 1630s a new society with new cultural codes and outlook had emerged in Scotland. It was a society led by godly session ministers and lairds, and their influence was sufficient to resist counter-actions by a London-based royal court. Any attempt to enforce a different pattern of churchmanship or culture was going to lead to conflict and, in the late 1630s, such a conflict exploded, with far-reaching repercussions.

THE SOLEMN LEAGUE AND COVENANT, 1638

When, in 1637, King James' successor, Charles I, and the archbishop of Canterbury William Laud attempted to force the Church of Scotland to use the *Book of Common Prayer*, they sparked an armed insurrection. Most famously there was a riot in St Giles' Cathedral in Edinburgh. When the dean of the cathedral, James Hannay, began to read from the new Prayer Book, legend claims that a local woman, who was named Jenny Geddes, hurled her stool at his head and shouted: "Dinna say Mass in my lug!" ("Don't say Mass in my ear!"). There is some debate as to whether this woman actually existed or whether the rioters were local apprentices in women's clothing.[13] What is definite is that a riot followed and Jenny Geddes passed into legend. Today the cathedral contains two nineteenth-century plaques commemorating the dean and Jenny and, in 1992, forty Scotswomen presented St Giles' Cathedral with a bronze sculpture representing her three-legged stool. (Merilyn Smith's bronze stool now stands on a plinth not far from the cathedral's Welcome Desk; something of an irony given the "welcome" that Jenny gave to the new Prayer Book!)

Charles I's 1637 Prayer Book was not Catholic, but in the fevered atmosphere of the late 1630s – with feelings running high in England against a royal-sponsored attempt to impose High Church Arminianism on a church which had a significant number of Calvinist-inclined clergy and members, where distrust against royal "tyranny" was close to combustion, and in Scotland where reformed Presbyterianism had long resisted royal attempts to impose episcopal structures and control – the Prayer Book was the last straw. It was symbolic of a church liturgy and style that was anathema to many in the godly and reformed camps. As far as they were concerned it was "Catholic" and that was as a red rag to a bull.

In addition, Charles intended to finance his Scottish church reforms by taking back lands which had once been held by the Catholic Church in Scotland (the Act of Revocation). These had been sold off to private landowners during the Reformation. This plan alienated those whose landholdings were threatened. This then added to anger at Charles' ecclesiastical policy.

In February 1638 most of the Scottish nobility and one-third of the Scottish clergy signed the National Covenant which had the explicit aim of restoring the purity of the kirk. Such a restored purity would be Presbyterian in its nature and thoroughly and austerely reformed in its style and content of services. The Covenanters declared that they would only accept changes to the Scottish church which had been approved by the General Assembly of the kirk. The General Assembly then declared episcopacy abolished.

Composed by Alexander Argyll Henderson, who in 1639 became one of the ministers at St Giles', and by Archibald Johnston of Wariston, who was a member of the congregation at St Giles', the Covenant continued the tradition of revolt. Parchment copies of the document were produced to be circulated for signature in every burgh and parish across Scotland.

The idea of the Scottish Covenant could trace its roots back to the sixteenth-century agitation against the rule of Mary, Queen of Scots. It was then that George Buchanan, a Gaelic scholar from Killearn, and one of Europe's most talented Renaissance thinkers, asserted that the ancient Gaelic kings of Scotland had not been divinely appointed. Rather, they had been elected. This meant that they were subject to the law of Scotland and not above it. This opened up a radical possibility: if a monarch broke their "contract" with the Scottish people (in a way that caused them to be regarded as a tyrant) then it would be legally acceptable to depose that monarch.

With many Scots signing the National Covenant, Charles I had lost control north of the border. The Covenanters would effectively serve as the government of Scotland for nearly a decade, although over time they would divide into different groups. And they would send military support to the Parliamentarians during the Civil Wars south of the border. The Scottish tradition of godly rule was to have profound repercussions across Britain.

THE BISHOPS' WARS, 1639 AND 1640

The Covenanters issued orders across Scotland authorizing recruiting and training for war. At the same time an appeal called on Protestant Scots living abroad (where many served as mercenaries) to return and fight for the Covenant. Among the many who responded was Alexander Leslie, who was appointed as the commander of the Covenanter forces.

Charles' responses to the revolt in Scotland only served to underscore his weakness. The first army he sent north was so inadequate and poorly equipped and led that it made little impact. Those royal troops that did enter Scotland were soon driven back by the Covenanters. As a result, in June 1639 Charles negotiated the Treaty of Berwick. On one side the Covenanters demanded that the king would ratify all acts of the Glasgow Assembly that had followed the signing of the Covenant and this included the abolition of episcopacy, the acceptance that all church matters in Scotland would be settled at the General Assembly of the Kirk, and that all civil grievances would be settled in the Scottish Parliament. Also, all royal forces would withdraw from Scotland and those Scottish bishops who had attempted to implement Charles' policy would be returned to Scotland for punishment. Charles was prepared to allow church matters to be decided by the General Assembly but refused to accept the acts passed at the Glasgow Assembly. The Covenanters were aware they were not as militarily strong as they appeared and what emerged was a compromise by which Charles agreed to authorize a General Assembly of the kirk at Edinburgh in August. This would be followed by a calling of the Scottish Parliament to debate the other issues. In addition, both sides agreed to disband their armies. The most controversial issues were only vaguely addressed and not resolved.

In 1640 King Charles attempted a second campaign against the Scots, but once again the army he raised was inadequate and he was short of money. He reluctantly called an English Parliament which then refused to vote him funds since many MPs sympathized with the Scots and opposed Charles' church policies and his style of royal government. In desperation, the king appealed to Spain for a loan and the queen appealed to her brother, the king of France, and to the pope. These appeals to Catholic powers did little to enhance Charles' Protestant credentials at home.

The Covenanters quickly mobilized their armies and suppressed Royalist clans in the Highlands. While this was happening, the main

Covenanter army – led by General Leslie – marched into England. They avoided English defences on the border and swiftly advanced toward Newcastle. At the Battle of Newburn, in August 1640, the English were defeated. Leslie's artillery units were better led (by Alexander Hamilton, who had served under the great Protestant hero Gustavus Adolphus of Sweden on the Continent) and his troops were better disciplined. The English abandoned Newcastle to the Covenanter army and fell back to Durham.

The king was forced to negotiate a truce at Ripon which allowed the Scots to occupy Northumberland and Durham and to be paid £850 a day from the English government to cover their expenses. As if this was not enough, the Scots were to be reimbursed for what they had paid to prosecute the war. For Charles it was a disaster.

The Second Bishops' War was finally concluded by the Treaty of London in August 1641. The Scots commissioners sent there to negotiate were welcomed by English godly sympathizers. Charles was forced to accept the end of episcopacy in Scotland, no punishment of those who signed the Covenant, the prosecution of Scottish Royalist bishops in Scotland, the return of any Scottish goods captured during the war, and the payment to the Scots of £300,000 as compensation for the wars. The English Parliament described this as "brotherly assistance", which revealed where their sympathies lay.[14]

At the same time, Charles was forced to summon what would later be known as the "Long Parliament" to ratify the treaty and because he was seriously short of money. What had started as a local conflict over the nature of godly rule in Scotland was about to engross the rest of the British Isles. For the kirk, God was more king in Scotland in 1640 than Charles; and the question of who was really in control of the whole country was about to explode on to a wider stage.

4

A Godly War?

The victory of the Scots over King Charles I in the Bishops'
Wars left Charles seriously short of money. As a result, he could
no longer persist with his policy of ruling without Parliament
so in November 1640 he very reluctantly called one. It was the
second time that year[1] that he had been forced to recall Parliament
in the hope of persuading it to grant him much needed money.
This second "Long Parliament" was to become embroiled in the
accelerated move toward godly rule – as defined by those who
were dissatisfied with current religious policies.

THE LONG PARLIAMENT AND THE FIRST STEPS
TOWARD GODLY RULE

Called the "Long Parliament" because it continued to sit through
the First and Second Civil Wars, it sat until December 1648, when
it was purged by the army. This purged Parliament (or as it became
known the "Rump" of the Long Parliament) was then finally
expelled by Cromwell in April 1653, as the country drifted into
a personal rule by the new Lord Protector. Although sidelined,
the Long Parliament was reinstated in February 1660, after the
death of Cromwell and the collapse of the Protectorate, and it
was not formally dissolved until March 1660, shortly before the
Restoration of Charles II.

John Pym led the attack on the king in the new Parliament,
although he was careful to attack the king's advisers first, rather
than the king himself. That would follow in due course. During
1641 a number of laws were passed to ensure that a monarch could

never again rule without Parliament: the Court of Star Chamber was abolished (see Chapter 2); ship-money and forced loans (used by Charles to raise money without calling a Parliament) were also abolished; the Triennial Act ensured that Parliament would be called at least once every three years.

What concerns us especially, however, are the actions that ran according to the Puritan agenda. Archbishop Laud was the *bête noire* of the Puritan opposition in Parliament and he was denounced and impeached within just a few weeks of the Long Parliament starting its meetings. He would eventually be executed in 1645. A bill for the abolition of episcopacy was introduced to the Long Parliament in May 1641 and episcopacy was finally abolished in October 1646. It had fallen foul of both the Independents who considered it corrupt and "popish", and also of the Presbyterians, who wanted their own system of church government brought in to replace it. Despite this, Charles refused to compromise in his support for episcopacy ("no bishop, no king" King James had said) and was still arguing for it as late as 1648 during the last attempt at a negotiated settlement between him and Parliament. But episcopacy was doomed (at least in the short term) as it was considered incompatible with godly churchmanship and was compromised by how it had been used to bolster High Church Arminianism in England and (with less success) in Scotland. During the years of the Commonwealth (1649–53 and 1659–60) and Protectorate (1653–59) most of the deposed bishops lived quietly in retirement and kept their heads down. At the same time many other clergy, who had held office under the old order, were prepared to serve the new order as a way of keeping a church job (a "benefice"). Only a minority refused to acknowledge the new church (this was especially so during the Interregnum, 1649–60) and these often sought a post with Royalist families as private chaplains, while some became schoolmasters or private tutors.

Once the country collapsed into civil conflict the pace of godly change would pick up as the saints increasingly took hold of the levers of power, even when they could not agree among themselves about exactly what course to take.

The drift to the First Civil War

The matter that finally led to the outbreak of the Civil Wars between Charles and Parliament was the question of which of them should control the army raised to defeat the Irish Uprising of 1641. We will return to this uprising in Chapter 6 but suffice it to say at this point that the matter was crucial since whoever did assume command would find themselves in charge of a force sufficient to overawe their rivals in England, in addition to deploying that army in Ireland.

Charles refused to allow Parliament's Militia Bill to become law. This is because it would have given Parliament control over the army and navy. He then went on to provoke Parliament still further, in January 1642, when he attempted to arrest five MPs whom he regarded as the main source of opposition to him. In the growing unrest, Charles and the royal family left London. In response, Parliament ratcheted up the crisis when it decreed that its decisions were legally binding *without* royal assent. In short, it could rule without the agreement of the monarch; a dramatic step. Civil War broke out in August of 1642. It was a conflict which further radicalized those who believed that the time had finally come to implement a programme of Bible-based reform in Britain. They were not dominant at first, since many of the king's opponents were far less radical, but the situation was to escalate as the war continued and as radicals came increasingly to the fore.

On the other hand, the king did all he could to try to undermine Parliament's authority, when he summoned an alternative Parliament to meet with him at Oxford. About one-third of the MPs and most of the House of Lords left Westminster to join him there in 1643. But it was never to provide a truly viable alternative to the group meeting in Westminster and, from 1645 onwards, special (so-called "recruiter") elections were held in order to make up the numbers of MPs at Westminster.

As the war progressed, Parliament became increasingly divided into two broad factions. On one hand were the "Presbyterians", who hoped for a negotiated settlement with the king. On the other hand, were the "Independents" who increasingly came to believe that only a military victory would resolve the crisis. As the conflict escalated, all attempts at negotiation with the king failed and, since neither Parliamentarians nor Royalists seemed capable of landing a knockout blow, neither could achieve a decisive victory. Finally, in December 1643, Parliament formed an alliance with the Scottish Covenanters. There had always been a significant amount of common ground between them, rooted in their objections to the High Church Arminianism of the king and his bishops. At first this alliance looked like it would tip the balance in favour of Parliament. However, the intervention of the Scots (who had their own agenda) only served to aggravate the divisions which already existed *between* the English Parliamentarians.

In 1645, the Independent faction within Parliament was successful in its demands for a radical overhaul of the Parliamentary army. The result – the efficient and effective New Model Army – then went on to decisively defeat the Royalists. This brought to an end the First Civil War. In 1646, facing defeat, King Charles surrendered to the Scots rather than to the forces of Parliament. Events quickly revealed that he intended to divide his enemies; but the Scots eventually handed him over to Parliament for the sum of £400,000. Then, at the end of December 1647, most of the Scottish army marched north and crossed back across the river Tweed. The king's Scottish guards were replaced by English Parliamentarian guards and he was now a prisoner of Parliament.

The fault-lines that Charles had worked on enlarging (in the hope of breaking up the coalition against him) centred on the thorny issue of the kind of church that should be established in the nation. Although the conflict had started through a combination of political, constitutional and religious factors, it would be the nature of godly rule that would become the epicentre of the next earthquake. And in this upheaval the saints were anything but united.

Godly rule during the Civil Wars:
Parliament and a struggle for the soul
of the nation

What we might call the "Peace party" (in favour of a negotiated settlement) finally became defined as the "Presbyterian" group in Parliament. Confusingly, the members of this group were not necessarily Presbyterian with regard to church organization. What united them was a willingness to draw closer to Parliament's Scottish allies since the Scots were willing to negotiate with the king. The Scots were prepared to do this as they hoped that a Presbyterian religious settlement could be achieved in England that mirrored that which had emerged in Scotland (especially after the Second Bishops' War). This willingness to negotiate then came to be an identifier of the group, with some being "Political Presbyterians" rather than religious ones.

This Presbyterian faction was opposed in Parliament by the "War party" of the Independents, and then later by the leaders and spokesmen of the New Model Army.

There were mixed reasons why MPs found themselves in one camp or the other, but a significant one lay in the matter of what form the church should take. This was not entirely surprising since the Presbyterians favoured a national church system based on a Scottish-style Presbyterian model. While this was far from what Charles wanted, there were at least points of contact with him since it still envisaged a national system with an established hierarchy of sorts. As a consequence, the English Presbyterians were inclined toward negotiation with the king; and the Scots even more so since they felt that their settlement in Scotland was fairly secure and so felt more confident in their negotiations over wider issues. In contrast, the Independents argued for a greater separation of church and state and a far greater degree of autonomy for local congregations. They were far less certain of achieving any such accommodation with Charles and, if they failed, then it would be his system that would be directly imposed on them in England. As the war progressed, this group became increasingly radicalized; and behind them stood the even more radical demands of the

Separatists – outside of Parliament and also well represented in the New Model Army.

Few MPs consistently supported one side or the other and we should not think of these groups as anything like formal political "parties". And there were also those who sought to bridge the gap between the War and Peace parties but who were increasingly squeezed out as positions polarized.

THE SOLEMN LEAGUE AND COVENANT
AND ITS BREAKDOWN

In order to tip the fighting balance in the war, the Long Parliament negotiated an alliance with Scotland. This was because by 1643 there was a real danger that the Royalists might win the war. This resulted in the Solemn League and Covenant, of September 1643, being agreed between both Houses of Parliament and the Scottish commissioners who had been sent south to negotiate. By this agreement Parliament promised to reform the Church of England along Presbyterian lines in exchange for military assistance.

In January 1644 the Army of the Covenant marched into England to fight Charles. It was a game changer and tipped the advantage heavily toward Parliament. In return, Parliament ordered that the Covenant was to be agreed by every Englishman who was over the age of eighteen. The names of any who refused to sign it were to be sent to Parliament. Clearly, the Scots' assistance was coming at a price. To the heirs of John Knox it seemed that a reformed nation of the two kingdoms was now a real certainty. To those who had a different view of how the church should look there was now real alarm. Signing the Covenant became mandatory for all who held any Parliamentary command. This lasted until 1648, when the agreement broke down and Charles made his own alliance with the Scots forces.

The reforms to the English church were discussed at the Westminster Assembly, which first met in July 1643 in the Henry VII Chapel in Westminster Abbey. It comprised ten members of the House of Lords and thirty members of the House of Commons, along with 120 clergymen (often referred to as "divines"). They came from across England and Wales and twelve Scottish commissioners also attended the Assembly.

With the signing of the Solemn League and Covenant between Parliament and the Covenanters in September 1643, its role was to plan the reform of church government and to consider the unification of the church in England and Scotland. These discussions continued throughout 1643–46. Things did not go well, as Presbyterianism was strongly opposed by Independent ministers and was totally unacceptable to Separatist Baptists, and the like, who wanted toleration of their congregations. John Milton commented that, "New presbyter is but old priest writ large."[2] For Milton the proposed new system threatened to overshadow both secular authorities *and* individual consciences. It looked as if freedom of belief in England was about to fall under the control of the Presbyterian sessions. This did not seem much of an advance from priestly control as exercised by Catholicism or High Church Arminian beliefs and practices as enforced by Archbishop Laud, his bishops and the Star Chamber. On reflection, it seems that Milton overstated the case. Presbyterian ministers in Scotland were far more controlled by the laity in their congregations than Milton suggested; they were called by the local church and had their performance regularly assessed by the members of the parish; ministers had to cooperate with lay elders who outnumbered them in the meetings of those who oversaw the running of the sessions.[3] They certainly were not priests whose role put them beyond contradiction. But one could understand his concern at the imposition of a new national system of church government.

In the end the Scottish Covenanters were deeply disappointed by the limited compromise that eventually emerged. In March 1646 a decision was finally reached to set up a *limited* Presbyterian system in England. This church system would be subordinate to Parliament. It would be made to conform to "the word of God", a rather imprecise term of reference; furthermore leading Parliamentarians called for allowing leeway for those of "tender consciences" who had difficulty with the proposed system.[4] This all gave room for much more interpretation of how the system would work than the Scots had envisaged. Even this limited system did not take off and Presbyterianism did not seriously expand beyond London and the South East; along with pockets in Lancashire, Cheshire and Derbyshire.

While this system was emerging (or rather failing to do so) the Assembly also discussed the form of services and the nature of belief that should be promulgated. In October 1644 a *Directory of Worship* was published which was intended to replace the *Book of Common Prayer*, which had been abolished early in 1645. The final *Westminster Confession of Faith*, with scriptural proofs of its principles, was approved by both Houses of Parliament in April 1647. This was then followed by the General Assembly of the Scottish kirk in August. Alongside it were published two catechisms (statements of belief) and a document called the *Form of Presbyterial Church-Government*, which were approved by Parliament in November 1647. This latter document presented a summary of the principles of the reformed doctrines that were now being articulated. The Scots' General Assembly approved the catechisms in July 1648 and they went on to be ratified by the Scottish Parliament, alongside the Confession of Faith, in February 1649. By that time, however, the Presbyterian plan had fallen apart in England and these legal ratifications were falling well behind the curve of events.

In 1648, King Charles (frustrated at his continued imprisonment since 1647 in the custody of the New Model Army, and with negotiations for a settlement going nowhere) cut a deal with a section of the Scottish Covenanter movement. From his prison in Carisbrooke Castle on the Isle of Wight, he turned again to the Scots. Some of the members of the Covenanters' General Assembly signed a secret treaty with him in December 1647. This was called "The Engagement" and by it Charles promised that he would support the establishment of Presbyterianism in England for a period of three years, in return for military support from the Covenanters. For those in support of the treaty it seemed to offer the possibility of kick-starting the process of creating a national church, since the outcome of the Westminster Assembly had lacked the thorough-going rigour that Covenanters had hoped for.

Not all among the Covenanters agreed with the treaty that had been agreed with the king. Indeed, a large group, known as the "kirk party", opposed it because Charles refused to take the Covenant personally. This hardly gave cause for confidence in his commitment to the project. In addition, they feared he would not honour the treaty if he was restored to power. There was good reason for these reservations since Charles was really committed to the restoration of the bishops.[5] Despite this, the "Engagers" defeated the kirk party in a skirmish at Mauchline Muir; they went on to organize an army to march into England during the Second Civil War (1648–49).

The most experienced Scots Generals – Lord Leven and David Leslie – refused to lead this army as they were not convinced by the strategy of the Engagers. As a consequence, the command of the invading force was given to the Duke of Hamilton, who lacked their military experience. As it was, Cromwell defeated the Scots at the Battle of Preston in August 1648, and Charles I was executed in 1649.

The Westminster Assembly continued to sit but its great days were over. It was never formally dissolved; however, it ceased to exist once Cromwell expelled the members of the "Rump Parliament" in 1653. The reforms of the Church of England that had been partially implemented by the Westminster Assembly remained in force throughout the Commonwealth and Protectorate but during this time there was much that undermined this system as increasing numbers of Separatist congregations sprang up in the wake of the sweeping away of both royal and episcopal power. Its decisions were finally revoked at the Restoration in 1660.

After the execution of Charles I in January 1649, the leaders of the Scottish kirk persuaded his son, Charles II, to accept the Solemn League and Covenant by the Treaty of Breda (1650). This led to the Third Civil War. This Presbyterian alliance was unpopular with Anglican Royalists and was clearly only made by Charles II due to his desperate need for significant military allies. The defeat of the Royalist-Scots alliance at the Battle of Worcester in September 1651 finally put an end to all attempts to impose Presbyterianism on England. It was already fatally weakened because attempts by the Presbyterian "Peace party" had already seriously alienated the New Model Army (which they had attempted to disband and, further, they had ignored the soldiers' demands for outstanding pay and the settlement of other grievances) which had finally taken action to drive them out of Parliament in Pride's purge of December 1648.

AN ARMY OF SAINTS?

Parliament's armies were originally recruited from regional associations but this led to problems as these soldiers were often reluctant to campaign away from their local areas. The answer was the creation of the New Model Army. The old, and ineffective, army high command was swept away and Thomas Fairfax was appointed captain-general and commander-in-chief of the new army in January 1645. Oliver Cromwell was officially appointed lieutenant-general of horse (and second-in-command of the army) in June 1645.

The new force soon proved its worth. It defeated the Royalists at the Battle of Naseby, in June 1645, and brought the First Civil War to a close in 1646. It soon became a force for change that outpaced that planned by more conservative Members of Parliament. Indeed, many of its officers and men would soon show themselves more radical than their own commanders. To the former, the army offered the possibility of imposing a really radical settlement on the nation. As we shall see, those within it such as the Levellers and Fifth Monarchy Men were thoroughly radicalized and became, for a while, the source of the most revolutionary proposals. Many regarded themselves as "saints in arms" and the ones who could force a godly settlement on the nation which offered hope of real social change. They were to be disappointed – but that is to get ahead of our story.

As the war progressed, a significant number of those on the Parliamentary side came to explicitly view themselves as God's agents and to note "how God infuses and inflames into the hearts of his people, to show themselves ready and cheerful to come forth to help the Lord…"[6] In the same way, Cromwell, described the Parliamentary side at the 1644 Battle of Marston Moor as, "the godly party". This was enhanced by the novel way (in the context of the 1640s) by which Cromwell recruited and promoted on the basis of religious qualities and expertise, rather than social class. As Edward Montagu, earl of Manchester, disapprovingly commented, "he [Cromwell] would give them the title of godly, precious men" and thought that the work of the war should not rely on the Scots or military prowess but, instead, on "the godly to this purpose".[7] Indeed, so strong a sense of religious identity did this encourage, that Richard Baxter (a preacher with some Presbyterian sympathies who later opposed the growth of what he regarded as "sects" within the Parliamentary army), later claimed that he had been offered the post of chaplain to the officers of Cromwell's Eastern Association because they planned to constitute themselves as a "gathered church".[8] He later regretted not taking up the post as he had lost an opportunity, as he saw it, to oppose republican sectaries.[9] The outlook of these officers was not unique. It was recorded at the time that "the Saints should have the praises of God in their mouths and a two-edged sword in their hands."[10] The distinctive godly character of such units was remarked on at the time by the Parliamentary newspaper *Special Passages*.[11] These men were the ones described by Cromwell, in 1643, as the "plain russet-coated captain that knows what he fights for, and loves what he knows".[12]

Others – such as the earl of Manchester and Richard Baxter – were less happy. As well as the threat to the class system, there was the mounting evidence that many of these were religious radicals and the charge of "Anabaptist" was levelled at them. To which Cromwell replied that they were simply, "honest men, such as fear God",[13] which rather ducked the question of their theology! The reality was that many of them undoubtedly were Baptist Separatists (though they would have resisted the tainted label "Anabaptist"). Cromwell was forced to admit as much when two army officers were arrested and disciplined, in 1644, for Baptist sympathies by a senior Parliamentary officer who was Presbyterian in outlook. To which Cromwell asserted that it did not matter that they were "Anabaptists", what mattered was their willingness to serve the cause.[14]

In time, though, Cromwell was to discover that some of these men had political minds of their own and political radicalism accompanied their religious radicalism. To start with, however, their political activism was in line with his own thinking. It was the officers of the New Model Army who (after the king's defeat in the First Civil War) presented the *Heads of the Proposals* to King Charles in the summer of 1647, independently of Parliament, as a basis for a constitutional settlement. These were radical but constructive demands: Royalists would be banned from public office for five years; the use of the *Book of Common Prayer* would no longer be mandatory; episcopacy could survive but with the power of bishops much reduced; an end to enforcement of church attendance; freedom to hold religious meetings outside of the established church; the Solemn League and Covenant to be revoked; Parliament would set a date for its own termination and there would then be biennial elections; Parliament would appoint state officials and military officers for the next ten years. These negotiations with Charles failed.

Over time the radicalism grew and then the army leadership became alarmed at its own men. The more radical members of the army rank and file soon decided that their military leaders (such as Oliver Cromwell and Henry Ireton) lacked sufficient radicalism and in the Putney Debates of 28 October to 11 November 1647, the most radical of these ideas were debated with the high command of the army (see chapter 7). These demands – articulating the views of regimental representatives, called "Agitators" or "Adjutators", and later those of the "Levellers"– continued to be published in documents called *Agreements of the People*, issued between October 1647 and May 1649.

GOD'S "MERCIES" REVEALED

With the collapse of royal authority and buoyed by Parliamentary victories, there was an understandable tendency for the saints to interpret these successes as signs of divine approval, often termed "mercies". This guided Cromwell's thinking. The victory at Marston Moor (1644) revealed "a great favour from the Lord" to "the godly party";[15] those at Islip and Bletchingdon (1645) were due to "the mercy of God" and Cromwell commented that, "God is not enough owned. We look too much to men and visible helps";[16] of the victory at Naseby (1645) he wrote that, "this is none other than the hand of God";[17] of the victory ("mercy") at Long Sutton he asked, "is it not to see the face of God!"[18]

The understandable tendency to view success as signs of God's Providence had a way of driving events forward and countering any objections. It fostered the rather circular argument: if this is how things are developing, then this must be how God is leading us, and this must be God's will. When combined with an intense sense of personal "election" (to salvation) and a belief in the heavenly origins of dreams and visions and revelations, this both gave assurance of the rightness of the cause and tended to ensure that decision-making was dominated by those who believed that they had a direct insight into the will of God. Manchester remarked that Cromwell's troops contained those "that call themselves the godly" and included some who claimed to have seen visions and received revelations from God.[19] Without getting into a debate over whether they had or not (impossible to know from our current perspective) this certainly gave opportunities to the naturally enthusiastic, the self-confident, and the fanatical, alongside the insightful and reflective, in a way that drove radicalism forward.

GODLY RULE ON THE GROUND: THE IMPACT ON ORDINARY PEOPLE

Those who wanted a spiritual transformation in the nation found that not everyone was sympathetic to their aims. There remained much support, throughout all classes of society, for the old Prayer Book liturgy which people had grown up with. The *Book of Common Prayer* continued to be used in private services, even if now frowned on in regular church use. At the same time, episcopalian tracts continued to be published and disseminated in defence of the traditional church structures.

However, whenever the most zealous units of the New Model Army were active in an area these practices, alongside any other practices considered sinful, came under attack. The most famous examples of such godly rule in action had to wait until the 1650s but had already started during the wars. For example, at Peterborough in 1643, the cathedral pulpit and organ were destroyed; soldiers dressed in looted surplices and danced in the aisles; crucifixes were pulled down and Prayer Books destroyed. At Lincoln Cathedral elaborate carvings were defaced and horses stabled in the church. Parliamentary cavalry similarly stabled their horses in Bristol Cathedral. In 1644, at Cambridge, the *Book of Common Prayer* was once more the target as were any church carvings considered idolatrous imagery. That same year, Cromwell, hand on his sword, disrupted the choir-led service at Ely. These were typical targets of aggression by the godly: the use of the *Book of Common Prayer*, religious images; the use of organs in church services; choirs used in church services. The latter did not equate with a hatred of music; instead it was opposition to its use in church. As far as they were concerned all these features were aspects of "popery".

The case for a godly republic

After the bitterly fought Second Civil War, in 1648, radical New Model Army officers forcibly purged Parliament of those they considered the king's supporters that December and brought about Charles I's trial and execution in January 1649, for inflicting a second war upon the country. This led to the establishment of a republican Commonwealth in England from 1649–53 and after that a Protectorate, which lasted until the death of Oliver Cromwell and then the end of his son's short period of rule.

As well as being a constitutional earthquake, this was a crucial step in the pursuit of godly rule and it differentiated this period of history from previous Christian government. For, with the death of the king and the proclamation of a republic, a time of experimentation was launched in which different groups of the saints would combine and compete for the role of deciding just what godly rule meant in practice. This was in contrast with the previous political arrangements whereby monarchs assumed that they were the ones who decided the will of God when it came to government and, inasmuch as they delegated it to others (i.e. to Parliament), it was with the proviso that they, the monarchs, were the fount of its authority and only they, in turn, could provide this legitimacy because they alone were God's anointed. With the death of "God's anointed" the question of authority was up for grabs and – amid the raw power politics of factions within Parliament and the army – the views of the gathered churches, as well as of those claiming personal prophetic authority, became part of the complex mix of factors deciding policy.

There had been hints of this possibility from the very start of the wars for some key players. As early as 1642, Cromwell (while recruiting at Huntingdon) had threatened that if he met the king in combat then he would fire his pistol at him as at any other opponent.[20] For those who later recalled this treasonable statement it was clear that for Cromwell "the liberty of the gospel" (however that was defined) was more important than monarchy.[21] The seeds of republicanism lay dormant in such an attitude even if, at the time, it merely meant opposition to a *particular king* who was behaving in a *particular way*, and not to monarchy in general.

By the winter of 1648–49 frustration over negotiating any settlement with the king that he would adhere to, combined with divisions within Parliament, the radicalism of the army and the sense that God's Providence was leading a certain way, convinced key members of the Parliamentary leadership that the execution of Charles and the establishment of a republic was the only way to break with the past. The fact that all the evidence suggested (and still does) that this lacked popular support cut no ice with those who now had a sense that they were walking a path preordained by God. A contemporary informant who knew those who were debating the death of the king claimed that they saw themselves "called to great services" [by God] and so were "excused from the common rules of morality", since they saw a precedent in the form of Old Testament characters, as "such were the practices of Ehud [who killed the Moabite king, Eglon[22]] and Jael [who killed Sisera, the commander of the Canaanite army of King Jabin of Hazor[23]]..."[24]

Radicalism had a logic and dynamic of its own which propelled it forward. It was in such an intense atmosphere that the Army Council debated the claim of one, Elizabeth Poole, who in December 1648 and January 1649 claimed to have received visions from God that at once assured God's support for the role of the army in saving the nation, *but* also asserted that the king should be imprisoned but not executed. That the Army Council took time on two occasions to meet with her and discuss her "visions" indicates both the doubts they were experiencing as they contemplated the execution of Charles and also the role that visions and revelations could play in government deliberations by 1649.[25] But Charles I *was* executed and a year later, in 1650, Cromwell was to describe it as "the glorious actings of God".[26] One account claims that Cromwell and the other regicides were together in a prayer-meeting when Charles was executed, for they saw themselves as the instruments of God's will.

On 17 March, 1649 the Rump Parliament passed a momentous Act which abolished the monarchy. Just two days later they passed an Act which abolished the House of Lords. Then, on 19 May 1649, they passed an Act which declared that England was now a republican Commonwealth.

The pressing question now was how would the godly discern the will of God? For now that Charles was dead, only God was King.

5

Hunting Down the Enemies of God

Duging the Civil Wars, British society was in turmoil. Recent research has, for example, made it clear how high the casualty figures in the conflict were. Comparisons of the Civil Wars with the two World Wars of the twentieth century have produced suggested figures for war-attributed deaths (as percentages of the entire British population) of 11.5 per cent for the Civil Wars, 3.04 per cent for the First World War and 0.64 per cent for the Second World War.[1] These make the impact on the British population of these seventeenth-century wars "greater than any other conflict in British history".[2] Other assessments, though lower, are still shocking, suggesting war-related deaths of about 3.6 per cent of the population; compared with a First World War figure of around 2.6 per cent of the population.[3] These figures do not take into account the catastrophic figures for Ireland. The key point is that even the lowest estimates reveal the enormity of the conflict; the suffering was immense.

It is not surprising, therefore, to discover that in such a period of political, religious, social and economic upheaval, and dislocation, many people sought scapegoats for the crisis that was tearing the country apart. In the context of the seventeenth century there would inevitably be a spiritual character to these attempts to discern the causes of distress. And, at a time when there was an intense struggle going on to establish the "correct" Christian character of the nation, there was a strong tendency to categorize enemies as agents of the Devil. In the case of Catholics and those regarded as "popish sympathizers" these would frequently be labelled by the godly as "Antichrist" or his allies, in an attempt to apply biblical terms of condemnation to contemporary contexts. As the godly fell out among themselves, in the 1650s, this term would also be applied to others of a similar – but for various reasons unacceptable – outlook among the saints.

However, if some enemies could be categorized as Antichrist's allies, it is not surprising that some others might be regarded as being directly in league with the Devil. These particular enemies were not acting in collaboration with an appointee of the Devil (i.e. Antichrist), rather they were in a direct personal relationship with the Devil himself and were workers of evil in the world. These were "witches". And in a period of time when many people believed in magic and the idea that spells and incantations might have effects on the life, health, and experiences of others, such people were greatly to be feared. They were the Devil's answer to the godly: committed, active, and at work in the world, but for evil rather than for good. As Britain became increasingly polarized in the 1640s it is small wonder that the single largest British witch hunt occurred as civil conflict escalated and as the ascendancy of the godly occurred. It was an aspect of godly rule that arose from the combination of a particular puritanical mindset with the peculiar circumstances of mid-seventeenth-century Britain. For, to some of those who considered themselves the representatives of the kingdom of God, the time had come to seek out, confront, and destroy those who had taken up spiritual arms against God and his saints, and who were active agents of the Devil.

This chapter examines the explosion of witch hunting in the 1640s, which accompanied the upheaval of the British Civil Wars. While this was part of a European trend in witch hunting that lasted from c.1450–1750 (resulting in between 30,000 and 50,000 executions across Europe),[4] the surge in violence in this decade in East Anglia was truly remarkable. It has been calculated that the astonishingly high number of 60 per cent of all those (usually women) executed for witchcraft in Britain between 1550 and 1751 died between 1644 and 1646.[5] Most of these were due to the activities of "Witchfinder General" Matthew Hopkins, and his associate, John Stearne, in East Anglia.[6] However, the surge (at a much lower level) extended beyond this period. In Scotland it lasted until 1727 and was only officially stopped across Great Britain in 1735.[7] It spread to New England (1647–63) and broke out again in North America, at Salem, Massachusetts, in 1692–93. In these North American examples, those who drove the hunts came from Puritan communities whose outlook mirrored that found in Britain and who used methods pioneered by the East Anglian witch hunters of the 1640s.

THE WITCH HUNTING PHENOMENON IN THE EARLY MODERN PERIOD

Despite a lot of assumptions to the contrary, witch hunting was not a medieval occupation. When, in 1969, the historian Hugh Trevor-Roper published his classic study, *The European Witch-Craze of the Sixteenth and Seventeenth Centuries*,[8] its title exemplified the findings of historians that this was indeed a product of a very particular set of circumstances, in a specific time period. While there *were* medieval examples of witch hunting, its intensity occurred in what historians describe as the "Early Modern Period" and the greatest numbers occurred in the seventeenth century (ironically as a more scientific understanding of the world was slowly emerging).

The Christian church inherited both Roman and Germanic anxieties about the use of malevolent (*maleficent*) magic. In addition, ancient folklore beliefs, found in Europe, about night-flying evildoers, who inflict suffering on others by supernatural means, are common to a wide range of cultures across the world. These beliefs had a particular appeal as a way by which misfortune, disease, and disaster might be explained in a pre-scientific world. To this existing folklore, much later Christians added the belief that such people joined with the Devil in a pact which included worshipping him and in taking part in "*sabbats*" whose activities were parodies of the Christian liturgy.

It should be added at this point that the New Testament has very little to say about witches and witchcraft,[9] and it was certainly not a preoccupation in the Christian scriptures. Seventeenth-century believers would have been more aware of it from the Old Testament, where they would have found twelve uses of the term. As well as general condemnations of the practice, without much further detail, they would most notably have known it from 1 Samuel 28, where King Saul visited a woman, who brought up the prophet Samuel from the dead so Saul could consult with him (and Saul was condemned for this). The main additional detail that they would have been aware of was the association of witches with "familiar spirits" mentioned in 1 Samuel 28:7, 2 Kings 21:6, and 2 Chronicles 33:6, which suggested a relationship with a demonic character.

Given this limited biblical focus on witchcraft it is not surprising that while magic, spells, and sorcery were condemned in some medieval law codes, the hunt for witches was not a major preoccupation of the church. Indeed, St Augustine suggested that witchcraft principally consisted of idolatry and illusion used to mislead others. This indicated that the sin lay in the will of the person involved, not in their ability to actually work magic. Indeed, the medieval text *Canon Episcopi* (included in canon law from the 1140s and probably originating in the tenth century) condemned those (women in the text) who believed that they could fly through the night in the service of the pagan goddess Diana. It went on to state that these were delusional dreams, sent by the Devil, and that it was a heretical belief to believe that these activities actually occurred. The text concluded by explicitly condemning those who thought it was possible to change their form (a common accusation in later witch trials). Consequently, it actually condemned the belief in the reality of witchcraft. This outlook influenced church thinking until the later medieval period when there was a dramatic revision of outlook with regard to the perceived reality of witchcraft.[10]

Outlooks began to change in the later fourteenth century, when the idea started to grow that witchcraft might be a reality rather than a heretical illusion. This trend accelerated in the fifteenth century when witch hunts occurred in Savoy and in Switzerland. By the early sixteenth century about five hundred of these trials had occurred. This was in sharp contrast to the lack of witch hunting activities earlier in the Middle Ages. The change was reflected in (and then given further encouragement by) the papal bull entitled *Summis desiderantes affectibus* (Latin: desiring with supreme ardour) of 1484. It concurred with the claim by the Dominican Inquisitor, Heinrich Kramer, that cases of witchcraft had occurred in the Rhine valley and elsewhere and it urged local authorities to cooperate with inquisitors in rooting it out. It was not radically different to earlier pronouncements but it became part of a growing trend when, in 1487, the same Dominican published a book entitled *Malleus Maleficarum* (Latin: hammer of witches), in which he condemned witchcraft as worse than heresy and drew public attention to the "problem". The book was highly misogynistic and claimed that witchcraft derived from the carnal lusts of women which drove them to sexual interaction with the Devil, and that witches could do actual physical harm (*maleficium*) to others. The book was officially condemned by the Catholic Church but it went on to be very influential in the Renaissance courts of Europe in the sixteenth and seventeenth centuries as interest in witch hunting dramatically increased.

As interest in the danger posed by witchcraft grew during the sixteenth century the distinctive characteristics of witchcraft came to be promulgated: a pact with the Devil; meeting in *sabbats*; the presence of imps in animal form ("familiars") as part of diabolical rituals; and night flying. Alongside this developed the alarming notion that the enormity of the crime meant that those accused should not be accorded the normal safeguards of the law and that this also applied to those who defended them. This idea became associated with the French Protestant Jean Bodin (1530–96), who was a jurist, a political philosopher, a member of the *Parlement* of Paris, and professor of law in Toulouse. The growth of such notions of acceptable illegality meant that when moral panics occurred – such as in East Anglia in the 1640s and at Salem, Massachusetts, in 1692–93 – they became extremely hard to stop.

The growing trend of witch hunting hit some areas worse than others. These included: the Spanish Netherlands (modern Belgium); the Rhineland and Southwest Germany; Lorraine in France; parts of Switzerland; and Scotland. In total, about three-quarters of all the witchcraft trials took place in the Catholic-ruled parts of the Holy Roman Empire, although the Catholic nations of Portugal, Castile (and Spanish-ruled Italy), along with Orthodox Eastern Europe, saw hardly any.

Where the panic took hold the death toll could be very high indeed: 900 burned in Lorraine between 1581 and 1591; 393 burned in Ellwangen, Germany, between 1611 and 1618; 200 burned in Baden, Germany, between 1627 and 1630; 600 burned in Würzburg, Germany, between 1628 and 1631; 1,800 burned in the Swiss canton of Vaud between 1611 and 1660. Catholics and Protestants alike contributed to these horrific figures.[11]

The occurrence of high-profile and highly lethal witch hunts were affected by a number of factors. First, there was increased social and religious tension following the Reformation. Second, the acceptance of the use of torture massively increased convictions in places such as Germany and Scotland. Third, economic disruption, accompanied by political conflict, encouraged hunts for those held responsible. Fourth, the emergence of stronger secular governments led to them policing spiritual matters that were once the preserve of the church. In contrast to this last factor of increased governmental control, the breakdown of social order could also allow a panic to emerge, accompanied by a desire to remove marginalized and socially stigmatized members of the community. In such a situation the emergence of professional witch hunters with an incentive to ensure high conviction rates accelerated the process. Larger panics tended to start with socially (and economically) vulnerable victims (often female) and then worked their way up the social scale as the hysteria spread and this then could draw in more men as victims. Scores were settled and money made by confiscating the property of those convicted. Some, who were probably mentally ill, denounced themselves. What is certainly clear is that there was no single cause of such a widespread phenomenon that affected so many diverse communities.[12]

Nevertheless, despite the strange geo-social patterns (there were many more victims in the Catholic area of what is now Belgium compared with the nearby Protestant area of what is now the Netherlands, and numbers were higher in Protestant Scotland than in Protestant England) and the fact that most died at the hands of co-religionists (i.e. Catholics killed fellow Catholics and Protestants fellow Protestants), the fact that the crescendo of denunciations and violence occurred when Christendom was tearing itself apart in religious conflict is clearly too great a juxtaposition of factors to assume it was a mere coincidence. The fact that most died at the hands of co-religionists suggests that, in some cases at least, it was prompted by a search for an enemy *within* a particular community (at a time of wider religious conflict between religious groups) whose activities could be used to explain crises affecting that community. This is certainly a reasonable line of enquiry when exploring the particular convulsions that afflicted Britain.

THE ENGLISH BACKGROUND

In 1542 the English Parliament passed the Witchcraft Act, during the reign of Henry VIII. This was the first law in England to define witchcraft as a "felony" and so to be punishable by death. It was repealed five years later, in 1547, under Edward VI, but was later restored by a new Act which was passed in 1562, under Elizabeth I. The new Act reduced the death penalty to only those cases where it was alleged that harm had been caused. This was added to in 1604, during the reign of James VI and I. Predictably, in the reign of a monarch who took a great interest in witch hunting, this addition broadened the terms of the 1562 Act so that invoking evil spirits or communing with "familiars" (see above) was also punishable by death. This broadening of the capital provision made possible later executions where no harm to others was proved but where the accused was found guilty of entering into a pact with the Devil (often through confession gained by forms of torture, or by fantastical "proofs" discovered on the body of the accused). It also introduced the death penalty for anyone found guilty twice of what were considered to be minor acts of witchcraft.

The 1562 and 1604 Acts transferred the trial of witches from the church to the secular courts. On one hand, this allowed the use of the death penalty (hanging not burning).[13] On the other hand, it gave the accused the benefit of common law criminal procedures; although this broke down somewhat in East Anglia during the 1640s.

Before this there had been other notable witch trials, most famously those of the Lancashire "Pendle witches" in 1612, when ten people convicted of witchcraft at the Summer Assize held in Lancaster Castle were hanged. They included eight women and two men accused of laming, causing madness, and sixteen unexplained deaths. These convictions were made possible by the confessions of the accused, combined with the "witness" of nine-year-old Jennet Device who claimed to have seen the use of familiar spirits, clay dolls used to kill, *sabbats*, and flying.[14]

Lancaster was again in the news in 1634 when twenty people were found guilty of witchcraft. As in 1612, this rested on confessions and a ten-year-old child's confession of "witnessing" shape-shifting, killing people by sticking thorns in images, and attending *sabbats*. In this case the judges were sceptical and refused to pass death sentences and some of the accused were sent to London where no "witch's marks" were found on them and the child admitted to lying. This scepticism over the reliability of evidence would be sadly lacking in other trials.

THE SCOTTISH BACKGROUND

At the same time as new legislation was appearing in England, the Scottish Witchcraft Act of 1563 made both the practice of witchcraft and also consulting with witches capital offences. In 1590, the North Berwick witch trials occurred in Scotland. King James VI, became involved himself, since he had developed a fear of witches due to his belief that witches had planned to kill him earlier that year, when he experienced storms while sailing to Denmark to fetch his bride, Anne. When James returned to Scotland, he heard that witchcraft trials were happening in North Berwick and personally interrogated the suspects. When Francis Stewart, fifth Earl of Bothwell, was accused of being a witch, he fled and was subsequently outlawed as a traitor. James went on to establish royal commissions to hunt down witches. He recommended torture in dealing with suspects (in contrast to English practice); and then, in 1597, he wrote a book entitled *Daemonologie* about the threat posed by witches.

The high-profile concerns in Scotland about witches continued after James transferred to London in 1603. Throughout the troubled years of the 1640s the General Assembly of the kirk and the Commission of the kirk pressed hard for more energetic enforcement of the Witchcraft Act of 1563. This had now become part of the Covenanter concern with enforcing godliness. In 1649, this led to blasphemy, the worship of false gods, and abusing of parents becoming capital offences. At the same time, a new Witchcraft Act was passed (1649). This both ratified the existing Act of 1563 and also extended it to make it a capital offence to consult with "Devils and familiar spirits".[15] In this process a much older concern had been extended and developed as part of the godly rule of the saints in Scotland.[16]

As a result of James' royal obsession with witch hunting in Scotland, and then the later concerns of the Covenanters, witch trials were far greater in number and also resulted in far more executions than in England. As a consequence, these Scottish trials had more in common with the witch trials of France and Germany.[17] The lack of strong governmental machinery in Scotland, contrasting with that in England, exacerbated this trend through local witch trials leading to executions. In this, Scotland was again comparable with Germany which also lacked centralized political control. This can be demonstrated by the fact that the number of death sentences passed by the courts in Scotland (with a less developed jury system and with the use of torture, especially in pre-trial investigations) was always far greater than that of England (with a more developed jury system and avoidance of torture).[18] In fact, it has been calculated that for every English witch executed, three died in Scotland; this despite the fact that the English population was four times the size of that of Scotland.[19]

The one great exception to that rule occurred during the 1640s and the exceptional character of this occurrence actually reinforces the overall pattern. But what happened during such a short period in East Anglia makes it stand out from the English norm.

The impact of Matthew Hopkins,
"Witchfinder General"

Matthew Hopkins and his associates were responsible for the deaths of somewhere in the region of three hundred people (mostly women) between 1644 and 1646.[20] Hopkins was the son of a Puritan clergyman from Great Wenham in Suffolk, whose reforming zeal was such that when his parish was examined in 1645 as part of a Parliamentary commission into the destruction of "superstitious" or "idolatrous" items, it found there was nothing that needed reforming. Clearly, there had been a zealous removal of anything that smacked of medieval Catholic piety. This gives an important clue regarding the cultural and intellectual milieu in which Hopkins grew up. That Hopkins, and his associate, John Stearne, used the language of military campaigns suggests that they saw (or chose to present) their actions as a spiritual equivalent of the campaigns being carried out at the time by the armies of Parliament. This is less surprising given that their activities took place in the heartland of Puritan support for the Parliamentary Eastern Association. This is not the first time that it has been surmised that Hopkins embodied the resentment of the godly at their treatment prior to the 1640s and to imagine that his character revealed the distinctive attributes of "Puritan godliness and self-motivation".[21]

By the early 1640s, Hopkins was residing in Manningtree, Essex. From Essex his activities extended into Suffolk, Norfolk, Cambridgeshire, and Huntingdonshire; and beyond this into Bedfordshire and Northamptonshire. The first trials occurred at Chelmsford, in Essex, where Hopkins and his associate, Stearne, were involved in a series of accusations which resulted in the arrests of twenty-three women on charges of witchcraft. Of these, nineteen were eventually hanged. It should be noted here that none were burned and this was the general practice in the British Isles: hanging not burning.

The two men then extended their activities in the company of women investigators called "prickers". Hopkins' technique consisted of "proving" that those accused were guilty of a pact with the Devil more than that they had caused any actual misfortune by use of magic (*maleficium*). This was not the usual practice in the British Isles where the focus was usually on hurt done, not consorting with the Devil.[22]

The strategy in East Anglia consequently shifted attention away from particular acts and onto the (otherwise unprovable) nature of the accused's thoughts and secret activities. In order to "prove" that these had occurred, Hopkins developed a number of techniques. Sleep deprivation was used to extract confessions (i.e. the accused implicated themselves). Lack of blood from a cut was identified as another "proof". The "swimming test" was used by which the accused was considered guilty if they floated (the water rejecting someone who had renounced their Christian baptism). The final "proof" was the discovery of a "Devil's or witch's mark" on the accused which it was alleged was the place at which the witch's familiar drank blood. Moles or birthmarks were used as "evidence" of such features. The test was extended to any area that did not react to pain since these were allegedly invisible marks. These were probed for on the body of the accused by the prickers. Finding such a witch's mark (a so-called "witch's teat") or one which was insensitive to pricking increased conviction rates in England, and in Scotland where the practice was also employed. When this practice was questioned (as in Geneva) acquittals, not surprisingly, occurred.

In the unsettled years of the Civil Wars, Hopkins and his associates were part of a process which rapidly produced results and convictions. However, he also ran into opposition. The Parliamentary newspaper, *Moderate Intelligencer*, in September 1645, expressed doubts over the condemnation of those who were no more than "silly Women that know not their right hands from their left" and "poore old women". It was similar concerns that had caused Parliament to send a Commission of Oyer and Terminer to Bury St Edmunds, Suffolk, in order that an assize judge should examine the evidence, rather than the justices of the peace who had been responsible for other East Anglian trials. This did not prevent the hanging of eighteen witches (sixteen women and two men, including Rev. John Lowes, the Vicar of Brandeston, Suffolk) but still revealed that disquiet was growing regarding previous methods used in East Anglia to extract confessions. Locally, John Gaule, the vicar of Great Staughton, Cambridgeshire, was not convinced by the methods used and preached against the hunts and, in 1646, summed up his concerns in a book entitled *Select Cases of Conscience touching Witches and Witchcrafts*. The next year Hopkins and Stearne retired (probably in the face of this mounting opposition) but by this time between two and three hundred people had been hanged. Indeed, so intense was this witch panic that some two hundred people were brought to trial, this frequently leading to execution, over a period of just six months in 1645.[23]

In the same year that he retired from witch hunting (1647), Hopkins died. A myth states that he was himself swum as a witch and died in a savage piece of poetic justice, but in fact he died of tuberculosis and is buried in the churchyard at Mistley, in Essex.

We know a great deal about the methods employed in these hunts because Hopkins wrote his own account in *The Discovery of Witches*, and Stearne wrote up his own in *A Confirmation and Discovery of Witchcraft*. Both were clearly influenced by the *Daemonologie*, written by King James.

Overall, the trials in England were not typical of the European hunts, since in England the charges were usually concerned with the practice of malevolent magic (*maleficium*) rather than actual contact with the Devil (which was more of a feature in Scottish witch trials). On the other hand the idea of witches' familiars played a key role in England, whereas this rarely appeared in Continental trials.[24] A major feature of English trials generally was the absence of the use of torture (unlike in Scotland) and this usually "prevented the development of chain-reaction hunts",[25] whereby those tortured named others and the situation spiralled out of control. The size of the East Anglian death toll is almost certainly linked to the use of forms of torture there (e.g. sleep deprivation) and so this exception proves the overall rule. For example, the octogenarian Rev. John Lowes was swum in the castle moat at Framlingham, then deprived of sleep for several nights, before being forced to run around the room until exhausted. And this to a man in his eighties whose only believable crime was being an unpopular "contentious man" with a record of harassing others through litigation.[26]

Overall, these East Anglian hunts have been considered atypical of the general pattern of English witch hunts since, in contrast to these other trials, those in East Anglia stressed pacts with the Devil rather than the neighbourly disputes leading to accusations of harm that tended to be such a feature of other English witchcraft accusations. This has been suggested to have been caused by Hopkins introducing Continental concepts to his cases.[27] However, their atypicality has been questioned, by reference to the fact that 87.2 per cent were women (where the records indicate gender) as is usual, most were poorer members of society who faced longstanding accusations of being implicated in acts of witchcraft, and many *were* accused of causing harm following altercations with neighbours. Furthermore, it has been suggested that the high profile of familiars and of the Devil in the East Anglian trials points to the development of these ideas within a well-established English tradition concerning familiars (first recorded in a case from Yorkshire in 1510). These are otherwise unrecorded in less-well-documented cases, and so there may have been (by the 1640s) an already established belief that pacts with the Devil existed.[28]

Overall, though, it still seems fair to conclude that the unusual nature of the East Anglian trials and executions still stand out and are understandable not just through the stresses caused by three years of war and the application of established concepts, but also by reference to something peculiar to the religious worldview of Hopkins and East Anglia in the 1640s. Which brings us to our final consideration.

WHEN GOD WAS KING: THE PLACE OF WITCH HUNTS IN THE CREATION OF GODLY RULE

There was no official sanction for the mid-seventeenth-century witch hunts. These were not government policy and they did not form part of a Puritan programme. Overall, it can be argued that there was no inherent link between puritanism and witch hunting, since the hunts occurred under widely different religious regimes and were certainly not a defining feature of godly rule. Officially, the Puritan divines (those influencing theology and outlook) had little interest in the hunting of witches.

Nevertheless, the evidence in a large number of cases (most strikingly East Anglia in the 1640s) indicates that prosecutors tended to be Puritan and sceptics Anglican.[29] Neither should one forget the way in which the Covenanters enthusiastically developed the approach that they had inherited from King James; these Scottish saints certainly saw it as an aspect of godly rule. In addition, the 1640s panic occurred in a "hot-spot area" of Puritan ideology (the region of the Eastern Association), at a time of political crisis (with a royal army at times threatening Cambridge) and was driven by a man who had grown up in a Puritan intellectual milieu in which references to the Devil and his works played a major part in forming outlooks. Many of those who appear in the East Anglian records reveal "a basic awareness of the threat offered to the godly commonwealth by the devil."[30] This was exacerbated by Parliamentary propaganda in the period 1642–45 which used apocalyptic language to describe the war and framed enemies as agents of the Devil. Neither should one ignore the presence of Puritan-inclined clergy in the witch investigations in Essex and Suffolk and the unusual presence of two Puritan divines in the Commission of Oyer and Terminer sent to Suffolk in 1645. Clearly, godly rule was making its own contribution to the crisis.

In conclusion, the East Anglian witch hunts both *shared* features common to the hunts that occurred across Europe and Britain, while at the same time possessing *their own* peculiar dynamic. And the peculiar dynamic in this case was part of the mentality of godly rule. The same will later be shown to be true of the North American witch hunts. They too were part of the godly experience and owed a great deal to the factors that drove the search for godly rule in other areas of life and in government. It is just that witch hunting was not exclusively the preserve of the puritanical outlook. But of it, it was certainly a part.

6

The "Rule of the Saints" in Ireland

As a result of the 1649–53 campaign of Parliamentary forces in Ireland, it has been calculated that perhaps as many as 500,000 Catholic Irish died, out of a total Irish population of 1.5 million. Those in charge of these forces saw this as a direct outworking of godly rule on a rebellious Catholic population that were "beyond the pale" (itself an expression that originated in the Protestant settlement of Ireland and described those Irish living beyond the areas of English-orientated settlement in Dublin). This chapter explores how the "rule of the saints" could lead to something that today has been described as ethnic cleansing and genocide. Cromwell wrote, early in his campaign, that, "I rejoice to exercise the utmost severity against them". That declaration itself was couched in a statement that insisted that the Irish had nothing to fear if they gave up resistance and the open confession of Catholicism. But what Cromwell regarded as reasonable and restrained on his part amounted in reality to the most brutal campaign of the British Civil Wars.

THE ENGLISH (AND SCOTS) IN IRELAND

The English crown had always treated Ireland as a foreign colony and the English involvement, that went back to the twelfth century (1169), had resulted in a complex state of affairs which theoretically claimed that the English crown had authority over all the island. However, in reality, this left power in the various hands of native Irish (Gaelic) lords, Anglo-Irish aristocratic settlers, and enclaves of royal power where royal appointees exercised some direct authority for the crown. This latter area was little more than the area running from Dublin to Dundalk and stretching inland for no more than forty miles. Apart from this area, only Cork, Galway, Limerick, Waterford, and the royal fortress at Carrickfergus were directly under English authority.[1] This began to change in 1534 when Henry VIII took on the direct government of Ireland and in 1541 changed his title from "Lord of Ireland" to "King of Ireland". Responding to Irish rebellions and resistance to religious change in England (the vast majority of the population in Ireland remained determinedly Catholic), the Tudor rule in Ireland continued to be, "complex, piecemeal and spasmodic", without any coherent plan.[2] In the last ten years of the reign of Elizabeth I the struggle for control intensified when Hugh O'Neill, the Gaelic lord of Tyrone, launched a rebellion of Gaelic and Anglo-Irish lords against the English crown. Through an immense effort the English government defeated it. With its defeat, Gaelic Ireland and Catholic Ireland came under increasing pressure as English rulers sought to finally stamp their authority on the island and to impose the English Protestant church on Ireland. The latter – though established by law – faced fierce resistance from a Catholic population still loyal to its own church that had been driven underground but continued to maintain a network of papal-appointed bishops and priests despite the loss of their cathedrals and parish churches. In Ireland national resistance to English rule went hand in glove with Catholic resistance to Protestantism.

In 1607 the defeated O'Neill and his followers fled abroad ("the flight of the earls") and the English crown took the revolutionary step – which disregarded the rights of Irish landowners – of seizing the land in six Irish counties and distributing it to a mixture of English and Scottish settlers, the city of London (still remembered in the place-name Londonderry, but Derry to Irish nationalists), army officers and some Irish. This accelerated the policy of so-called "Plantations". Sporadic land transfers had happened before, in the wake of uprisings,[3] but this was a radical new phase that commenced after 1607. It turned the formerly Gaelic stronghold of Ulster into a Scots/English colony (over half the settlers were Protestant Scots). This policy created a divided Ireland, in which the loyalist (to the English crown) Protestant settlers of the "New English" ("*Nua Ghaill*") and the mixed Anglo-Irish, but still Catholic, loyalists of the "Old English" ("*Sean Ghaill*") faced the majority of the population who were Catholic and did not accept the legitimacy of English rule. These were the Gaelic "Old Irish" ("*Gaedhil*"). Until 1641 the Catholic loyalists (the Old English) still hoped to share power and an involvement in government with the newcomers in Ulster. In this they managed a balancing act between political allegiance to Charles I and religious allegiance to the pope. But it was one they found increasingly difficult as the crown did not fully accept the difference between them and the Old Irish, and the settlers of the New English demanded that only Protestants should enjoy the benefits of full citizenship.[4] By a late-fifteenth-century Act, known as "Poynings' Law",[5] the Irish Parliament in Dublin was made subservient to the English Parliament. Then, during the early seventeenth century, the Irish constituencies were altered in order to favour the election of English and Scottish Protestants. As a result, there was an artificially manipulated Protestant majority in the Irish Parliament.

As the 1640s dawned, the group of loyal Catholic Irish (the Old English) found their political and religious liberties increasingly under threat. Sir Thomas Wentworth, lord-lieutenant of Ireland, strove to increase revenue for the cash-strapped Charles I and to reduce the influence of the Catholic Irish nobility. This included extending plantations into Connacht (Connaught) and Leinster and confiscating estates wherever an opportunity arose, in order to make way for more Protestant (often Scots) settlers. Between 1631 and 1640 these policies accelerated and it was this Protestant intolerance (by the High Church crown and the distinctly godly Scots/English settlers) that drove the loyal Catholics of the Old English to make common cause with the Old Irish in the Irish Rebellion of 1641.

The Irish Rebellion of 1641: a backstory of unfinished business

In 1641 an economic recession and a poor harvest combined with resentment at land seizures to ignite the Irish Rebellion. It had not gone unnoticed how successfully Scotland had resisted King Charles I in the Bishops' Wars. There was a great irony in this, for it meant that the revolt of the Scots godly against the High Church Arminian Anglicanism of the king now encouraged an Irish and Catholic revolt against the same king and against the Scots/English settlers, many of whom were drawn from the ranks of the godly.

The rebels quickly captured Charlemont, Dungannon, Mountjoy, and other English-held strongholds. However, the attempt to seize Dublin failed when too few rose in revolt and all non-residents (i.e. Catholics) were compelled by the authorities to leave Dublin. This failure meant that a swift seizure of power then turned into a bloody war.

The official proclamation of those leading the rebellion stated that the rebels had taken up arms in defence of the freedoms of the native Irish. No threat was made against the king or his subjects in Ireland. However, this did not stop violence escalating and targeting the settlers in Ulster. There the hated Protestants (settled on expropriated Irish land) were evicted and plundered. Their farms and houses were burnt and their livestock was seized. This soon turned into the indiscriminate killing of settlers. In November 1641 an infamous massacre took place at Portadown, County Armagh, where about one hundred men, women, and children were thrown off the bridge and drowned in the river Bann. News of these killings were soon publicized in England and the numbers killed – though high – were hugely inflated in a serious of widely read pamphlets.

Soon most of Armagh, Down, and Tyrone were controlled by the rebels. In November, Leinster too was in open revolt and the coastal town of Drogheda was under siege. James Butler, the earl of Ormond, was made the overall commander of government forces in Ireland, but his army failed to relieve Drogheda and was defeated. By the spring of 1642 the revolt was blazing across the whole of Ireland.

It was then that the opponents of King Charles at Westminster accused the government of complicity in the uprising and refused to allow the king to raise an army to crush it. Instead, Parliament voted for the Militia Bill which placed an army under its control. It was this tussle with the king over the raising of an army to send to Ireland which acted as the final escalator into civil war in England.

Parliament also passed the Adventurers Act, in March 1642. This promised land in Ireland to any "speculators" who provided money to finance the army. Meanwhile, a Scots Covenanter army was sent to Ireland in order to protect the Protestant settlers (many of whom were Scots Protestants). The saints of Scotland were now coming to the rescue of the godly in Ireland (and indeed to the rescue of Protestants generally, of whatever persuasion).

As the war in Ireland developed, those in arms met at the Confederate Assembly at Kilkenny. Here the Old Irish (Catholic and anti-English) formed an alliance with the Old English (Catholic and formerly pro-English). This then turned into the drawn out eleven-year so-called Confederate War, which continued until Ireland was finally subjugated by Cromwell and other Parliamentary generals in 1649–53.

The war was bloody, complex and indecisive. It was made more confusing still by the fact that civil conflict had erupted in England pitting those fighting the Confederates in Ireland also against each other in England! The Confederates laid siege to Dublin, but the Royalist commander, Ormonde, handed over the city to the English Parliament which had sent a fleet to the port. In 1647 the Confederates were defeated at Dungan's Hill, Meath, by these new arrivals. Another Confederate army in Munster was also defeated at Knocknanass, Cork. In January 1649, the Confederates signed a deal (the Second Ormonde Peace) and placed their armies under Royalist command. This, ironically, put them under the command of the earl of Ormonde, who had earlier surrendered Dublin to Parliament, to avoid its capture by the Confederates. This realignment in 1649 was because they now both felt they had a common cause against the English Parliament, which they both regarded as the greater threat.

The situation became even more complex when Charles I was executed in January 1649, just as the Confederates and Royalists were sinking their differences. For, thoroughly disgusted by the execution of Charles, the Ulster Scots also then joined the coalition of Confederates and Royalists against the newly declared English Commonwealth in Westminster. Scots settlers in Ulster were horrified by the execution of the king just as in Scotland generally and condemned "the insolencies of the sectarian party in England"[6] for their violation of the Solemn League and Covenant in killing the king, and also abandoning Presbyterianism in favour of the toleration of a variety of different religious practices (though not Catholicism, of course). The Scots in Ulster then proceeded to besiege the pro-Parliament English garrison in Derry/Londonderry.

In response, the Parliamentary spokesperson, John Milton, bitterly denounced the Scots Protestants as "the pontifical see of Belfast".[7] This situation created a strange anti-Parliamentary group including Catholic Irish, Irish Royalists of various persuasions and Presbyterian Ulster Scots. Not all Confederates accepted the new alliance as they felt that it did not address Catholic grievances and conflict broke out between them and those who had accepted it. But although this internecine fighting added to the death toll, it was about to be dwarfed by what was coming, for the commander of the army of the godly – Oliver Cromwell himself – was on his way to Ireland. On his arrival he was already very much aware of all the atrocities perpetrated against Protestants in 1641; this was the backstory that was always there as he campaigned and justified his actions in Ireland. For it was unfinished business, and consisted of the punishment "owed" to the Catholic Irish. For Cromwell, that punishment was about to arrive in the form of the army of saints who had brought down the king and were in the process of enforcing the rule of God in England. Now it was the turn of Ireland and for Cromwell, as his later comments revealed, he was convinced that he was a sword in the hand of God. His crossing of the Irish Sea was symbolic of the Old Testament crossing of the river Jordan by the Israelites, leading to the conquest of the land of Canaan.

CROMWELL ARRIVES AND SETS OUT
THE AGENDA OF THE SAINTS

In March 1649, the English Parliament authorized Cromwell to lead an army to Ireland. A Parliamentary victory over the main Royalist army at the battle of Rathmines meant that Cromwell could land unopposed at Dublin, in August 1649. He brought with him siege artillery and about 6,000 veteran troops. The army he commanded was well resourced and was the most formidable military force in Ireland. This army of saints – fresh from defeating the king – was about to radically change the situation in Ireland. And Cromwell soon made it clear that his agenda included the final subjugation of the island.

Cromwell was determined to avenge the (hugely inflated) numbers of those settlers killed in the 1641 rebellion, to annihilate organized Catholicism, and to remove the last vestiges of royal power. This would, indeed, be a godly crusade and he was explicit about his aims.

In a speech in Dublin, Cromwell laid out his agenda:

for the carrying on of the great work against the barbarous and blood-thirsty Irish... for the propagation of the Gospel of Christ, the establishing of truth and peace...[8]

Before leaving Bristol, he had told his soldiers that they were like the Israelites who had destroyed the idolatrous inhabitants of Canaan.[9] This was a theme in line with the ethno-religious sentiments of a Parliamentary declaration in February 1642, "that the country [Ireland] will be replanted with many noble families of this nation, and of the Protestant religion".[10] The ungodly would be destroyed and the godly established in their place.

When, later, Cromwell insisted he only killed those taken in arms and that only those who resisted had cause to fear, these statements sit uncomfortably with the Old Testament language he used to describe his role as if it was the conquest of Canaan and the putting to the sword of the heathen who were, after all in his view, "barbarous and blood-thirsty". There seems little

85

room in this language for flexibility. And when one adds that Cromwell was quite open about killing all members of the Catholic clergy, one suspects that he had a definition of righteous godly judgment which was elastic enough to include the slaughter of non-combatants while, in more sober mood, he would clearly state that this was not his intention (except for Catholic clergy, who had it coming). The problem was that Cromwell had a fairly broad view of who deserved death (including unarmed priests and friars) and an extirpatory mindset with regard to Ireland, which meant that, when he was angry, slaughter could expand to include those whose safety he promised to respect in his cooler moments. In short, Cromwell thought that the Irish were savage papists who were stained with the blood of Protestant settlers and it did not take much to tip him over the edge into slaughter. It was as if two Cromwells had travelled to Ireland: one was the godly hard man prepared to be merciful; the other was the angry ideologue, set on extermination of savages, who felt he was the sword of judgment in God's hand. Because he was never just the latter, one cannot say that he had a genocidal agenda because he did not. But because he harboured the emotional intensity of this latter attitude, it could tip him toward genocidal action and, when that happened, Cromwell would have his justification to hand in the sinful nature (as he saw it) of the Irish.

WAR CRIME OF THE GODLY?
THE DESTRUCTION OF DROGHEDA

From Dublin, Cromwell set about smashing Royalist strongholds on the east coast of Ireland. He did this by taking the walled towns of Drogheda and Wexford. At both towns the garrisons were massacred after the towns themselves had been taken by storm.

At Drogheda, in September 1649, Cromwell forbade his troops "to spare any that were in arms in the town". And so, as he recounted, "we put to the sword the whole number of the defendants." This included 1,000 defenders who took refuge in the main church of the town. When some in the steeple continued to fire down at the Parliamentary soldiers, it was burned beneath them. Cromwell coldly recounted how one Catholic defender screamed as he burnt to death, "God damn me, God confound me, I burn, I burn."[11] The brutal and dispassionate mention of such a detail in his despatch clearly reveals a lot about Cromwell's mental outlook. It is reasonable to suggest that in this terrible self-condemnatory screaming of a man burning to death, the general saw some kind of vindication of his action. It was as if this appalling episode somehow clarified the spiritual ascendancy of the Parliamentary forces and revealed the unworthy status of those immolated. And yet even Cromwell may have had a slight lingering doubt regarding this which needed to be dispelled. For, when describing the killings in the brutal words of "this is the righteous Judgment of God upon these Barbarous wretches, who have so imbrued their hands in so much innocent blood", he went on to justify it as a salutary example, which "will tend to prevent the effusion of blood for the future" and – perhaps more revealing still – he stated that, otherwise, such slaughter "cannot but work remorse and regret".[12] Did he have remorse and regret? If so, he was able to overcome it with the arguments that his actions were justified (since the defenders had refused to surrender) and was necessary (to persuade other garrisons to quickly come to terms).

Cromwell also noted that all identified as Catholic clergy were killed as a matter of course but he did not regard these as non-combatants. He later, in January 1650, responded to the Irish Catholic bishops by insisting that he had not killed any who were not in arms. The phrase "and many inhabitants" that concluded Cromwell's despatch regarding the death toll at Drogheda would seem to contradict this, except for the suggestion that this was added to the despatch by the Parliamentary printer and was not in the original communique.[13] But, remembering those Catholic clergy, it seems that Cromwell clearly had a fairly flexible definition of what it meant to be "taken in arms" and, perhaps, a selective memory of exactly who had died at Drogheda and later at Wexford.

This raises the vexed question of just how many died at Drogheda and how many of these were civilians. Clearly, most of those defenders who were taken in arms were killed and in this Cromwell can be argued to have been acting within the brutal conventions of seventeenth-century siege warfare where "no quarter" could be declared if a town fell after its defenders had earlier refused to come to terms and surrender. For example, the commander of English forces in Scotland, in 1651, ordered the killing of defenders at Dundee. Nevertheless, the tone of Cromwell's despatch reveals a cold determination which suggests that the lack of quarter was more than just following established procedure; there were also scores to settle in Ireland. But regarding the civilians, the matter is more complex still. Hugh Peters, the Parliamentary chaplain, suggested a total death toll of 3,552, while Cromwell at one point referred to 2,000 killed,[14] but this does not differentiate soldiers from civilians. For, although there may not have been a general massacre of civilians at Drogheda, many certainly died. Maybe somewhere in the region of 1,000 civilians were killed.[15] This latter number arises from the subtraction of a figure of about 400 survivors from a garrison of 3,000, to put the civilian dead at about 1,000 (hence Peters' total death toll of about 3,500).[16] But Cromwell also suggested, at one point, that the garrison numbered "near 4,000,"[17] so the room for disagreement remains, since it is possible to make the total number killed refer only to those of the garrison taken in arms. Later Irish Catholic Church sources, however, dating from the 1660s, claimed that 4,000 civilians had died and that it was "unparalleled savagery and treachery beyond any slaughterhouse".[18] This number is almost certainly too high.

On balance it seems clear that *many civilians* were killed and, while the "no quarter" order might have been legally justifiable in seventeenth-century terms and even thought necessary to encourage other garrisons to surrender, Cromwell and his soldiers "were also stoked up by a lust for vengeance, a desire fuelled by the grotesque pamphlet literature on the massacres that had appeared since 1641".[19] In short, the evidence points to a war crime of shocking proportions.

THE TRIUMPH OF THE PARLIAMENTARY FORCES IN IRELAND

From Drogheda, Cromwell marched to Wexford. Here, in October 1649, during the negotiations for the surrender of the town an officer in the castle allowed the besieging army access to the town, perhaps because he feared a repeat of the fate of Drogheda. But it happened anyway. When the Parliamentary army stormed into the town that adjoined the castle there was another slaughter. This one was not ordered by Cromwell but he made no attempt to stop it. In the marketplace large numbers died at the hands of Cromwell's soldiers. A later petition from Wexford to the crown, after the Restoration, indicated that 1,500 civilians were killed *in addition* to the members of the garrison.[20] Cromwell's only comment, in his report to Parliament, was that almost 2,000 of the enemy died, and that they were now made "with their bloods to answer the cruelties which they exercised upon the lives of divers poor Protestants". God had "brought a just judgment upon them, causing them to become a prey to the soldiers".[21] As always, he had his "get out of jail card" to hand: they deserved it because of the 1641 killings. And it was God who had willed it and made the saints-in-arms the executioners of his "righteous judgment" and so there was no human blame attached to such servants of divine will. Who better than the godly to act in this way against the murdering papists of Wexford? And yet Cromwell was struggling to pin the historic atrocities on the slaughtered people of Wexford. All he could manage was to recount a story of seven or eight Protestants put to sea in a leaking boat, who drowned in the harbour and a vague accusation of some Protestants deliberately starved.[22] If true, this was terrible – but the events are uncertain and small in number, whereas the later butchery at Wexford was a matter of record.

Cromwell's army campaigned across Leinster during the autumn and winter of 1649. His victories had dramatic knock-on effects as the anti-Parliamentary Protestant forces operating in southern Munster gave up the Royalist cause and came over to Parliament. Then, early in 1650, Cromwell captured the Confederate capital at Kilkenny, in Leinster. This was followed by the fall of Clonmel and, after a long siege, the fall of Waterford. His successes spread fear of him far and wide and, no doubt, many had heard of Drogheda and Wexford.

To those who condemned his brutality and assault on religious freedom (Cromwell, as an Independent, believed in tolerance of religious difference) he retorted:

> *I meddle not with any man's conscience; but if by liberty of conscience you mean a liberty to exercise the mass, I judge it best to use plain dealing, and to let you know, the Parliament of England have power that will not be allowed of.*[23]

Freedom only stretched so far. It encompassed the different views among the godly but did not include Catholics. This was little wonder, since it did not stretch even as far as fellow Protestants of High Church Anglican inclinations. And once again, in an accompaniment to the above statement, he alluded to the judgment due on Catholics for the killings of 1641. At the same time he denied the intention of collective punishment. However, those Catholics who experienced his collectivist denial of the right to Catholic religious services would have differed at this point about the collectivist nature of his polices. Furthermore, it was clear that, try as he did to excuse it, the killing of Catholics generally was always possible to justify when it occurred, because 1641 allowed him a way of doing that. It was the judgment they had brought on themselves.

Finally, if Irish Catholics continued to resist, their fate would be "misery and desolation, blood and ruin", which Cromwell would then inflict on them with a completely clear conscience for, if they proved so obdurate, he would "rejoice to exercise utmost severity against them".[24]

Cromwell finally sailed from Ireland in May 1650. He left his son-in-law Henry Ireton in overall command of the English forces remaining in Ireland. The former Confederate armies (called *tories* from the Irish for "pursued man") turned to guerrilla warfare in the face of Parliamentary supremacy in conventional warfare, but it was to no avail. By the end of 1650 almost all of Leinster, Munster, and Ulster were back under English control. Fighting in Connacht continued throughout 1651. When Ireton died of plague, in 1651, the completion of the Irish campaign passed to others and it was completed in May 1652, when the last Irish forces, in Galway, surrendered.

The change to guerrilla warfare led to a massive increase in civilian deaths as Parliamentary forces carried out reprisals and destroyed crops and food stores as a weapon of war against the insurgents. As if this was not enough, the movement of English troops into Ireland brought plague to the island. The death toll rose inexorably.

"To Hell or to Connacht"

This is allegedly the choice that Cromwell gave the Irish Catholic population of Ulster, Leinster and Munster: that they must move to the barren western lands of Connacht or face death if they remained east of the river Shannon. There is no evidence that he ever actually said it, but it sums up the way he is remembered in Ireland for the brutality of what occurred after he left, as much as for what occurred while he was in Ireland. This later development involved discriminatory legislation and "the most catastrophic land-confiscation and social upheaval in Irish history".[25]

In the 1650s a number of penal laws were enacted against Irish Catholics. These included: the banning of Catholics from holding office in the Irish Parliament; the expulsion of Catholic clergy; making illegal the Catholic Mass; banning Catholics from living in towns; banning the use of Gaelic; and shutting traditional bardic schools. More devastating were the mass land confiscations. These targeted about 40,000 Catholic landowners who had taken part in the Confederate Wars, and were deported to the West Indies; other Catholic landowners in Ulster, Leinster, and Munster were expelled, but "compensated" with poorer land in the west of the island (in Connacht and Clare). The degree of land lost depended on the extent of a landowner's involvement in the rebellion. This opened up richer farmland for new Protestant settlers and contained the expelled Catholics between the Atlantic and the river Shannon. As a result, the number of Catholic landowners fell from about 60 per cent of the population to just 8 per cent.[26] These expulsions helped Parliament pay debts it incurred fighting the wars in Ireland since it used the land as rewards for those owed money.

The Act for the settlement of Ireland was passed by the English Parliament in August 1652. All those transplanted were to move by 1 May 1654. The penalty for not transplanting was death by hanging. Hence: "To Hell or to Connacht." A one-mile-wide strip of land, known as the "Mile Line", was established around the perimeter of Connacht and Clare. This was reserved for military English/Scots settlers and was designed to hem in the Irish. The Irish were forbidden to live in the towns of Connacht. Those Irish already holding land in Connacht and Clare also had their estates reduced and they were often subject to being moved to a different area. Some of the indigenous Irish landowners in Clare were transplanted to Galway, Mayo, and Roscommon. Landless Irish were allowed to settle on state-owned land so long as it was further than ten miles from the river Shannon. Or they could remain where they were to act as labourers for the Cromwellian settlers.

Some of those who were dispossessed by these government actions joined the *tories* in a continued guerrilla war against new settlers, or "planters" as they were called. The government offered large rewards for the capture or killing of these *tories*. The first to be settled on the land were ex-members of the army and they were then followed by the adventurers who had put up money to fund the Irish campaign. The last of these adventurers were finally settled in May 1659. This completed the transplantation. All in all it was a shocking policy of dispossession, ethnic cleansing, and cultural subjugation of a native people. And, not surprisingly, it was chaotic and accompanied by changing administrative decisions over this piece of land or that particular group. In all this chaos the Irish were at the mercy of the English authorities of the Cromwellian state.

THE CASUALTIES OF THE WAR OF THE SAINTS

There are no definite figures for how many Irish people died between 1641 and 1653. The closest contemporary estimate was calculated by William Petty, in a survey completed in 1672. In that survey he calculated the death toll to be 618,000. This was about 40 per cent of Ireland's pre-1641 population of about 1.5 million. These included figures for the Wars of the Confederates, as well as the Cromwellian campaigns. Of these dead, he thought that over 400,000 were Catholics, of whom he calculated that 167,000 were killed directly by war or famine, with the remainder killed by war-related diseases.[27] Comparative studies remind us that, while the destructive impact of these particular wars was the key reason for the occurrence of famine in Ireland, there were also severe food shortages, bordering on famine, throughout much of Europe in the period 1648–51.[28] Nevertheless, the shortages in Ireland were far more severe than most suffered elsewhere, and most of these Continental examples were, themselves, also the products of avoidable human conflict. For example, earlier in the Thirty Years' War of 1618–48, the population of Germany is estimated to have fallen from sixteen to ten million – due to much the same combination of atrocity and pillaging as caused such devastation in Ireland.

Returning to the estimate from 1672, Petty's figure is probably too high. This is because many thousands of the missing people that he noted had probably either left Ireland for exile on the Continent or had been transported to the West Indies in penal servitude. Nevertheless, the human cost was clearly enormous. In 1653, Colonel Richard Lawrence reported that: "the plague and famine had swept away whole counties so that a man may ride 20 or 30 miles and not see a living creature, either man, beast or bird."[29]

Modern historians' estimates of the death toll range from between 20 and 40 per cent loss of population due to the conflicts, between 1641–51, compared to death tolls of 3.7 per cent in England and 6 per cent in Scotland.[30] However, even if we take the lowest projected figure, of somewhere in the region of 200,000 Irish deaths, this would still represent a loss of over 10 per cent of the estimated population of Ireland. This is still staggering and comparable with the Potato Famine of the 1840s. There is, however, the real likelihood that the death toll was actually much higher than 200,000. Furthermore most of these died after 1649, as a consequence of the rule of the saints.

The bitterness left by the campaigns in Ireland ran deep. For, in contemporary Irish poetry, it was Cromwell who, "*do chriocnaigh Eire*" ("finished off Ireland"). The old Catholic gentry, looked askance at the republican and lower-class English who had deposed them, the "*scum na sagsan*" ("English scum"). And Catholics generally now felt they had been reduced to a status, "like worms – trod upon by a mean and regicide colony" which was made up of "little phanatick scabs". For Catholics, their condition after Cromwell was, "worse than the Christians under the Turks or the Israelites in the bondage of Egypt".[31] It was a terrible legacy of godly rule.

7

Social and Political Justice for the Common Man? The Levellers

T here are many ways in which the events of the seventeenth century have left their mark on the modern world. One of the most moving can still be found at Burford parish church in Oxfordshire. Here a plaque on the wall of the church records these words,

To the memory of Three Levellers
Cornet THOMPSON
Corporal PERKINS
Private CHURCH
Executed and buried in this Churchyard
17th May 1649.[1]

On the day that I visited with my family, several years ago, we were not the only ones to lay flowers below it in memory of those executed by firing squad on that distant May morning. Indeed, since the 1970s, Burford has held an annual Levellers Day to commemorate the event (held on the Saturday nearest the date of the executions).[2] The Levellers have not been forgotten. But what has often been forgotten, as their legacy has been recalled and celebrated by modern democrats or those wishing to trace the roots of modern British radicalism and the Left in contemporary politics, is that the demands of the Levellers lay very much within the outlook and values of the godly of the seventeenth century. For, while their principles continue to resonate within the world of contemporary secular politics, the Levellers were drawn from among the ranks of the saints-in-arms. And this, *as well* as their political grievances, has to be explored if we are to fully understand this radical group within the New Model Army (alongside their civilian sympathizers in the late 1640s). For they were very much of the opinion that the kingship of God should be revealed in a politically revised social order that shocked and dismayed many of their officers and the Parliamentary government. In this they both looked toward future political developments, while still being firmly rooted in the world of the Civil Wars.

WHO WERE THE LEVELLERS?

The first thing that must be said is that they were not "Levellers"! They never willingly called themselves this and were very well aware that it was a title and an accusation that was coined by their enemies and used against them. In so doing, their opponents took a term that had first appeared as a way of describing rural rebels who espoused the tearing down ("levelling") of hedges in the anti-enclosure Midland Revolt of 1607. The name implied that they wished to abolish property rights and impose equality of wealth through some kind of revolutionary redistribution. They did not. In contrast to the movement known as the "Diggers" (see Chapter 8), the Levellers opposed common ownership, unless it came about through the agreement of landowners.[3] They certainly did not espouse a communist-style expropriation of wealth or a collectivization of land holdings. In contrast with such ideals, the Levellers were individualists not collectivists. It was justice (as they saw it) that they demanded and not the levelling of society.

In contrast to their adopted name, the Levellers did not originally have any kind of collective title. The Leveller leader, John Lilburne, referred to those of his persuasion as "Levellers so called" and tended more to use the term "Agitator" which had become used within the New Model Army to mean something like "Representative" or "Articulator". However, from 1649 onwards, leading members started using the term to describe themselves simply because that was the one being used by others to identify them.

In addition, they were never a homogeneous group in any way reminiscent of a modern political party. And although this loose group of allied activists issued a series of political demands, they never produced one simple manifesto of beliefs. Nevertheless, they did draw together a large number of people around a general set of demands which provided a rallying point and a common set of general values; and they were skilful at both creating a sense of common purpose and in articulating grievances. They also used identifiers such as sea-green ribbons and sprigs of rosemary to signal allegiance and were energetic and astute in their presentation of petitions and the dissemination of pamphlets in order to spread awareness of their demands. They also published a newspaper, *The Moderate*, between July 1648 and September 1649.

The Levellers became an active force toward the end of the First Civil War (1642–46) and were most influential in 1647, before the outbreak of the Second Civil War (1648–49). By 1650, in the face of determined government opposition, and following the failure of a number of mutinies in the summer of 1649, their influence rapidly declined.

Their origins lay in a growing dissatisfaction felt by a number of Parliamentary supporters as the First Civil War drew toward its close. Leading critics, who soon became spokesmen for the movement, were John Lilburne (*c*.1615–57), Richard Overton (died 1664) and William Walwyn (*c*.1600–81). The movement first appeared among educated and middle-ranking (mostly London-based) civilians. In October 1645, Walwyn published *England's Lamentable Slaverie*, in response to the arrest of Lilburne who had condemned the wealth of MPs while soldiers fought and suffered lack of pay. From the early days of the movement, a meeting of minds occurred between these dissatisfied civilians and the more radical elements within the New Model Army.

This came to fruition in 1647, when representatives (known as "Agitators") were elected in army regiments to convey grievances to Parliament concerning: arrears of pay; Parliament's plans to disband some of the Army; and further plans to despatch the remainder of the army to Ireland in order to suppress the rebellion that had been ongoing there since 1641. This culminated in June

1647 with the publication of the Agitators' demands in a document entitled *A Solemn Engagement of the Army*, which forced the army leadership to set up an army council, in which representatives of ordinary soldiers could discuss matters with the high command, the so-called "Grandees". While some in the army leadership were contemplating a watered-down settlement with the king (expressed in a document known as the *Heads of the Proposals*), the Levellers, both civilian and military, threw their weight behind their own radical proposals – *An Agreement of the People* – which, as we shall shortly see formed the basis for a great army discussion at Putney, near London, in the autumn of 1647.[4]

THE LEVELLERS' DEMANDS

The Levellers grouped around a bundle of demands including: religious toleration; legal reforms in order to make access to the law easier for ordinary people; an extended franchise; individual rights guaranteed by a written constitution; a government that was answerable to the people; and free trade.

Walwyn's *England's Lamentable Slaverie* argued that Parliament should be directly accountable to the people. In July 1646 Walwyn and Richard Overton published *A Remonstrance of Many Thousand Citizens*, which demanded: the dissolution of the present House of Commons and fresh elections; the abolition of the House of Lords; religious toleration; equality before the law; and the ending of the trade monopolies which benefited powerful sections of society. Alongside this, it argued for the removal of "the Norman yoke". This was a common idea among seventeenth-century radicals that "free-born" Anglo-Saxons had seen their rights eclipsed at the Norman Conquest of 1066. Ever since then, it was claimed, monarchs and their allies had subjugated the free-born people of England and excluded them from full political participation. This was a fiction, since nothing like this had existed before 1066, but it was a popular belief among those eager for radical change as it suggested that, far from arguing in favour of political novelties, they were really just attempting to restore traditional English freedoms. It was a potent and useful myth, even if historically false.

Collaboration between civilian and military radicals in October 1647 and again in May 1649 produced the closest the Levellers came to a clear-cut manifesto. Entitled *An Agreement of the People*, among other things it called for: equal Parliamentary constituencies; biennial Parliaments; abolition of the House of Lords; freedom of religion; and equal application of the law to all. In its final form in May 1649 (now entitled *An Agreement of the Free People of England, tendered as a Peace-Offering to this distressed Nation*) it was refined by the civilian Levellers, Lilburne, Overton, and Walwyn, after what they saw as a failure of the army leadership to engage honestly with the process of discussing it. Their revolutionary proposals included: the vote for all men over twenty-one (apart from servants, beggars, and Royalists); annual Parliaments; equality before the law; restriction of the death penalty to murder only; abolition of imprisonment for debt; abolition of tithes to the Church of England; taxation in proportion to wealth; and abolition of conscription. By the time it was published, all the civilian Leveller leaders had been imprisoned and a couple of weeks later the army mutiny at Burford was suppressed. Consequently, this most radical version of their demands coincided with the collapse of the movement. It would leave a lasting memory, but had no other contemporary effect.

What the Levellers never succeeded in doing was squaring the circle between their demands for a greatly extended franchise and, at the same time, the protection of property rights. For, as their opponents were quick to point out, giving political power to poorer people was likely to lead to demands for some kind of redistribution of wealth. And, even without this, their demands for equality of the franchise horrified the elites in a rigidly hierarchal society who (probably rightly) interpreted this as the prelude to the collapse of their economic as well as political domination of the nation. Cromwell and the godly among the Independents might believe that by grace all stood equal before God but they certainly did not think that this kind of radical equality of worth applied to men as they stood in relation to voting for Parliament!

THE LEVELLERS AND THE KINGDOM OF GOD

The Levellers were men of their time and their political views were framed within a set of Christian godly parameters. This is all too easily ignored by twentieth- and twenty-first-century sympathizers who tend to describe them in solely secular terms. In one sense this is understandable since most of what they stood for involved political rights and obligations that are equally at home in the secular world of modern democratic politics. This is further emphasized by the fact that Leveller writers such as Richard Overton had a tendency to express ideas in terms of political rights based on Natural Law. So, he could write in 1646, in *An Arrow Against All Tyrants*, "For by natural birth all men are equally and alike born to like propriety, liberty and freedom." While he expressed the view that, "God by nature has made him free", the emphasis still remained on rights due to the natural state of equality that all had by birth and, therefore, all should experience in terms of political rights. To Overton, therefore, all possessed "a natural, innate freedom".[5]

However, this was only one strand among the narratives of Leveller thinking. For John Lilburne, also writing in 1646, drew on the Old and the New Testaments in order to justify his political views in *London's Liberty in Chains*. In this pamphlet Lilburne made clear that human political rights are based on a Christian view of creation in which God created all as equal, but tyranny is a result of sinful humanity; a state rectified by Christ who came to restore humanity to the former state of "its first perfection, beauty, splendour and glory". For Lilburne, the campaign for improved political rights was rooted in a Christian understanding of God and humanity. On one hand there is, "The omnipotent, glorious, and wise God, creating man for his own praise," while on the other hand this divine creation was done in such a way as to establish humanity with the caveat, "But made him [man] not Lord, or gave him dominion over the individuals of Mankind, no further than by free consent, or agreement..."[6] This Leveller radicalism is firmly rooted in Christian understanding and sharpened (without actually saying so) by the concept of personal election and empowering faith that was such an integral part of the godly mindset. As a result, one can argue that Lilburne's political outlook arose directly from his personal faith in the sovereignty of God as expressed in the personal experience of individual believers. Lilburne's outlook was rooted in the Calvinist experience that made many extremely confident in their election and in their status. This is not surprising as his earliest base was in a Particular Baptist church. Ironically, it had exactly the same effect on Cromwell but caused him to interpret his successes as evidence of divine approval, even as he was opposing the demands of the equally empowered Lilburne. Lilburne himself came out of a Puritan tradition which had earlier seen him criticize Archbishop Laud and High Church Anglicanism and which caused him to spend so much time imprisoned in the Tower of London that his wife even named one of their children "Tower"! It should be noted, however, that this Calvinist phase waned in his later writings and he ended life as a Quaker.[7]

It is not surprising, therefore, as Christopher Hill once noted, that, "the Levellers were never a united, disciplined party or movement, as historians find to their cost when they try to define their doctrines with any precision."[8] Or to put it another way, it is not surprising that they did not sing from the same doctrinal hymn sheet since, "they had no fixed membership and no one hymn sheet!"[9] But even Overton, with his greater emphasis on Natural Law than Creation Right, was a General Baptist (for at least some of his life) and his seemingly more rational and secular tone should not distract us from the sense of the potential general election, by grace, of all humanity that came from an Arminian (General) view of Christ's sacrifice and offer of salvation. From this it was but a short step to argue for universal political rights.

In the same way, William Walwyn first became involved in politics through campaigns for religious tolerance because he was originally an Independent and later a Separatist, who believed in the formation of congregationalist fellowships outside of the established Church of England. In the early 1640s he made this case in a pamphlet entitled *The Humble Petition of the Brownists*.[10] The term "Brownists" indicated those of a Separatist outlook (named from a sixteenth-century proponent of Separatism). The majority of the passengers on the *Mayflower* in 1620 were Brownists; so much so that, "In the American colonies, Brownism became a name for Separatists, especially those who had emigrated from Holland in the 1620s."[11] The Levellers believed strongly in the separation of church and state and, therefore, the freedom of believers to choose their own form of church and style of worship. Again, one can see how a theological position became the foundation for a political position. For, if an individual could choose their church and form of worship, why not their government too? Socially conservative Independents such as Cromwell never followed their theological position to its logical political conclusion, but the Levellers did.

The Levellers further explicitly stated on a number of occasions that their commitment to *social justice* arose from expressions of Christian love and service to God. That *social justice* should accompany *political justice* is clear from Leveller demands; but it would not lead to an enforced redistribution of wealth, rather it led to policies designed to assist the poor, such as abolition of tithes. In this they could be accused of having rather more concern for small tradespeople (from whose ranks they drew their support) than the very poor. They were more concerned with individual political rights and a fairer society than one in which a radical inversion of the economic order had occurred.

While both Overton and Walwyn were accused of "atheism", this was almost certainly due to their questioning tendency, accompanied by some unorthodox theology,[12] rather than anything that today would be described as "atheism". Interestingly, Walwyn's political radicalism also caused one anonymous pamphleteer to compare him to "that Arch-Anabaptist" Thomas Müntzer, who had influenced thinking during the sixteenth-century German Peasants' War. On their part, both Walwyn and Overton challenged the reliability of the atrocity propaganda that contemporaries aimed at the Anabaptists at Münster, describing it as, "That lying story of that injured people… the Anabaptists of Münster" and questioning, "Who writ the histories of the Anabaptists but their enemies?"[13]

Finally, it should again be asserted that the Levellers' emphasis on the rights of individuals to participate in a more democratic form of government was entirely consistent with their experience of the involvement of ordinary members of a congregation in the life and decision-making of the "gathered churches".

THE LEVELLERS IN ACTION:
THE PUTNEY DEBATES, 1647

The Leveller proposals, as outlined in the earliest version of *An Agreement of the People*, were debated at the so-called Putney Debates which occurred between October and November 1647. Putney, on the south bank of the river Thames, was at this time a village situated a short distance from London. At these debates the leaders – the Grandees – of the army, Cromwell, and his son-in-law Ireton, tried to control what they considered to be the extremism of the Levellers. They were particularly incensed over a proposal that the franchise should be extended to all adult males. The Leveller Colonel Rainsborough controversially asserted that, "the poorest he that is in England hath a life to live as the greatest he; and therefore... I think it's clear, that every man that is to live under a government ought first by his own consent to put himself under that government."[14] This was an explosive demand in the mid-seventeenth century and, considering that this did not come to pass until 1918,[15] one can see just how far ahead of its time it was as a political aspiration. Now the Levellers' definition of the franchise requirement did vary and later excluded servants, Royalists and those receiving poor relief (at the time of the third edition of the *Agreement* in May 1649), while in October 1647, in the lead-up to the Putney Debates they had simply called for "all the freeborn at the age of twenty one years and upwards, be the electors" (in *The Case of the Armie Truly Stated*).[16] Either way, however, they were radical by the standards of the time – though it must be noted that they never once considered giving the vote to women.

Parliament was as alarmed as the army elites over the implications of the radicals' demands and so denounced the *Agreement*, which was described as being destructive to the government of the nation. In order to prevent any recurrence it then ordered Fairfax to discover who had authored the document.

On 15 November 1647 there was an attempt to gain wider support in the army for the *Agreement* by assembling at Corkbush Field, near Ware in Hertfordshire. This was thwarted by the army leadership through the threat of force, and when Colonel Rainsborough attempted to present General Fairfax with a copy of the *Agreement* he was ignored. Most of the members of the seven regiments at the assembly agreed to sign a declaration of loyalty to the army leadership. Officers who refused were arrested. When two other regiments arrived with the motto "England's Freedom, Soldiers' Rights" stuck in their hats, one regiment was faced down by Fairfax, while the other had Cromwell ride among them with drawn sword to ensure that the mottos were removed. Three mutinous ringleaders were sentenced to death – and in a practice later seen at Burford, lots were drawn and one, Private Richard Arnold, was executed on the spot as an example. Had the regiments stood together and opposed the Grandees, they could have overwhelmed them; but lacking the single-minded resolve of their Grandee-commanders the Levellers did not pursue their radical demands.

THE LEVELLERS IN ACTION:
THE WHITEHALL DEBATES, 1648–49

After the collapse of the mutiny at Corkbush Field, the outbreak of the Second Civil War in 1648 caused the divided New Model Army to sink its differences and face the new threat posed by the king in alliance with the Scots. But the dissatisfaction had not evaporated.

Two new documents were produced by Levellers in the late spring of 1648. The army Agitators produced one called *The Armies Petition, or a new Engagement*, while their civilian allies produced *A New Engagement, or Manifesto* and also refined some of the demands they had earlier published. With the king finally defeated, another series of meetings took place in Whitehall in December 1648 between Levellers, some Independents, and the army Grandees. By that time "Pride's Purge" had removed Presbyterians from the Long Parliament and the king was due to face trial. Lilburne hoped that Parliament would agree to the (now extended) *Agreement* before the forthcoming trial so that it would form part of a comprehensive settlement of the nation. He was to be disappointed. Senior army officers insisted on amending it before placing it before Parliament and were probably only playing for time anyway. When it was finally put to Parliament, it was postponed until after the king's trial and never again discussed.

THE LEVELLERS IN ACTION: THE 1649 MUTINIES

The execution of King Charles I in January 1649 had not quietened those soldiers unhappy with the way that politics in England were developing. The regicide might have been the single most revolutionary action of the Parliamentary opposition to the contemporary status quo but it was not accompanied by similar radicalism in the transformation of politics. The Leveller demands were far from being met. Dissatisfaction was exacerbated by the fact that Parliament was still reluctant to settle the matter of back-pay owed to the army. To many among the ranks of unpaid soldiers, the new supremacy of the Independents in Parliament did not seem radically different to the situation under the Presbyterians which had fed their unrest back in 1647. At the same time, both civilian and military members of the Leveller movement were demanding elections for a more representative Parliament than the "Rump" that had been left after the purge of Presbyterians in December 1648. Parliament was now very much overshadowed by Cromwell and the army leadership – Pride's Purge was, in effect, nothing more than a military coup that had removed those MPs who had continued to support a negotiated settlement with the king, and it had made possible the king's trial and execution. The coup did not settle what the future representative nature of Parliament should be, and the Levellers were growing increasingly dissatisfied with the state of affairs.

The matter was made more explosive by the plans for an expedition to Ireland (see Chapter 6). For many in the army this was the last straw. Not only were they unwilling to take part in such an expedition while pay remained in arrears but some also felt that their use in Ireland, while the political state of England remained unresolved to their satisfaction, was unacceptable. It increasingly looked as if the army was being used by the Parliamentary leadership without an acceptance of its very particular nature and purpose. Having been raised to resist the king and pursue a "settlement of the nation", many in the army were not prepared to be used, as they saw it, as mere mercenaries to do the bidding of the Grandees of the army and the state. Such soldiers saw themselves as a political force in the land and were not prepared to be taken for granted.

Trouble flared in April 1649. When lots were used to decide which regiments would go to Ireland, three hundred men of Colonel Hewson's infantry regiment refused to obey orders and further stated that they would only travel to Ireland if Leveller demands were met. In response they were dismissed from the army without their back-pay being paid. Resentment spread and toward the end of April soldiers in Colonel Whalley's regiment mutinied, took possession of the regimental colours, and made their headquarters in the Bull Inn at Bishopsgate, London. Only when confronted by Fairfax and Cromwell did they back down. One of their number, Robert Lockier, who had earlier acted as an Agitator within the regiment and who was considered to be the mutiny's ringleader, was executed by firing squad at St Paul's Cathedral on 27 April 1649. At his funeral, thousands of mourners wore the Levellers' colours of the sea-green ribbon and also wore rosemary (for remembrance) in their hats, in a show of strength reminiscent of that that had been shown at the funeral of Colonel Rainsborough the previous year.[17] The uprising spread further to Salisbury, Wiltshire, where Colonel Scrope's regiment of horse mutinied and elected new officers in defiance of being selected for service in Ireland.

The Salisbury mutiny sparked an escalation of the crisis. In a radical play for control of the army by its rank and file, the mutineers demanded the implementation of the Levellers' *Agreement of the People* and the reinstatement of the elected Army Council that had been formed in 1647. Similar declarations were soon to be issued by four other New Model Army regiments.[18] While this was happening, William Thompson issued a Leveller manifesto at

Banbury, Oxfordshire, with the title *England's Standard Advanced*, and he led a mutiny of local troops in support of the imprisoned John Lilburne and his *Agreement of the People*. The mutineers from Wiltshire then rode north to join him at Banbury.

However, the army leadership of Fairfax and Cromwell moved quickly. At the head of loyal regiments they prevented the various mutineers from joining up and surrounded a large group at Burford, whom they surprised in a night attack. Somewhere in the region of 340 prisoners were locked in the church at Burford. Evidence of their time in the church can still be seen there today, but most notable is the carving in the lead of the font which reads, "Anthony Sedley 1649 prisoner".[19] There is also a Nine Men's Morris board carved into one of the tombs by one of those held there for several days.

On Thursday 17 May 1649, three of the ringleaders were taken from the church and shot against the churchyard wall. The other mutineers were made to watch from a vantage point on the roof of the Lady Chapel. Four had been sentenced to death, but at the last minute they were made to draw lots; one pulled out the lot inscribed "Life given by God" and he was reprieved and made to preach to the survivors and publish a pamphlet repenting the mutiny. The remaining mutineers were pardoned. The churchwardens were left to pay for the cleaning of a church which for several days had been a prison for hundreds of men.[20] William Thompson was killed near Wellingborough, Northamptonshire, after having himself shot dead two of the troopers pursuing him. His brother had been one of the three earlier executed at Burford.

THE END OF THE LEVELLERS

With the establishment of the Commonwealth, following the execution of King Charles I, the Levellers quickly clashed with the newly appointed Council of State that was tasked with running the new republic. In March 1649 a new Leveller tract was published with the provocative title of *England's New Chains Discovered*. As its title implied, it embodied the disappointment that the Levellers felt at the lack of real political freedom that they had hoped would accompany the final overthrow of the monarchy. For publishing this pamphlet, Lilburne, Overton, Walwyn, and other Levellers were imprisoned, sparking the failed mutinies that culminated in the siege at Burford. Levellerism was now in decline as a political force; its high-water mark of influence had come and gone.

Although Lilburne was acquitted of high treason at a trial in October 1649, in 1652 he was in court again, on charges of criminal libel against a member of the Council of State, a treasonous offence. He was exiled, but returned in 1653 when he was again arrested and imprisoned for life. While held at Dover Castle he described in his pamphlet *The Resurrection of John Lilburne* that he had given up political activities and converted to Quakerism. He died in 1657.

One Leveller leader, John Wildman, maintained that the reason for his own arrest, in March 1649, was down to the hostility of London Independent congregations who he had criticized for their lack of Christian holiness, since he had given up active politics. He was released in the autumn of 1649.

A BRIEF RESURGENCE

With the establishment of the Protectorate under Cromwell in 1653, there was a slight revival of Levellerism. Many on the left of the godly felt that this near-monarchical regime was a betrayal of all that they had fought the Civil Wars for. There then followed a number of failed conspiracies aimed at overthrowing the regime. These involved ex-Agitators, along with those who had once been active Levellers. They were not the only disappointed saints, since (quite separately) the very different group of the Fifth Monarchy Men were also plotting to bring down the man that they felt had taken the place of King Jesus at the head of a godly commonwealth. All failed.

For the Levellers this resulted in the re-arrest of John Wildman in 1655. He had conspired with both republicans and Royalists against Cromwell. He was not the only one to do so, since Richard Overton too became involved in Leveller-Royalist conspiracies and was briefly exiled, only to return and then vanish from history. Wildman, though, was released in 1656 but continued to be involved in complex conspiracies involving a bewildering array of disillusioned Levellers and Baptists, alongside Royalists and representatives of Catholic and Spanish interests. After the Restoration he was imprisoned, 1661–67, for more republican intrigues and then again, in 1683, under suspicion of involvement in a plot to assassinate King Charles II and his brother, the Duke of York. Wildman was then involved in the Monmouth Rebellion against James II (and VII in Scotland) in 1685 which resulted in his fleeing to the Netherlands. There he became involved in the cause of the Protestant William of Orange, who eventually overthrew the Catholic James II in the "Glorious Revolution" of 1688. Wildman was knighted in 1692 and died the next year. He had travelled a long way from the radicalism of the late 1650s.

THE LEGACY OF THE LEVELLERS

From the 1970s the British Labour movement has publicized the role played by the Levellers. In a 1976 pamphlet, based on a talk given on the newly instituted Levellers' Day, the Labour MP Tony Benn suggested that the seventeenth-century Levellers would have a lot to say about contemporary issues ranging from the huge inequality in financial power to the recall and replacement of MPs. The Levellers were no longer "hidden from history". The matter has been well summed up by a recent reassessment of modern use of the Leveller legacy: "This was not an act of returning to a distant past but creating a particular sort of living present. This theme continues into the twenty-first century."[21]

In 1988 the band the Levellers was formed; their genre being variously described as "alternative-rock", "folk-punk" or "folk-rock". The titles of their first recordings – *An Agreement of the People* and *All the Free Commons of England* – made clear how they took inspiration from the seventeenth-century radical movement. In 2010 they returned to the Glastonbury Festival and in 2013 they headlined at Camp Bestival festival in Dorset. A film, entitled *A Curious Life*, about the band was released in 2014. The "Rolling Anarchy" symbol (three sickles placed so as to form the letter "A") is often used by the band. Often surrounded by the words of the French anarchist philosopher, Pierre-Joseph Proudhon, "Whoever puts their hand upon me to govern me is a usurper, a tyrant, and I declare them my enemy," the anarchist-leaning nature of the band is clear.

These two currents of remembrance serve to illustrate something of the complex legacy of the Levellers: radical activists... proto-democrats... libertarians from oppressive government... proponents of freedom for the common man and woman... One suspects that, as God-fearing members of the army of saints, they would have been less convinced by the anarchist track that their legacy has taken. For they came from a period of history when their belief in the liberty of humanity was inspired by their understanding of the nature of the kingdom of God.

8

A Very English Kind of Communism… The Diggers

Today, St George's Hill in Weybridge, Surrey, is an immaculately kept area of extremely expensive homes, golf and tennis clubs, whose residents have included the Beatles' drummer, Ringo Starr. The golf course has been described as "a golfing gem".[1] Its Residents' Association describe it as, "a distinctive and unique location in understated and tranquil surroundings."[2] In the spring of 1649, however it was anything but "tranquil". For it was then that this prime piece of Surrey real estate became the focal point of a radical experiment in rural communism; an experiment that ended after violent intimidation organized by local landowners.

The rise of the "Diggers" or "True Levellers"

If the Levellers were uneasy at the label they carried, then it must be said that the group who occupied the common land at St George's Hill had no such reservations. In fact they were pleased to refer to themselves as the "True Levellers".[3] For if the Levellers demanded political reform in order to achieve individual political rights and others called for freedom of conscience in matters of religion, the Diggers called for nothing less than the reordering of the system of land ownership in the country. In any period of history this would have been revolutionary, but in 1650 when about 83 per cent of the English population lived in the countryside,[4] and wealth was still measured primarily in terms of land and agricultural products, the idea of the communalization of agriculture was truly shocking.

Yet in the context of 1649 this may have seemed achievable to this most radical of groups. The execution of the king in January of that year and the abolition of the House of Lords soon afterwards seemed to signal a massive change in the social order. Alongside the upheaval of the recently concluded Civil Wars and the politicization of large numbers of men through membership of the New Model Army, there was a general air of "anything might be possible" among the most optimistic of those dissatisfied with the current state of society. After all, episcopal authority had gone, Presbyterian authority had been thwarted, significant minorities in the population were actively involved in the governance of Independent congregations of the Church of England or in Separatist Baptist fellowships, and even the "Rump" of the "Long Parliament" – in an act passed in May 1649 – declared the new republic of England to be "a Commonwealth".[5] The latter term (not invented by the Rump but drawn from the godly and Parliamentary lexicon) had connotations of community sharing and cooperation in a new Christian political order. It is true that for many of those who used it, the term was little more than a veneer to cover the reality of a republic achieved through non-legal means. Sir Arthur Hesilrige (1601–61) – a political and religious radical, who in the 1650s fell out with Cromwell – later rather lamely expressed this view: "force was much upon us. What should we do? We turned ourselves into a Commonwealth."[6]

However, to the Diggers the term was pregnant with possibilities. They were soon to find that, in the face of entrenched and powerful opposition forces, these would be still born. But that is to get ahead of the story.

All of this historical context is worth reiterating because we need to understand the Diggers' motivations if we are to really understand their character and their role within this turbulent period of history. For the Diggers, as much as the Levellers, have been prised away from the godly context of the 1640s and 1650s by many modern writers and presented as if they were modern *secular* agrarian anarcho-communists. While there are some grounds for this modern tendency, such a characterization goes much too far.

The rise of the Diggers coincided with the end of the Civil Wars and a series of bad harvests. Exacerbated by the economic and trade dislocations caused by years of warfare, unemployment and food shortages affected many communities. As a response to these conditions a number of areas experienced civil unrest with hungry people seizing grain stores by force and tearing down hedges because these symbolized the property rights of wealthy landowners. At the same time there was heightened discontent in the army and the most high-profile activities of the Levellers, culminating in the abortive Whitehall Debates of December 1648 and the Leveller-inspired army mutinies of the spring and summer of 1649.

Among those involved in this rural unrest a number adopted the term "Leveller", even though they had no real connection with the likes of Lilburne and his associates, both civilian and military, as they sought to negotiate an extension of political rights. Nevertheless, it was in this context that agrarian Levellers or "True Levellers" began to assert themselves. Lilburne and his allies were quick to deny any association with them since they did not espouse the wealth redistribution or abolition of property rights which were being articulated by the "True Levellers". In fact, the franchise arrangements being proposed by the political Levellers meant that many of those drawn to the ranks of the "True Levellers" would have been disenfranchised by the Leveller proposals, which did not include the poorest in society.[7] The "True Levellers" therefore represented what we might call the left wing of the amorphous Leveller movement and a wing that was less interested in the constitution than in the practical reordering of rural society and property rights. This section of the movement soon began to articulate their beliefs in a series of publications so typical of this age of pamphlets.

In December 1648 *Light Shining in Buckinghamshire* was published by agitators who had been active in a number of anti-enclosure riots that had occurred in the county between 1647 and 1648. These enclosures were the latest manifestations of rural change that had been sweeping the country since the early sixteenth century. At their simplest they involved the hedging in of land by local dominant landlords in order to maximize their control of the land. This was at its most controversial when it involved the hedging in (effectively the privatization) of "common land" which had previously been subject to some form of common ownership and use. As in the later Enclosure Movement of the eighteenth-century "Agricultural Revolution", this process disadvantaged those unable to produce documentation detailing their rights to the use of this land but advantaged those wealthier citizens whose possession of legal documentation (plus social clout) enabled them to take these areas of land into their own private ownership. This was exacerbated if the enclosure was accompanied, as it often was, by the switch in land use from cereal production to sheep rearing or dairying, as these tended to employ fewer from the ranks of the landless labouring class in the village community. This loss of rights to graze animals or otherwise enjoy the benefits of the common land was made worse when enclosures also took in "waste" which had previously been available (for grazing of animals, collection of firewood, siting of cottages) by anyone in the village community. It should at this point be pointed out that "common land" was never available for just anyone to use. It was not that "common"; rather it was land with specific and traditional connections with specific and identifiable local communities.

What is clear is that enclosure of land was highly unpopular among the most poor and vulnerable in the village communities and it could also lead to nasty shocks for some better-off members if they found themselves on the losing side in a battle with a powerful local landowner who could afford both legal representation and the buying-in of hired-muscle to intimidate others. When this was accompanied by favourable judgments in courts dominated by allies of these wealthier people, this could make opposing the raising of hedges very difficult indeed. And so acts of rebellion often led to the tearing down (levelling) of these very hedges. In so doing, the levelling of actual hedges soon became synonymous with the levelling of other – social, legal, and ideological – barriers which sought to hedge in the rights and privileges of some, and keep out others. It was in this way, during the anti-enclosure Midland

Revolts of 1604–07, that both the terms "leveller" and "digger" first appeared; the former implying the smashing of hedges and the latter the filling in of ditches.[8] They were revolutionary terms and well bedded into the popular vocabulary by the 1640s.

Those who published *Light Shining in Buckinghamshire* quoted the Bible in making their case for the overthrow of the nobles and the redistribution of wealth; and they promised the rich that "God will visit you for your oppressions."[9] In this they continued a tradition traceable to the culmination of the Midland Revolt in which one activist – John Reynolds of Desborough, Northamptonshire – claimed authority granted him by King James and "the Lord of Heaven" to destroy enclosures. He became known as "Captain Pouch" from the contents of a leather satchel which he claimed contained proof of his authority. Incidentally, when captured and hanged, the contents of the satchel were said to be no more authoritative than a piece of green cheese.[10] The relevance of this story to those who published *Light Shining in Buckinghamshire* is that both came from a Christian milieu that saturated their outlook with scriptural insights and values. To Captain Pouch, his authority from the "Lord of Heaven" was part of his mental outlook and appeal, just as the writers of *Light Shining in Buckinghamshire* turned to the Bible for their justification. To properly understand the nature of the Diggers' ideology alongside the tendency to secularize them in many modern works it is necessary to bear in mind the religious impulse that ran through the movement.

Light Shining in Buckinghamshire was not the only product of this group; its sequel, unimaginatively titled *More Light Shining in Buckinghamshire*, appeared in March 1649. Keeping in touch with the mood of the times, this second pamphlet appealed for assistance to the regiments of the New Model Army. It is noticeable that these Buckinghamshire radicals were happy to openly confront both Parliament and the army Grandees, whereas the more famous group which settled on St George's Hill were keen to engage with state representatives and to try to persuade them of the justice of the Digger cause.[11]

At the same time as things were stirring in Buckinghamshire, a number of similar cases of unrest were striking in other areas of the country, although it is now difficult to trace whether they were coordinated or coincidental. What we can say is that during 1649–50, a number of Digger communities sprang up with the intention of occupying common land and waste. The plan was to cultivate them communally and to encourage others to do the same. In this way the landless could benefit from the land and the social order of rigid private property would be shaken.

GOD AND THE DIGGERS... WHAT DID THE DIGGERS REALLY BELIEVE?

In their reflections on what they perceived as being wrong with the state of rural society, the Diggers had begun to articulate what, a century later, Adam Smith would first popularize as "the labour theory of value" before Karl Marx would shape the concept to his critique of nineteenth-century capitalism. This states that the value of an object comes from the effort (labour) put into it by a worker and that this should not be diverted to profit another person. For the Diggers this was a relatively new and expanding economic experience, since between 1500 and 1650 the number of independent smallholders (who had once kept control of the products of their labour) had been shrinking and was being replaced by an expanding class of hired labourers who worked for wages (to the benefit of their employers). In the mid-seventeenth century it was still possible to remember, or at least have some awareness of, the fact that this had not always been the case. The writings of the Digger leader Gerard Winstanley reflected a changing world in which wage labour was increasing rapidly. Indeed, it has been calculated that by the 1680s two-thirds of the English population were landless labourers and, "by that time England had acquired a rural proletariat".[12] As Winstanley put it, "The rich by their covetous wit got the poor to work for small wages, and by their labour got a great increase, for the poor by their labour lifts up tyrants to rule over them."[13]

For the Diggers the answer was clear: take common land into communal ownership so that this problem of wage-driven labour could be avoided. Since they considered that the earth was a "common treasury", these True Levellers took direct action to cultivate available waste and common land. Their ultimate aim was that this would begin a national process by which all such land would eventually be restored to its rightful owners. In this way the common people, instead of the king and gentry, would regain control of both the land and their labour and its value. By concentrating on common land, waste land, and the royal and gentry parks that had been seized from Royalists, they could offer the hope of a rural land revolution without necessarily threatening the landholdings of middle-ranking members of the rural community. This seemed to offer tenurial change without compulsion. No longer would "rich men receive all they have from the labourer's hand".[14]

This was all very anarcho-communist and one can see why some modern writers stress the modernity of Winstanley's economic analysis. But his thinking went deeper than this and it was a metaphysical construct that was rooted in Christian theology. In this he was not alone. The first critic of the St George's Hill Digger community described one of its leaders, William Everard, as being "once of the army but was cashiered, who termeth himself a prophet..."[15] Now this might just have been a throwaway line that meant nothing more than Everard was a visionary leader. But there are reasons why we should not dismiss it so lightly. In January 1649, in the pamphlet entitled *The New Law of Righteousnes*, Winstanley had promised that the economic order would change soon, since Christ would rise in his people and lead them to a more righteous relationship with each other. There is more than a hint of contemporary millenarianism about this statement even if he never meant anything quite so cosmically transformational as the Second Coming of Christ, which the Fifth Monarchy Men preached was imminent (see Chapter 9). This is clear from phrases he used such as, "it is the fullness of time" and the "restorer of the earth" would soon "make the earth a common treasury" again.[16] Even the slightest acquaintance with Old Testament prophecy and also with the incarnational[17] and eschatological[18] language of the New Testament will pick up echoes of it in these words of hope in future transformation of the world order. Galatians 4:4, in the

Geneva Bible states, of Christ, "But when the fullness of time was come, God sent forth his Son…" And in a reference to Christ's Second Coming, Ephesians 1:10 states,

> *… in the dispensation of the fullness of the times, he might gather together in one all things, both which are in heaven, and which are in earth, even in Christ.*

It is reasonable to assume that Winstanley had such verses in mind as he penned *The New Law of Righteousnes*. There is, for example, plenty of evidence that some Anabaptists preached a form of communism; to the extent that this belief was explicitly rejected in the Thirty-nine Articles of the Church of England. And there were clearly "End Time" features in Winstanley's words when he stated that one who entered into communal enterprises, "doth join hands with Christ to lift up the creation from bondage, and restores all things from the curse".[19] This was an explicit reference to the Fall as described in Genesis, which led to the earth being cursed and human beings alienated from the act of labouring. Genesis 3:17–19 describes God's judgment on Adam:

> *"Because thou hast obeyed the voice of thy wife, and hast eaten of the tree, (whereof I commanded thee, saying, Thou shalt not eat of it) cursed is the earth for thy sake: in sorrow shalt thou eat of it all the days of thy life.*
> *Thorns also and thistles shall it bring forth to thee, and thou shalt eat the herb of the field.*
> *In the sweat of thy face shalt thou eat bread till thou return to the earth: for out of it wast thou taken, because thou art dust, and to dust shalt thou return."*

What Winstanley was prophesying was nothing less than the restoration of the earth and of fallen sinful society through the implementation of a communal ownership of the land. This was as eschatological as it was socio-political. Once the Diggers had settled on St George's Hill, their manifesto – *The True Levellers Standard Advanced*[20] – claimed that all the scriptural prophecies about the "restoration of Israel" (referring to justice and freedom from want) involved digging. It seems that he and the early Diggers entertained the far-reaching thought that the process they were starting would be part of the restoration of the whole of fallen creation. No wonder Everard was described as one "who termeth himself a prophet". And, unless we draw this conclusion, some of the Digger statements sound simply bizarre. How else should we interpret, "True religion and undefiled is to let everyone quietly have earth to manure",[21] unless it has a deeper symbolic as well as a practical meaning. It is surely too prosaic to conclude, as Christopher Hill appeared to, that this was primarily about the means to feed cattle over the winter and so to have sufficient fertilizer for the land. In contrast to Hill's claim that, " 'Manuring' is the crucial word in Winstanley's programme",[22] it could be asserted that the crucial words really were, "True religion and undefiled", for it was this that was represented by the Digger programme and which promised more than just a reorganization of crop routines and cattle management. For Winstanley, the Second Coming of Christ was not to be looked for in a dramatic event such as "Christ coming in the clouds" as traditionally taught but rather as Christ "rising up" within the saints and, through this, restoring humanity from its fallen state and society from its enslavement to private ownership. This was clear from his 1648 pamphlet *The Saints Paradice*, which predated his Digger activities. It is almost as if the act of digging was a symbolic event that would trigger supernatural agency. Something of this is clear in such statements as,

> the curse then shall be removed from the Creation, Fire, Water, Earth and Air... There shall be no barrenness in the earth or cattle, for they shall bring forth fruit abundantly. Unseasonable storms of weather shall cease...[23]

This End Time expectation must be set alongside Digger practical experiments in planting crops suitable for sandy soil, increased use of manure and encouraging seizure of royal estates and common land.

This rather neatly brought together the themes of the curse of the land in Genesis and the curse of society through the Norman Yoke theory (as espoused by the Levellers), for the same word (i.e. "curse") could be applied to both. For Winstanley wrote, in *A Declaration from the Poor Oppressed People of England* (1649), how the ancestors of the modern gentry had gained the land and dispossessed others "by the sword" and that "though you did not kill or thieve, yet you hold that cursed thing in your hand by the power of the sword…"[24] In addition, he identified Charles I as embodying the "666 mark of the beast" of the Book of Revelation but whose death presaged the restoration of creation by God. He also believed (a belief illegal since 1648) that all humanity would be saved.

The "prophetic" nature of Winstanley's motivation is further emphasized in the way in which he described how the words "work together, eat bread together" were received in a visionary experience. Describing these words as coming to him "in a trance", as some modern historians have done,[25] is understandable, but any seventeenth-century member of the godly would have used a different term. This was "receiving a word from the Lord", this was the kind of "prophesying" that so irritated the High Church Arminians as they looked askance at the saints of the Independent churches and the gathered congregations. There have even been suggestions that many early Quaker communities in the Midlands had Digger connections, but that this early history was suppressed by later Quakers.[26] It should be noted that prophetic utterances were a notable feature of this earlier period of Quakerism, and Winstanley duly would become a Quaker.

The establishment of the Digger communities

We first hear about the most famous of the Digger communities in April 1649. On 16 April a report was made to the Council of State (ruling the country alongside Parliament since the execution of the king in January of that year) concerning the Digger community at St George's Hill. This and the one later established at Cobham Heath were led by Gerrard Winstanley and William Everard. They renamed the first one "George Hill" because they rejected the saints of the established church. This was very much in line with the mindset of the godly. The Diggers believed that the poor sandy soil could be made fertile by God's assistance and by improved agriculture such as manuring. Somewhere in the region of fifty men and their accompanying families joined the George Hill settlement.

The commander of the New Model Army, Sir Thomas Fairfax, interviewed Winstanley and Everard, but concluded that they were basically harmless and advised local landowners to use the courts to remove them. Everard soon left the community.

In court the Diggers were accused of being "Ranters", a sect associated with sexual promiscuity and without any real political significance. This was false and Winstanley had earlier criticized Ranters regarding their behaviour. This was typical though of the kinds of accusation levelled at Anbabaptists. Facing eviction by the army and continued intimidation organized by local landowners, they were forced to relocate to Little Heath, near Cobham, in August 1649. However, in the face of rising hostility this community too was abandoned, in the spring of 1650.

Another Digger community was established at Iver in Buckinghamshire, which may have been related to the group who produced *Light Shining in Buckinghamshire*. Another community was established at Wellingborough, Northamptonshire, which produced its own manifesto, the *Wellingborough Declaration*, in March 1649. There were further Digger colonies in Barnet, Hertfordshire, Enfield, Middlesex, Dunstable, Bedfordshire, Bosworth, Leicestershire, Gloucestershire, and Nottinghamshire. Another was sited at Coxhall in Kent.[27]

In March 1650, representatives from the Surrey Diggers were arrested in Buckinghamshire. They carried a letter signed by their leaders, including Winstanley. It encouraged the spread of Digger colonies and asked for gifts of money from sympathizers, to assist the Surrey Diggers. The Parliamentary newspaper, *A Perfect Diurnall*, carried a report to the effect that those arrested had travelled through Surrey, Middlesex, Hertfordshire, Bedfordshire, Buckinghamshire, Berkshire, Huntingdonshire, and Northamptonshire before being arrested. Clearly, Digger ideas had been spread far and wide. But it was to no avail; the movement was doomed.

THE END OF THE DIGGERS

All the Digger settlements faced hostility from local landowners. Those in Surrey faced the triple sanction of legal action, refusal to buy their produce, and open violence. It all ended there in April 1650, when the Diggers' cottages were burned down and their crops destroyed. Other Digger communities also succumbed. In April 1650, the Council of State ordered the arrest of the leaders of the Wellingborough Diggers, who were then held in Northampton prison.

In 1651, faced with the failure of his revolutionary vision, Winstanley wrote a tract entitled *The Law of Freedom* in which he proposed state action to bring in the necessary rural reforms. He even dedicated it to Oliver Cromwell, but the plea was ignored. By this time he had drifted away from millenarian hopes.

Winstanley had come a long way since his first tract of 1648 (*The Mystery of God*), when he advanced a "dispensationalist"[28] belief that he was living in the last-but-one dispensation and awaited the imminent restoration of creation by the action of God. Something of this survived as late as 1649 as, in *The True Levellers Standard Advanced*, he pondered Revelation 12:13-14 where the rule of one called "the dragon" and "the serpent" would last for, "a time, and times, and half a time". Seventeenth-century Christians differed widely in how they interpreted the meaning of this verse and what its length implied. But in 1649 Winstanley was convinced that the time was almost up and that momentous events were imminent. However, that confidence passed and this accompanied his complete abandonment of all traditional forms of religion, including prayer to an external God (God being within, he came to believe), traditional concepts of heaven and hell, and even the use of the term "God" itself – to be replaced by the term "Reason" because he disagreed with so much of what was implied by the former term. In 1676 he was buried as a Quaker, a sect which emphasized searching for God within themselves. By the time of his death, Winstanley had ceased to pursue the transformation of society by outward actions. God's kingship had become an inward matter and not an outward reordering of society.

9

"God's People Must Be a Bloody People!" The Fifth Monarchy Men

One of the most dramatic of the godly groups who came to prominence in the middle of the seventeenth century were the Fifth Monarchy Men. They were particularly active in the 1650s, during the Commonwealth and Protectorate periods. Their striking and unusual name derived from their belief that the time of the "Fifth Monarchy" was about to begin; that is the monarchy which – according to some interpretations of biblical prophecy – would succeed the previous historical "monarchies" (empires) of Babylon, Persia, Greece, and Rome and which would constitute the rule of Christ (after the Second Coming). Christ would reign on earth with his saints for one thousand years (a millennium) before the final judgment and the creation of a new heaven and a new earth.

The story of this movement reveals perhaps the most direct application of the godly belief in the rule of the saints, and the hopes of those determined to establish a form of government and society in which, as they saw it, God truly would be King on earth. As the "prophetess" Anna Trapnell put it, in 1654, in a pamphlet entitled *The Cry of a Stone*:

> *Oh King Jesus thou art longed for,*
> *Oh take thy power and raign...*[1]

These members of the godly were determined to implement a theocracy of the saints ruling for and then alongside Christ himself.

CHRISTIAN MILLENARIANISM: A BRIEF OVERVIEW

A core belief of Christianity looks forward to the Second Coming of Christ and the ushering in of the fullest manifestation of what is described as the "kingdom of God". The study of this belief is known as "*eschatology*" (End Times). In its broadest scope this covers beliefs concerning death, the resurrection of the dead, heaven, and hell; but is usually used to refer to the Second Coming of Christ. This future event is sometimes also referred to as the "*Parousia*". This Greek word means "presence" and it became particularly associated with the return of Christ. Another Greek word used in the New Testament to describe this End Time event was "*apokalupsis*" (apocalypse), meaning "revelation". In the New Testament, the Second Coming of Christ was also referred to in a Greek phrase which translates as "the Day of the Lord". Before we leave these key terms it should also be noted that the word *millenarianism*, or the alternative term *millennialism*, is also often used to describe this belief in Christ's return. This is derived from belief in the *millennium*, the thousand-year reign of Christ on earth after his return, prior to the final transformation of the created order.

Belief in the imminence of this event was a significant factor in the worldview of the early church. The fact that the Second Coming did not occur caused puzzlement and meant that the belief has been both reinterpreted and debated over the past two millennia. By the seventeenth century there existed a complex variety of beliefs about this doctrine and this built on a foundation of centuries of competing and conflicting interpretations. The seventeenth-century proponents of this belief drew on (consciously or unconsciously) a turbulent backstory. Eleventh- and twelfth-century crusaders had seen conflict with Islam as fulfilling prophecies. Other medieval groups too proclaimed millenarian beliefs, such as the Secret Flagellants of Thuringia in the 1360s, among others. The Bohemian Taborites, a radical section of the Hussite Movement (a forerunner of the Protestant Reformation) until their defeat in battle in 1434, preached the imminence of the Second Coming of Christ and the establishment of the millennium. In 1476 the so-called "Drummer of Niklashausen" (near Würzburg in Franconia, Germany), Hans Böhm, announced "messages" from the Virgin Mary, which included denunciations of the clergy and the arrival of the New Jerusalem, focused on Niklashausen. Thomas Müntzer (executed in 1525) preached in Zwickau, in Saxony, that the Second Coming was at hand but first there would be a period of terrible upheaval; then the elect would rise up and destroy the godless.

Millenarian beliefs became prevalent among sixteenth- and seventeenth-century Protestants who tended to identify the pope as the Antichrist referred to in the New Testament. Various attempts were made to identify the "mark of the beast" (666) in Revelation 13:18 as applicable to contemporary rulers and events. In 1597 the English writer Thomas Lupton, in a publication entitled *Babylon is Fallen*, named the year 1666 as the date of the Second Coming. He followed this, in 1610, with a second work entitled *A Prophesie That Hath Lyen Hid, Above These 2000 Years*, which reiterated the claim. However, in 1593, John Napier calculated that the key date would be 1688, in his book *A Plaine Discovery of the Whole Revelation*. These hinged on conflicting calculations, based on computations of numerical references (many obscure and mysterious) culled from various scriptural passages but particularly from the complex and difficult-to-interpret Book of Revelation, despite scriptural warnings that only God knows the day and hour.

What is clear is that the Reformation, through its removal of papal authority, had given rise to an explosion of radical millenarian ideas. At the same time, it caused such infighting within Christendom that each side accused the other of being the "Antichrist". And in such troubled times it seemed as if the known world *was* coming to an end. In addition, the Reformation's emphasis on a personal relationship with God, accompanied by expanding access to scripture in the vernacular among ordinary people, led to the emergence of some very varied interpretations indeed among some who were now deeply convinced of their personal spiritual insight and authority. This was especially so when disturbances to the social order allowed determined people to project their views on to wider society. The bloody events of the Anabaptist seizure of Münster in 1534, for example, soon took on a millenarian character. After its suppression, other millenarian prophets proclaimed the imminent arrival of the New Jerusalem in the 1560s. Such views continued to circulate among Anabaptist groups. Conflicts such as the Thirty Years' War and the British Civil Wars only added to this sense of being in the middle of apocalyptic events. This ensured that millenarian beliefs were very much in the Protestant (and in Britain the godly) mainstream and were certainly not just the preserve of certain fringe groups.

SOME KEY BIBLICAL TEXTS AND THEIR INTERPRETATION

A number of key biblical passages appear again and again in millenarian interpretations and were central to the outlook of the Fifth Monarchy Men.

One was that of the four beasts/kingdoms and their successor kingdoms that appear in the Old Testament book of Daniel 7, as revealed to him in a dream. The fourth beast had ten horns and, from these, an arrogant "little horn" appeared which would eventually be destroyed by God's chosen representative (the Messiah) and this would then result in, "the kingdom of the Saints of the most High" which would last forever (Daniel 7:18) and furthermore, "the Ancient of days came, and judgment was given to the Saints of the most High: and the time approached, that the Saints possessed the kingdom" (Daniel 7:22). Later Christians interpreted these beasts/kingdoms as the empires of Babylon, Persia,[2] Greece, and Rome.[3] From the Roman Empire, a later phase would emerge, then the arrogant little horn, and finally the return of Christ and the rule of the saints. But identifying the key second phase of the fourth empire (and the horns) proved difficult, with many different candidates suggested by Christian writers.

The concept of a four-staged succession of kingdoms also appeared in Daniel 2, in Nebuchadnezzar's dream. This took the form of a statue made from gold, silver, brass, and iron, with feet part iron and part clay. A stone "cut without hands" smashed these feet. Daniel explained that this destruction indicated the breaking of an apparently strong but diverse and brittle kingdom; then "shall the God of heaven set up a kingdom, which shall never be destroyed" (Daniel 2:44). Some (e.g. the *Geneva Bible* commentary) took this to mean that "all the kingdoms of the world are transitory, and that the kingdom of Christ shall only remain forever", but others were quick to identify particular rulers, such as Charles I, with these feet of iron/clay. The phrase "he [God] taketh away kings: he setteth up kings" (Daniel 2:21), also resonated with those supporting the regicide of 1649.

The Old Testament figures of the "fourth beast" and the "little horn" also became intertwined with Christian ideas about "Antichrist". The term Antichrist is found in the New Testament five times in the letters known as 1 John and 2 John, once in plural form and four times in the singular.[4] The wording of these particular references are such that today they are often interpreted as marking out a certain category of persons, rather than an individual; but the individual identification is still made by many Christians. Belief in an individual Antichrist figure also focuses on the letter known as 2 Thessalonians. Here the term "Antichrist" is not actually used and the terms found here (in the *Geneva* translation) are "man of sin", "the son of perdition" (2 Thessalonians 2:3) and "that wicked man" (2 Thessalonians 2:8). The conflation of this person with "Antichrist" and the "fourth beast" is understandable,[5] given that he is described as one who "exalteth himself against all that is called God, or that is worshipped: so that he doth sit as God in the Temple of God, showing himself that he is God" (2 Thessalonians 2:4).

In the complex terminology and imagery found in the study of prophecy the composite figure of the (singular) "Antichrist" has, and is, often conflated by Christian writers with figures found in the New Testament Book of Revelation. Here we find one termed the "beast coming out of the earth" (Revelation 13:11). The other figure is the different beast seen to "rise out of the sea" (Revelation 13:1), who is closely associated with one referred to as the "false prophet". All are enemies of God in the End Time.[6] The references to the sea, animal imagery, and ten horns, in Revelation 13:1-2, appears to link to Daniel 7, referred to earlier. The enigmatic "mark or the name of the beast or the number of his name" is given in Revelation 13:17–18 as, "six hundred threescore and six" (i.e. 666). There is also a reference to a woman (termed "great Babylon that mother of whoredoms, and abominations of the earth") sitting "upon a scarlet coloured beast, full of names of blasphemy, which had seven heads, and ten horns" (Revelation 17:1–6). The identity of the "whore", as of the "beast", divided and continues to divide interpreters.

Once the beast(s) and false prophet are defeated, according to Revelation, then those saints "which did not worship the beast, neither his image, neither had taken his mark upon their foreheads or on their hands" will be vindicated and it was seen that "they lived, and reigned with Christ a thousand years". After that was the general resurrection of the dead. (Revelation 20:4–5). This reign of Christ being the Fifth Monarchy from which the seventeenth-century group took its name. Again it echoes aspects of the prophecy of Daniel 7.

By 1650 the history of the church had seen many interpretations advanced regarding the identification of these figures.[7] This was despite the fact that the official consensus, following the writings of the fifth-century theologian Augustine, was that they were metaphors and not describing historical events.[8] Just to give some examples of those who dissented from this orthodoxy: before Augustine, a document known as *Ascension of Isaiah* (variously dated from the late first century AD to the beginning of the third century) thought Antichrist was Nero; Irenaeus (died *c.*202) suggested several possible candidates for Antichrist and thought that the ten horns of the beast represented the Roman empire which would eventually be divided into ten kingdoms (Tertullian, died *c.*220, thought something similar as did Jerome, died 420); Athanasius of Alexandria (died 373) thought that the heretical theologian, Arius of Alexandria, was associated with the Antichrist. Even after Augustine, Pope Innocent III (pope 1198–1216) accused Muhammad; Joachim of Fiore (died 1202) applied these prophecies to Islamic Saracens and antipopes; other medieval writers accused various popes of being Antichrist for various reasons;[9] in the thirteenth century, Eberhard II von Truchsees, Prince-Archbishop of Salzburg, insisted that the ten horns/kingdoms were the Turks, Greeks, Egyptians, Africans, Spaniards,

French, English, Germans, Sicilians, and Italians who were the inheritors of the Roman Empire, and he accused the papacy of being the "little horn"; the late-fourteenth-century John Wycliffe associated the pope with Antichrist.

Following the Reformation, the Augustinian orthodoxy broke down on the Protestant side and the prophecies were increasingly perceived as historical and predictive. The application of the term Antichrist/beast to the papacy in general was made by Martin Luther, John Calvin, Thomas Cranmer, and John Knox. Then, there were the views of Thomas Müntzer and the later Anabaptists at Münster that we explored earlier. Historical (meaning now and in the near future) interpretations of Daniel and Revelation were firmly back on the agenda. In England, the late-sixteenth-century writings of Cambridge-educated Thomas Brightman (1562–1607) and Joseph Mede (1586–1668) – alongside the German theologian, Johannes Alsted (1588–1638) – greatly influenced the Fifth Monarchy Men.

The identification with the papacy (alongside identifying *some parts* of Daniel with certain Roman emperors) was reflected in the commentary to be found in the much-read *Geneva Bible*.[10] Anyone reading these would be in no doubt as to the identification of the Catholic Church with Antichrist and the beast. Millenarian preaching, often by increasingly radicalized Presbyterian preachers, accelerated in the 1640s during the Civil Wars.[11] These preachers looked forward with enthusiasm to the imminent suffering to be imposed on those who had once persecuted the saints with apparent impunity. In this they saw the avenging sword of God about to fall on "this Babylonish company".[12] It was a view preached before Parliament and within the New Model Army.

A number of numerical calculations also occurred in consideration of prophecy. The amount of time that the beast/false prophet/Antichrist would have power over the earth was taken, from Revelation 12:14 as "a time, and times, and half a time". This verse referred to a period of time when a woman (the church?) is pursued by a dragon/serpent (the Devil), who eventually gives power to the beast from the sea, with ten horns and seven heads bearing blasphemous names. Some interpreted this as three and a half years (or 1,260 days) but there were widely differing views on this. Some read "days" as "years"[13] and by starting it in the fourth century AD, with the rise to power of the papacy (c.390), expected the downfall of Antichrist in the 1650s. The number of 1,260 days appeared also as a time when "two witnesses" of God would declare his message (Revelation 11:3), before being killed by the beast and lying dead for three-and-a-half days (Revelation 11:9). These repeated time periods clearly echoed similar time periods found in the book of Daniel and again led to varied interpretations.

Daniel 12:11 referred to when, "the daily sacrifice shall be taken away, and the abominable desolation set up, there shall be a thousand, two hundred and ninety days". Some took this period (three years and 195 days) as indicating the reign of Antichrist since "the abominable desolation" indicated blasphemous activities and the time period seemed the same as the more approximate one in Revelation 12:14. However, the *Geneva Bible* commentary considered it the period of time between Christ's death and his Second Coming but suggested it simply meant "the time shall be long of Christ's second coming, and yet the children of God ought not to be discouraged" (since a literal length would have culminated in c.1323). Daniel 12:12 then added, "Blessed is he that waiteth and cometh to the thousand, three hundred and five and thirty days". The addition of forty-five days (total 1,335 days) was interpreted by the *Geneva Bible* commentators as simply meaning nobody could calculate Christ's Second Coming and so be patient. But to many others the clock could be set running at the rise to power of *anyone* they labelled "Antichrist" and the Second Coming expected about three and a half years later.

To these established identifications, the Fifth Monarchists added their own as they sought to interpret the events of the 1640s and 1650s.

The core beliefs of the Fifth Monarchists

Many Fifth Monarchist beliefs were also held by others of a Puritan outlook in the seventeenth century. Among the Fifth Monarchists could be found both Baptists and infant-baptizing Independents (derived from Church of England congregations), Calvinists, and believers in free will. Where the Fifth Monarchists differed from many of their contemporaries among the godly was in their very literal application of prophecies to contemporary events (especially the execution of the king), in their identification of a date for the destruction of Antichrist, and in their extreme self-confidence in both the correctness of their interpretations and in their belief that they were the saints chosen by God to rule under Christ. They allied this with the belief that they were called to active insurrection designed to overthrow all worldly government and, through their own efforts, to be part of the process through which Christ's literal kingdom would be established on earth. Some were committed to violent acts. Their declaration of 1656, for example, resolutely declared, "God's people must be a bloody people."[14] The Fifth Monarchist, Mary Cary – in a book tellingly entitled *The Little Horn's Doom and Downfall* (1651), a title prompted by the prophecy of Daniel –wrote of her hatred for the rich and her willingness to fight them. In contrast, other Fifth Monarchists were active but non-violent. In short, while they sang from the same hymn book they were not all on the same page!

The identification of Charles with the "little horn" was not limited to Cary. John Canne, in 1649, asserted that Charles' death was the fulfilment of God's judgment on the fourth monarchy's "little horn", foretold in Daniel 7:9–10. Fifth Monarchist-inclined members of the army made a similar assertion in the 1650 Declaration of Musselburgh and went on to claim that they had "proclaimed Jesus Christ, the King of Saints, to be our King."[15]

Dating of the long-awaited events was influenced by a calculation that 1,656 years elapsed between the Creation and the judgment of the Flood and, so, 1656 was identified as a key year. Also, the 1,260 days of the witnesses, in Revelation 11:3, were interpreted as years, starting in AD 396 and the assumption of papal political authority and culminating in 1656. Then, 1657 was chosen as it was three and a half *literal years* since the start of the Protectorate (as in the 1,260 days of Revelation and similar in Daniel). This identification labelled Cromwell as the beast. This switching between *literal* and *symbolic* time periods was fairly arbitrary.

With regard to the form of government required in a theocracy of the godly, ruling initially on behalf of Christ, they were far from egalitarian. Some argued for an assembly elected by the "gathered churches". John Rogers wanted Cromwell to select godly co-rulers to make a modern Sanhedrin (the ancient Jewish ruling council), whereas John Spittlehouse wanted representatives chosen by the officers of the godly army and later changed this to a call for Cromwell, as a second Moses, to select men. Then, after the failure of the Barebone's Parliament (see below), many Fifth Monarchists thought that only they were loyal to Christ and so should rule for him. For, by the end of 1653, they were of one mind that Cromwell's Protectorate was *not* the one approved of by God or referred to in prophecy.

Meetings in Fifth Monarchist fellowships were characterized by prophesying and sharing of dreams and visions from God: "revelations". Their most famous visionary was Anna Trapnell who, in late 1653, spent eleven days semi-conscious and uttering prophecies. Sermons might last seven hours and involved a high level of emotion and contributions from the congregation. In keeping with many Puritan groups, liturgies and set prayers were unacceptable, as was organ music.

When it came to the kind of society that such a theocracy should aim to establish, they again were not of one mind. Some, like Mary Cary, loathed the rich and identified them as the prime enemy of the godly. Others envisaged the implementation of the Old Testament Law of Moses. Others advocated the abolition of all existing titles (but the elect would rule like kings), refused hat honour to social "superiors" and used the non-deferential terms "thee" and "thou" to them as Quakers did. Some favoured redistribution of land and work schemes to assist the poor, but most believed in private property, and none preached common ownership. It was envisaged that, eventually, taxation would cease. Most of all they looked for a divine transformation of health, weather, the fertility of crops, wealth, and social harmony, once the millennium was established.

THE RISE OF THE FIFTH MONARCHY MEN
AS A MOVEMENT

The Fifth Monarchy Men first formally appeared in December 1651. It was then that a meeting at the church of Allhallows the Great, off Thames Street in London, was addressed by Christopher Feake, John Simpson, and Henry Jessey. Following the execution of King Charles I, there had been high hopes among a large minority of the godly that the Rump Parliament would take steps to implement a godly programme of reforms. They were to be disappointed and, by 1651, a number began to doubt Cromwell's commitment to really radical change. While some were more intent on praying for change, there were others (such as those meeting at Allhallows) who were committed to bringing down the government in order to replace it with one more amenable to their demands. Not surprisingly this provoked hostile reactions from senior members of the government and the army and the leaders of a number of prominent Independent churches. Undaunted, the Fifth Monarchy Men continued their weekly meetings. These took place at Allhallows and a number of other churches and meeting places.

The group had two main centres. The first was in London. The second was in north Wales where the leaders were the preachers Vavasor Powell and Morgan Llwyd. There is also evidence indicating a scattering of other congregations in East Anglia and in south-western England (eastern Devon and Cornwall). In the north the group was less successful, although there appear to have been some small groups in Hull, Liverpool, and Manchester.

The movement had a noticeable number of supporters among tradespeople and artisans in towns. A large number of these were involved in the cloth trade which had suffered a downturn as a result of the wars and whose apprentices and journeymen appear disproportionately in Fifth Monarchist congregations. It is consistent with this character that the later Monmouth Rebellion of 1685 (which also attracted millenarian activists from godly congregations in Somerset and eastern Devon) was also largely supported by clothworkers and was certainly not the rustic "pitchfork rebellion" that it is sometimes portrayed as.

There was also a sizeable Fifth Monarchist following in the army and this included a number of officers, most notably Major-General Thomas Harrison. A number of ministers in Fifth Monarchist congregations had earlier served as either chaplains or officers in the New Model Army. Once again, as with the Levellers, the highly politicized (today we might say radicalized) members of the Parliamentary army were well represented. The navy of the Commonwealth period also contained a significant number, both officers and ordinary sailors. At a senior level the naval commissioners John Carew and Nathaniel Rich were members; and the leading naval administrator Sir Henry Vane was a sympathizer, as was Robert Blackborne, Secretary of the Admiralty. The aforementioned Fifth Monarchists Thomas Harrison and John Carew, were judges (officially titled "commissioners") at the trial of Charles I and both signed his death warrant. Clearly, the Fifth Monarchy Men were far from being an inconsequential group.

"AT THE EDGE OF PROMISES AND PROPHECIES"

As we have seen, the Fifth Monarchy Men were deeply disillusioned with the Rump Parliament. An example of their disappointment is provided by the Welsh preacher Vavasor Powell, who criticized its failure to renew the Act for the Propagation of the Gospel in Wales. Clearly, they concluded, to build a more godly nation the Rump should be replaced by a more determined assembly. The answer soon seemed at hand.

Cromwell too was tired of the Rump (which he dissolved in April 1653) but he and the Army Council of Officers were cautious about authorizing elections to a new Parliament since they concluded that it would probably return Presbyterians and Royalists, alongside those who were ideological allies. As an answer to this dilemma, Major-General Harrison suggested to Cromwell that there be a ruling body set up that was based on the Old Testament Sanhedrin of seventy members, who were carefully selected from among the saints. Being a Fifth Monarchist he believed that such an assembly – based on scriptural precedent – would be more likely to pursue a godly agenda and would thus be the prelude to the reign of Christ. He had Cromwell's ear as he had commanded the troops that had been used by Cromwell to eject the MPs of the Rump Parliament.

In the end it was a modified version of Harrison's idea which was finally accepted by Cromwell and the Army Council. Though modified, it was very much in line with the spirit of Harrison's proposal. In May 1653, within one month of the closing down of the Rump, letters from Cromwell and the Army Council were sent to Independent churches across England to nominate those they thought suitable for invitation to the new assembly. Many Fifth Monarchists now declared that God had raised up Cromwell as a new Moses and that he would lead the nation to its Promised Land. Other congregations too issued statements of support, and optimism was high that soon the reign of Christ would be revealed.

When the process of nomination was completed, 140 were selected for membership: 129 from England; five from Scotland; and six from Ireland. A number of them were from congregations with strong Fifth Monarchist sympathies. This parliament – which sat for just over five months – is now remembered as the "Barebone's Parliament", the "Nominated Parliament" or "Parliament of Saints". The first name is taken from the unusual surname of one of its members, Praise-God Barebone, who represented the City of London. Cromwell himself seems to have shared in the heady optimism when he declared to the assembled members, "You are as like the forming of God as ever people were... You are at the edge of promises and prophecies."[16] A theocratic assembly had been formed. It was indeed an assembly of saints. The rule of God through his elect seemed on the brink of happening. And with the institution of such an assembly it seemed to many (even Cromwell seems to have temporarily leaned that way) that the millennium was at hand.

The "Barebone's Parliament" met from July to December 1653. Never before had Fifth Monarchists been so influential in national politics. Although it has been calculated that under 9 per cent of the assembly were Fifth Monarchists,[17] they could find allies among other radicals on certain issues. But their influence would not last.

Fifth Monarchist Members of Parliament pursued a radical reform of the legal system and the non-interference of the state in church matters. With regard to the Anglo-Dutch War (1652–54) they hoped that the war would spread across Europe until Rome fell and the pope was overthrown.[18] But the Fifth Monarchists were a minority in the assembly and lost the votes that aimed to abolish tithes and restrictions on public preaching. Despite this failure, the radicals alarmed those of a more conservative disposition. After six months, the conservatives led by Major-General John Lambert organized a vote for the dissolution of the assembly in December 1653. The vote occurred while the radicals were absent at a prayer meeting. The move was supported by soldiers who denied the radicals access to Parliament, and Cromwell went along with it. He claimed not to have had prior knowledge of it. The rule of the saints was eventually replaced by the Army Council's "Instrument of Government" which led to Cromwell becoming Lord Protector.

DISAPPOINTMENT, REBELLION, AND DEFEAT

The Fifth Monarchists were devastated. One of them asserted that the Lord Protector, "tooke the Crowne off from the heade of Christ, and put it upon his owne".[19] These were strong words. Vavasor Powell asked rhetorically, "Lord, wilt thou have Oliver Cromwell or Jesus Christ to reign over us?"[20] In May 1653 preachers at Blackfriars had declared that they had been told "by revelation" of the urgent "necessity of Monarchy in this Nation but bestowed it… on a new Line [i.e. King Jesus]".[21] They believed that this would be initiated by a period of rule by them and that this would lead to a supernatural intervention by Christ. It would be miraculous action triggered by the divinely led rule of the saints.[22] To these assertions of the need for the establishment of the reign of Christ via a theocracy, Cromwell countered with, "A notion I hope we all honour, and wait and hope for: that Jesus Christ will have a time to set up his reign *in our hearts*."[23] That was not enough for Fifth Monarchists, who now plotted Cromwell's overthrow, in favour of King Jesus. The Fifth Monarchist prophetess, Anna Trapnell declared that those who did the bidding of the Protectorate were "of the Beast".[24] A Fifth Monarchist resolution of 1656 identified Cromwell as the "little horn" of Daniel's prophecy (earlier identified as Charles I).[25]

Leading members such as Feake and Simpson were imprisoned. Harrison was sacked from the army. Other Fifth Monarchist officers resigned. Two plots against the Protector failed in 1657 and again in 1659. After 1657 the ringleader, Thomas Venner, was imprisoned (he was released when the Protectorate ended in 1659).

If the Protectorate was deeply disappointing, then the Restoration of Charles II in 1660 was devastating to a sect committed to the rule of Christ alone. Those Fifth Monarchists who were guilty of regicide – Harrison, Jones, and Carew – were hanged, drawn, and quartered in October 1660. Others were imprisoned as the sect was driven further underground. On his way to his execution, a bystander shouted at Harrison, "Where is your Good Old Cause now?" Harrison replied, "Here in my bosom, and I shall seal it with my blood."[26] Other accounts suggest that he claimed that he would soon return with Christ to judge those who had judged him.

In January 1661 a Fifth Monarchist uprising took place in London over four days, led by Venner. Its battle cry was, "King Jesus and the heads upon the gates."[27] The revolt was crushed with the deaths of some twenty-two of the saints and the later execution of another twenty, including Venner himself who was hanged, drawn, and quartered.

In the face of tough government action and the failure of their prophetic hopes (the year 1666, for example, was not of cosmic significance) the movement faded away. Many drifted into the Baptist churches or Nonconformist Congregationalist fellowships.

1685: THE LAST EVIDENCE OF THE FIFTH MONARCHY MEN

There are reports of some Fifth Monarchist activity continuing into the 1680s. A few ended up being arrested for small-scale plots and there was a Fifth Monarchist among those who stole the Crown Jewels from the Tower in 1671. A small group of Fifth

Monarchists, including the son of Thomas Venner, took part in Monmouth's Rebellion of 1685 against King James VII and II and millenarian beliefs were noted among his West Country followers,[28] with a Fifth Monarchist tasked with raising London for the cause.[29] It was the last attempt to revive the "Good Old Cause" and even Leveller sea-green ribbons were reported as being worn by some of the rebel army. It ended in disaster at the Battle of Sedgemoor and was the last attempt to establish the rule of the saints, albeit under the unlikely leadership of the Duke of Monmouth.

10

Not Very Quiet Quakers!

O ne of the striking features of England in the late 1640s and 1650s was the way in which the lifting of social controls, with the collapse of episcopal and royal authority, combined with a sense of traditional norms being shattered through years of war and upheaval, to produce groups whose ideas and demands would have been almost unthinkable in the 1620s or 1630s. It was as if a huge and turbulent social experiment had been set in motion to see what people might think and how they might behave when restrictions are either lifted or appear might be lifted. The latter is, of course, important to remember since many of those whose challenge to morality, economics, and politics were the most radical quickly found that prisons, the stocks, branding for "Blasphemy", and other punishment had not departed from the country.

THE CURIOUS CASE OF THE RANTERS

Shortly after the collapse of the Leveller-inspired mutinies in the spring and summer of 1649 reports appeared of an amorphous group of people preaching doctrines and behaving in ways that, understandably, shocked and horrified many of their contemporaries. These people came to be commonly described as "Ranters". Ranters used varied terms to describe themselves since they clearly never had sufficient unity of purpose or outlook to ensure that one label was applicable. Labels such as "Levellers" (that term again) and "My One Flesh" were used, but it is the name "Ranter" – coined by their enemies – that has stuck. What is interesting is that the "leveller" label was used; it seems that the only people reluctant to use the name were some of the Levellers themselves! However, "Ranter" became an umbrella term used by contemporaries to describe a mixed group of self-styled prophets, preachers, and rebels against both contemporary morality and the social hierarchy. While it has been suggested that, rather like witches, they did not actually exist but were the projection of other people's anxieties in order to condemn the sins they feared within themselves,[1] there is clear evidence that something of a loose core of ideas and practices existed among those described by the term.[2]

We know something of their activities because they were attacked in a large number of pamphlets and newspaper reports which appear from 1649 onwards. While these largely recount their beliefs and behaviour as seen from the viewpoint of their enemies there is enough that has survived from the so-called Ranters themselves to suggest that these shocking and revealing reports did indeed represent something of what Ranters stood for. In addition, the corroboration of other reports by contemporaries – such as George Fox describing their rudeness and boasting of fornication, Richard Baxter recounting their blasphemous speech and whoring, Gerrard Winstanley condemning their sexual misconduct and excessive eating and drinking – reveal common features of Ranter behaviour. These activities stimulated something of a moral panic. This was particularly apparent among church leaders, MPs, and those entrusted with maintaining public order.

THE ORIGINS OF THE RANTERS

The Ranters never constituted one organized group or sect. Of all the radical groups – such as the Levellers and Diggers – they are the most difficult to tie down. In fact, they constituted more of a mood and an attitude than a movement. However, they themselves clearly recognized others with similar views and behaviour, and certainly organized themselves into local groups holding meetings. But this was not part of a national movement, more a widely reported mood. One thing does seem clear though and that is that most of their members had once been Baptists, although some were connected with a very loose group of people who had given up on all formal church membership and were described as "Seekers".[3]

Leaders and writers accused of being Ranters included: Abiezer Coppe, Lawrence Clarkson, Joseph Salmon, and Jacob Bauthumley. All of these had served in the army of Parliament. Some had served as soldiers, others as preachers. They came out of that same mobilized and radicalized milieu that had also produced many of the Levellers, Diggers, and Fifth Monarchy Men. In fact, the timing of the failure of the Levellers and the first appearance of significant Ranter activity is almost certainly not coincidental. The feelings of disillusionment, frustration, and helplessness that these defeats generated in the ranks of many lower-class citizens and ordinary soldiers may well have caused some of them to give up political activism and, indeed, give up on their society's norms generally. It was in such a mood of frustration and hopelessness that rebellion against all existing constraints and mores occurred. Coppe, for instance, bitterly recounted the killing of the Leveller mutineers in his pamphlet, *A Fiery Flying Roll*, of 1649. The same denunciation of the army for shooting its own appeared in the pamphlet, *A Rout, A Rout*, written by Salmon, again in 1649 after the crushing of the Leveller mutinies.

The beliefs of the Ranters

We know from the attacks mounted by their enemies that Ranters indulged in sexual promiscuity, in drunkenness and swearing, and in blasphemous speech. Coppe was accused of preaching naked and of fornication. A pamphlet written by John Holland in 1650, entitled tellingly *The Smoke of the Bottomless Pit*, described Ranters as believing that God was in every creature, there was no heaven or hell, the Bible was unreliable, good and evil were the same thing, sin did not exist since God made all things, and sexual liberty should be encouraged.

Those accused of Ranterism appear to have held to a loose common outlook which held that God was in everyone; in fact in every living being. Even in every object. So, Jacob Bauthumley wrote that God was in "this dog, this tobacco pipe, he is in me and

I am in him."[4] This abandoned the generally accepted Christian world and cosmic view that envisaged God as being in heaven, while sinful people on earth were separated from him by their fallen nature. It thus also abandoned the need for repentance and conventional salvation since there was, Ranters maintained, no separating divide which needed to be overcome in the first place. In London, a group linked to Laurence Clarkson called itself "My One Flesh" as a way of both emphasizing the unity of God with people and creation generally; and also among people. It may also have had connotations of sexual intimacy since it echoed the words of Jesus regarding marriage, "And they twain shall be one flesh: so that they are no more twain, but one flesh" (Mark 10:8). Given the reputation of Ranters for promiscuous sexuality it may also have parodied or even challenged the words of Paul, "Do ye not know, that he which coupleth himself with an harlot, is one body? for two, saith he, shall be one flesh" (1 Corinthians 6:16).

There were some similarities between Ranters and some early Quakers, given the fact that both emphasized the experience of God through the indwelling Spirit of God or the "Inner Light". After this, though, the Ranters diverged from most Quakers (though perhaps not all among the earliest, as we shall see) by arguing that any person who believed and experienced this personal connection with God was liberated from the need to follow the moral and social norms of contemporary society. And the Ranters went further, by claiming that this liberation meant that anything done by such a person could be justified and, indeed, the more extreme the violation of constraining norms, the more they proclaimed their liberty of status. For many this meant that all moral restraints could be ignored and actually openly flouted. It was for this reason that the Ranters became associated with sexual promiscuity, with drinking to excess, and with swearing. For them, not only did these things not matter but partaking in them publicly declared Ranter freedoms. They could even lead to spiritual liberation since they encouraged the partaker to no longer heed external restraints and moral codes. As Coppe expressed it, "God hath so cleared cursing, swearing, in some, that that which goes for swearing and cursing in them, is more glorious than praying and preaching in others."[5]

There was, to the Ranters, no such thing as "sin" or "sinfulness" since such concepts did not apply to the truly liberated person who had become united with God. The same applied to any form of organized religious structure, prayers, or study of the Bible. Since the Ranters claimed to have discovered complete inner liberty, they claimed they did not need any religious structure, activity, or guidance in order to know how to behave or to gain a relationship with God.

It is no surprise that the activities and claims of the Ranters outraged every shade of opinion in their contemporary society. The Rump Parliament responded to the moral panic that Ranters prompted by passing the Adultery Act in May 1650, and the Blasphemy Act in August 1650.

The Adultery Act carried the detailed title of, "An Act for suppressing the detestable sins of Incest, Adultery and Fornication" and introduced the death penalty for incest and adultery (with the exception of rape, which cleared a woman of blame), unless a man thought a woman was single or a woman's husband had been absent three years. For fornication the punishment was three months imprisonment for every such offence. Prostitutes (male or female) and brothel keepers were to be placed in the stocks, branded on the forehead with the letter B (for "Bawd"), and imprisoned for three years. A second offence carried the death penalty.[6]

The Blasphemy Act was formally "An Act against several Atheistical, Blasphemous and Execrable Opinions, derogatory to the honour of God, and destructive to humane Society." The words of the Act reveal something of both the activities of Ranters and the specific concerns of lawmakers in response. The law made it a crime to claim:

to be very God, or to be Infinite or Almighty, or in Honour, Excellency, Majesty and Power to be equal, and the same with the true God, or that the true God, or the Eternal Majesty dwells in the Creature and nowhere else.

This targeted two Ranter claims. The first was that they could be so united with God as to be, in effect, God. Some early Quakers strayed dangerously close to this position; or certainly so their detractors claimed. The second sought to counter the most extreme view of the Inner Light which might, in extreme circumstances, claim that the light in a person was so intense that God dwelt in them to the exclusion of others (i.e. they were effectively God).

The Act also targeted the outcomes of such beliefs as exemplified by the Ranters, by condemning,

> *whosoever shall deny the Holiness and Righteousness of God, or shall presume as aforesaid to profess, that Unrighteousness in persons, or the acts of Uncleanness, Prophane Swearing, Drunkenness, and the like Filthiness and Brutishness, are not unholy and forbidden in the Word of God, or that these acts in any person, or the persons [so] committing them, are approved of by God, or that such acts, or such persons in those things are like unto God.*[7]

It was exactly this that lay at the heart of Ranter claims and the controversies that they caused. For Ranters not only claimed that so-called sinful acts were not sins, they went further and declared that such activities were actually in line with God's will and revealed the inner experience of God to such a degree that such a person might be described as, "like unto God".

The Act went on to outline offensive behaviour in some detail and this included swearing and cursing, immoral acts that were listed at length, denying the reality of heaven and hell and salvation and judgment. With an eye to Ranter claims that the more a person did these things the more liberated they were, the Act explicitly repudiated the claim that "such men or women are most perfect, or like to God or Eternity, which do commit the greatest Sins with least remorse or sense."

For the first offence the punishment was sixth months in prison, extended to one year if the person could not put in place sufficient sureties of good behaviour. Punishment for a second offence was banishment for life. To refuse to go into exile or to return, was punishable by death.[8]

The extreme nature of these punishments (both in the Adultery Act and the Blasphemy Act) reveal the extent of the outrage and

144

the moral panic that was induced by the spread of Ranter beliefs following the first appearance of such beliefs and behaviour to a noticeable degree in 1649.

As with many such extreme reactions to a moral panic, these Acts were not easy to enforce and those for sexual misconduct were particularly difficult to use as a means to change the habits of the nation. For example, it is clear that persistent managers of brothels were not hanged as otherwise the practice would have been massively reduced, and there is no evidence of this. On the other hand, the Acts did demonstrate the commitment of the godly (even within the much maligned Rump Parliament) to attempt a transformation of public morals, both as a way of driving forward a programme of legislation acceptable to God and in response to the challenges thrown up by the upheavals of the 1640s. And prominent offenders were punished. The most publicly active of the Ranters were arrested and brought to trial. In this way, Jacob Bauthumley had his tongue bored through as the punishment for writing a book deemed blasphemous. Other leading Ranters, such as Lawrence Clarkson, Joseph Salmon, and Abiezer Coppe, were only released from prison as a result of writing recantations.

The significance of the Ranters

The Ranters posed no political or economic challenge to society. Although Coppe described God as "that mighty Leveller" and declared, "kings, princes, lords, great ones, must bow to the poorest peasants",[9] these were aspirations that left the achieving of this to God and did not include any practical political or economic programme to implement such a revolution. In this respect they stand out from Levellers, Diggers, and many early Quakers (who did pose political and ecclesiastical challenges to the status quo). Nevertheless, they are important as an historical phenomenon. At its simplest, they illustrate the extent of disintegration of religious and moral norms and values caused by the wars and attendant upheavals. They also point to the degree of disillusionment, hopelessness, and despair experienced by lower-class men and women that accompanied the failures of the most radical movements (such as the Levellers and Diggers) by the middle of 1649. To such people the world was certainly not being turned upside down by Parliament and so some decided to do it in a moral inversion of the established order. More controversially, they reveal the extreme edge of what could be possible (*though certainly not inevitable*) in a godly inclined society where personal experience of God, personal assurance of holiness, personal revelation, and knowledge ("prophesying") was accelerating challenges to formal, hierarchical, and liturgical religious expression. This certainly does not mean that Ranterism was a logical outcome of the revolution being enacted by the godly but it was, perhaps, not such a surprise that *some people* took the revolution in this direction. And this was especially so when the more powerful of the saints – be they MPs or army Grandees – frustrated those below them in the social hierarchy by shutting the door on real political, economic, and social change. The Ranters exemplified a form of "Eat, drink and be merry – in an extreme degree – for tomorrow is going to be very much like today and yesterday, for the socially and politically disadvantaged." Not exactly a catchy slogan but the evidence suggests that it sums up something of the causal factors leading to Ranterism. As one historian succinctly put it, "Ranterism articulated the ideology of a counter-culture; the society of masterless men and women: the vagrants, itinerants, cottagers and urban immigrants."[10]

While they existed, however, they certainly threw a large stone into the pond of the godly society that some, at least, were attempting to construct. And they justified the sense of anxiety felt by more disciplined and mainstream people. It is noticeable that Quakers and Diggers were often labelled as "Ranters" by those who disapproved of them. And they were very quick to deny the connection since they knew how the "mud" of such disapproval could stick and obscure their own aims. Much the same had been done with the label "Anabaptist". It is also likely that (subconsciously at least) the Digger and Quaker leaders recognized the very real dangers of Ranter excess influencing their own groups, unless it was firmly resisted. Given the free movement of ideas and people among and between such groups this was all too likely.

By the mid-1650s Ranterism was in terminal decline. By the end of the Protectorate it had effectively ended as a social phenomenon. The reasons for this were threefold: the draconian reaction of law enforcers; the return to relative stability after the end of the Civil Wars; and the existence of Quakerism into which a number of early Ranters (as well as some Diggers and Levellers) retreated. By desisting from the more extreme of their claims and behaviour these Ranters could be accommodated within a loose movement (i.e. early Quakerism) which also emphasized the Inner Light and the rejection of formalized religious activity, dogma, knowledge, and teaching. In addition, the fact that *some* early Quakers exhibited ideas and behaviour reminiscent of *some aspects* of Ranterism provided a "bridge" along which disillusioned or disappointed (or reconstructed and repentant) Ranters could travel, without having to return to (what was to them) an unacceptable level of religious orthodoxy. On the other hand, they would have to curb their behavioural excesses (the whoring, swearing, and drinking) as this was not a feature of Quakerism, even in its most volatile and varied early form.

THE BEGINNING OF THE QUAKER MOVEMENT

Modern Quakerism is characterized by meetings of quiet reflection and absence of formal liturgy, creeds, and biblical preaching. But in its early days many Quakers were anything but quiet! The movement later described as Quakerism grew out of the work and preaching of George Fox (1624–91). Fox underwent a religious conversion, in 1647, which radically changed his outlook on life. He became convinced that all worldly authority was corrupt and incapable of communicating the revelation of God to individuals. Consequently, one could only receive God's message through the Inner Light which was experienced by an individual within themselves.

By the late 1640s Fox's preaching in the Midlands and the northern counties of England had gathered small groups of followers scattered across the area. Many of these converts came out of Baptist churches. Others were Seekers. It is clear that Fox was appealing to a similar constituency to that which Ranters appealed to. From the behaviour of some early Quakers it is clear that some in their ranks would have been described as Ranters by outsiders. One can see how contemporaries found it hard to identify who was in which group and which label best identified any one of them at any one time. Clearly, membership boundaries were fluid and a significant part of religious society, on what one might describe as the "left" of the godly, was in a state of flux by the early 1650s.

At first these communities called themselves "Children of the Light", and then "Friends of the Truth". This declared both their conviction regarding the Inner Light and the confidence that through this they had apprehended the truth which eluded others. The famous label of "Quaker" was coined by Judge Bennett during Fox's trial for blasphemy, which occurred in 1650. The name was coined in mockery because Fox had enjoined the judge to "tremble/quake at the word of the Lord". Quakers preferred and prefer the description of "Religious Society of Friends", or just "Friends".

The beliefs of the Quakers

The key Quaker belief, as articulated by Fox, held that Christ can be experienced in anyone who believes and that this is experienced through the "Inner Light", which comes from personal meditation on God. This meant that personal inward reflection was a surer way to meet with God than study of the Bible or the involvement of priests or ministers. To a generation committed to scriptural holiness and adherence to the Bible as the word of God this attitude toward scripture was deeply offensive and disturbing.

Fox and the early Quakers also believed that through experience of the Inner Light it was possible for a person to achieve perfection in this life. The struggle that a believer went through in this process became known as the "Lamb's War", which echoed imagery from the Book of Revelation. Such a transformation was described by the term "convincement". For Quakers this inward experience of Christ replaced the expectation of the Second Coming of Christ in outward form that was held by almost all of the godly and was the driving belief of the Fifth Monarchy Men. And if Christ was to be so fully known internally then convincement could lead to perfect sanctification. The Quaker leader, Edward Burroughs, put it this way: "the saints of God may be perfectly freed from sin in this life so as no more to commit it."[11] This was not a Ranterish belief in nothing constituting sin anymore but, rather, a conviction that what was conventionally described as sin could be fully overcome. However, for those of a more Ranterish disposition there was a fine line between belief in being made perfect and the concept that holiness was so concentrated in them that they could be described as divine. This was certainly not what Fox and Burroughs meant but others, such as James Nayler, took the idea to dramatic and shocking conclusions.

This rejection of the effectiveness of conventional ways to relate to God caused Fox to reject all church hierarchy and religious ceremony. The very idea of paying clergy to preach was repugnant to these early Quakers and they dismissively referred to church buildings as mere "steeplehouses". It is therefore little wonder that early Quakers refused to pay tithes, since they advocated a total abandonment of the national church system. This set of beliefs set them on a collision course with every form of church existing in the seventeenth century, from Anglican churches, through Independent congregations, to Separatists such as the Baptists. In sharp contrast to their modern image of quiet pacifists, the early Quakers were well known for disrupting church services and interrupting preachers with denunciatory shouted comments.

Quakers stood out from many of their contemporaries in encouraging women to preach at Quaker meetings. This was because the Inner Light was believed to be accessible to all, regardless of their gender. This was socially radical and challenged the gender-related hierarchy of society. And this was not their only rejection of the norms of the day. They also refused to accept the legitimacy of lawmakers and their laws and Quakers refused to take public oaths. Their rebuttal of worldly authority was clearly demonstrated in their refusal to perform hat honour (removing hats) in the presence of "social superiors". As part of this egalitarianism they used the familiar terms "thee" and "thou" to generals and magistrates and annoyed them greatly by so doing. It was a form of social rebellion which was fully understood by those who were targeted. This Quaker egalitarianism expressed itself in words that looked toward a radical change to the social order. In 1658 Isaac Pennington expressed it in this way:

That which is high, that which is wise, that which is strong,
That which is rich, that which is full, that which is fat: the
Lord will lay low.[12]

The millenarianism of this is reminiscent of a Fifth Monarchist pamphlet but, unlike the Fifth Monarchists, the Quakers did not propose a programme of political action in order to trigger such changes. Instead, they looked solely to God and one can only assume a divine intervention brought about by the inner transformation of men and women, since most Quaker millenarianism did not look to an outward Second Coming.

Early Quaker communities also included those who exhibited behaviour similar to Ranters and to other enthusiastic members of the Separatist sects. This included experiencing trance-like states, high excitement, and ecstatic speech. This was their version of the "Prophesying" which occurred in a number of Puritan fellowships and which had so alarmed High Church Arminians in the 1630s. Some were reported as going naked as they travelled and preached. This too had Ranter overtones but without the sexual promiscuity that attended it in that group.

Unlike the Ranters, the simplicity, modesty, and piety of Quakers tended to earn for them the respect of some of their opponents, even though these were shocked by their lack of conformity to other expected features of godly behaviour and practice. Even Cromwell expressed respect for their sincerity although the disruptive behaviour of Quakers and the challenge this posed to social order drew sharper responses. Others were less patient still and there are many recorded incidents of Quakers being brutally repressed by those who disapproved of their practices.

The impact of the Quakers

In the early 1650s the movement was particularly influential in the north of England. It was there that Margaret Fell (1614–1702) was converted and became an influential supporter and organizer. She was of great assistance to the movement because she was the wife of Thomas Fell of Swarthmoor Hall in Ulverstone, Lancashire. He himself did not convert to Quakerism, but as a magistrate he was able to protect Quakers from prosecution and persecution. Margaret Fell married George Fox after her husband died.

Fox was particularly skilful at spreading Quaker ideas through the printing and dissemination of pamphlets. This took Quaker ideas to a wide range of people. In 1654 this was accompanied by Quaker preachers taking the message to the south of England and targeting key urban centres such as London, Bristol, and Norwich. In Essex the preaching in 1655 was led by James Parnel, known as the "Quaking boy" due to his youth. He was arrested and died in prison. It was a reminder of the dangers faced by early Quakers in the challenge they posed to society.

What alarmed most contemporaries was the threat to social order and hierarchy and the undermining of a national church structure. After all even when opposing Presbyterians, the Independents of the army and of Parliament still remained committed to the maintenance of a recognizable (although loosely organized) national church. And even Separatists were committed to the concept of "church" even if not as part of a national structure. Quakers were opposed to all of this and their rise in numbers caused alarm. Between 1653 and 1659 about one thousand Quakers were taken to court for refusing to pay tithes to the national church. And it should be remembered that the early members did not just quietly withdraw from their local churches and seek the Inner Light in the company of like-minded people. Instead, they openly disrupted services. Some hung notices on church doors that read, "Babylon's merchants", echoing the millenarian language that Puritans used against the perceived enemies of God's kingdom. In short, Quakers caused trouble, just as an earlier wave of Puritan enthusiasts had disrupted the choir services of the Church of England during the Civil Wars, and Jenny Geddes had thrown a stool at the service leader in St Giles' Cathedral, in 1637. For such determined members of the godly to now find their own services (in England at least) disrupted by Quakers must have come as something of a shock. The saintly advance guard of the rule of God on earth had found they were being outflanked on the left by a more radical movement still. And this disruption was not confined to the most radical of the Quakers; it was fairly common practice as they confronted what they regarded as false religion. This clearly prompted angry responses from those so disrupted. This was alongside the fear that Quakers simply represented Ranterism in a new form.

It is interesting to note that a pamphlet published in 1650, under the title *The Ranters Declaration*, was republished in 1655 with exactly the same illustrations on the front, but now bearing the title *The Quakers dream: or the Devil's pilgrimage in England*,[13] and promising to reveal how in their meetings occurred "Shriekings, Shakings, Quakings, Roarings, Yellings, Howlings, Tremblings in the Bodies…" The woodcut of a man and woman embracing, that in the Ranter version was titled "Increase multiply", now read "Free-will"; a preacher with a caption that once read "We have overcome the Devil" now read "walk answerable to the light within you"; men drinking and smoking with the title "No way to the old way" became "be thou merry", but the smoker has lost his pipe; and finally four naked women standing before a fiddler once did so by the title "Hey for Christmas" but in the Quaker version stood beside "Above ordinances". While the accusations varied, the idea was clearly that there was not much to choose between Ranters and Quakers. And the printer clearly thought that he could get away with associating nakedness with Quakers, which suggests it might have been grounded in more than just scurrilous mud-slinging. Clearly, Ranters and some early Quakers seemed linked.

The impact of this Ranterish wing of early Quakerism should not be ignored. The most striking example of this occurred in 1656 in Bristol and involved an early leading Quaker, James Nayler. Nayler had already attracted an enthusiastic group of followers whose devotion to him outraged other Christians. One of his followers wrote of him, "Thy name shall no longer be James but Jesus" and another described him as "Thou lamb of God". This was a combination of Quaker perfectionism and millenarian zeal, with a Ranterish twist, that was heresy to any mainstream Christian, including other Quakers. In 1656, on Palm Sunday, Nayler entered Bristol in a fashion that clearly imitated Christ's Palm Sunday entry into Jerusalem, as his followers laid branches before him and called out "holy, holy, holy".[14] Nayler's punishment reveals the shock of his contemporaries at these actions. He was imprisoned, branded on the forehead with "B" for Blasphemy, his tongue was bored through, he was whipped through London and Bristol, placed in the pillory, and subjected to indefinite confinement. Fox disowned Nayler. In response to such examples of excess, Parliament agreed a new Confession of Faith that all must subscribe to, and heavy fines were brought in for disrupting services or refusing to attend church. After the Nayler affair, Fox openly discouraged links between Quakers and more radical groups.

Quakerism was noticeable among members of the New Model Army. Here its attitude toward authority was recognized as a threat to discipline, and General Monck in Scotland and Major-General Henry Cromwell in Ireland cashiered Quakers from the regiments under their command. Despite prosecutions, Quaker ideas rapidly spread across Britain and preachers carried the belief to the Netherlands and Germany and also to the English colonies in North America. It has been estimated that there were somewhere in the region of 60,000 Quakers in Britain by 1660.[15] This meant that they constituted about 1.1 per cent of the British population (of approximately 5.3 million) and this had been achieved in just over ten years. It was an impressive achievement, although this sharp rise did not continue.

In 1659, following Cromwell's death, the growth in Quaker numbers and their high profile became unintentionally part of the process that led to the Restoration, as many in authority feared an outbreak of sectarian unrest and looked to the re-establishment of a strong centralized government in order to prevent it occurring.

QUAKERS AFTER THE RESTORATION

After the Restoration of 1660 a number of Quakers were arrested and this seemed to herald a new crackdown on the group. In response, Fox issued what became known as the Peace Testimony. This committed Quakers to non-violence under all circumstances. It was a clear attempt to remove any hint of subversion or revolutionary activism from the Society of Friends. From then onwards the kingship of God was to be found primarily within the individual, although also expressed in social action. But anything resembling a threat to the government and social stability was off the agenda. As a result, they are one of the few sects dating from the period of the Commonwealth to survive into the twenty-first century.

11

Cromwell and the Rule of God

For the godly, determined to implement the kingship of God in Britain and Ireland in the seventeenth century, there was no clear model of how this should be done. As they read the Old Testament there were several ways in which Israel, God's Chosen People, had been governed. A theocracy had developed when the Israelites left Egypt, mediated between God and the people through Moses. Then under his successor, Joshua, God's people conquered and settled the Promised Land of Canaan. Next, under tribal elders and Judges, the people faced various crises. After this, kingship was requested by the people of Israel and Saul was anointed by Samuel. Despite problems in this form of government, due to individual human weakness, the heroic rule of King David set a pattern for how future kingship would be judged and even how God's promised messiah could be envisaged. The reign of King Solomon oversaw the building of God's temple in Jerusalem and accompanied a time of enlarged influence and power for Israel. Then the rule of some good and some bad kings finally led to the conquest of Israel by its enemies and exile in Babylon. After the return from the exile in Babylon a theocracy again emerged, centred on a rebuilt temple.

On this basis, it was clear that there was no prescribed governmental system that could be lifted from the Old Testament, and clearly in the scriptures God had worked through some very different systems that varied from theocratic mediators to royal dynasties. This meant that the godly of the seventeenth century could rather pick and choose, according to circumstances and their own individual outlook. For those disillusioned by the Stuarts and convinced that the execution of Charles I should be accompanied by the establishment of a republic there were Old Testament passages that could be referred to which clearly presented the establishment of kingship as a response to human weakness and a deviation from the pure theocratic rule of judges appointed by God:

But the thing displeased Samuel, when they said, Give us a King to judge us: and Samuel prayed unto the Lord.
And the Lord said unto Samuel, Hear the voice of the people in all that they shall say unto thee: for they have not cast thee away, but they have cast me away, that I should not reign over them.
As they have ever done since I brought them out of Egypt even unto this day, (and have forsaken me, and served other gods) even so do they unto thee (1 Samuel 8:6–8).

On the other hand, the highly positive way in which King David was described, his heroic and God-approved military victories, and the way in which this enhanced the concept of kingship meant that kingship was not irrevocably compromised as a form of government:

Then David knew that the Lord had established him King over Israel, and that he had exalted his kingdom for his people Israel's sake (2 Samuel 5:12).

And when thy days be fulfilled, thou shalt sleep with thy fathers, and I will set up thy seed after thee, which shall proceed out of thy body, and will establish his kingdom.
He shall build a house for my Name, and I will establish the throne of his kingdom forever (2 Samuel 7:12–13).

For thou, O God, hast heard my desires; thou hast given an heritage unto those that fear thy Name.
Thou shalt give the King a long life; his years shall be as many ages.
He shall dwell before God forever; prepare mercy and faithfulness, that they may preserve him (Psalm 61:5–7).

That human kingship was acceptable as a form of rule, under God's overlordship, is clear from these passages. However, it should be noted that in the *Geneva Bible*'s commentary on the last passage the compiler was quick to undermine this monarchical interpretation by suggesting that actually "this chiefly is referred to Christ, who liveth eternally not only in himself, but also in his members". While this was, no doubt, a sincere attempt by the commentator to apply this passage to a wider application and to see in it principles that went beyond its immediate context, a desire to defuse this positive view of human kingship is apparent. It gives an insight into a godly mindset which, even as it admitted that human kingship could enjoy God's favour, rather sidelined this interpretation in favour of a messianic (rather than political) interpretation and even focused it on the godly themselves. What had started as a statement of support for righteous kingship swiftly became restated as actually referring to the rule of Christ through his saints: "his members".

THE PROBLEMS FACING CROMWELL

The way in which the godly rule of the saints should enable the rule of God as King to be established was not at all clear. Little wonder that Cromwell is recorded as saying, in 1647 at the Putney Debates, that he was not "wedded and glued to forms of government".[1] It is clear that "Cromwell was not wedded and glued to *forms* of government because he was wedded and glued to the *ends* of government".[2] And these ends, as he saw them, were building up both the church and state as God revealed his will through events and through his saints. But there was no predetermined structure.

Cromwell was not alone in this flexibility. And so, as we shall see, Cromwell and various of those who had defeated the king could envisage (often conflicting with each other as they did so), at different times, the replacement form of government being: a republican Commonwealth governed through a Council of State and the Rump Parliament; a radically reformed Parliament with a new franchise; some kind of accommodation with a reformed Stuart monarchy; the semi-theocratic assembly of the Barebone's

Parliament; the Protectorate and military rule through the major-generals; then various Protectorate Parliaments; and finally, a tentative suggestion of a new dynasty (King Oliver I?). Each option could claim it represented both a practical solution to a current problem that was justified from the Bible, while riling and provoking others within the ranks of the godly who considered this option a betrayal of everything they had fought for. Not an easy situation.

This meant that Cromwell, for example, might envisage himself (and be proclaimed by *some* others) as, variously: a conquering military hero and judge in the likeness of Joshua; a law-giving and mediating Moses-figure; a semi-royal governor under God like Zerubabbel; and even perhaps a new King David or Solomon who was going to enlarge the godly kingdom and the cause of Protestantism across Europe. All these governmental models in one man, in one short and intense decade: but which was the one approved of by God?[3]

SHOULD ONLY GOD BE KING? "TAKE 1"

In 1651 Cromwell is reported, by a contemporary,[4] to have concluded, "That now the old king being dead, and his son being defeated, he held it necessary to come to a Settlement of the Nation." To this the Speaker of the House of Commons replied that it was beholden on them to do so since "God hath given marvellous success to our Forces under your command…" and it was required that Parliament should "improve these mercies to some Settlement such as may be to God's honour, and the good of this Commonwealth". Major-General Harrison added that this proposed Settlement should encompass "both of our Civil and Spiritual Liberties; and so, that the mercies which the Lord hath given-in to us may not be cast away".[5] But it was not clear what shape such a settlement should take. Nor how to ensure that it encompassed a political and social transformation *and* a spiritual one that settled the shape of the church.

By 1651 Cromwell and the Parliamentary forces had triumphed over all their enemies. Charles I had been defeated in two civil wars and beheaded in January 1649. Cromwell and the other

Parliamentary generals had brutally crushed the Irish opposition (of various kinds) in 1649–53. Then, in June 1650, Charles (later Charles II) landed in Scotland after earlier doing a deal with the disgruntled Scots (angry at the execution of his father and the failure of Presbyterianism in England). In return for Scottish support, Charles signed the Covenant shortly after landing and agreed to impose a Presbyterian settlement on the realm. Cromwell then routed the Scots at the battle of Dunbar, in September 1650, but in January 1651 Charles II was crowned at Scone and launched an invasion of England. That led to the battle of Worcester in September of 1651 (exactly one year after Dunbar) and the final crushing of Royalist hopes at the hands of Cromwell and the New Model Army. Writing to John Cotton, the minister of the Puritan church in Boston, New England, Cromwell expressed the excitement that many others around him must also have felt: "Surely, sir, the Lord is greatly to be feared, as to be praised." And he raised the question and its apparent answer: "What is the Lord a-doing? What prophecies are now fulfilling?"[6] That prophecies were being fulfilled seemed clear. The millenarian nature of the comment is striking; exactly which prophecies did he think were coming to fruition? In the absence of anything more specific in his letter and in line with his equally non-specific language to the Barebone's Parliament in 1653, it is reasonable to assume that he meant it in the most general terms, that God was about to do (unspecified) wonders. Cromwell was not a Fifth Monarchist and did not indulge in the detailed application of specific prophecies. Nevertheless, he was confident that he stood on the cusp of a monumental movement of God.

The republic of the Commonwealth had been saved by the victory at Worcester; and by 1651 the question was pressing over how this new form of government should develop. The execution of Charles I had resulted in what we would now describe as regime change, but there was no consensus over what was going to replace royal government when it came to detail. Officially, authority lay with the Rump Parliament and the Council of State made up of the leading representatives of the Parliamentary cause. Cromwell himself, though the leading Parliamentarian, was only captain-general of the army, a member of the Council of State and of several key Parliamentary committees. He was officially simply the "most powerful official of the government".[7] His titled pre-eminence lay ahead, but in the period 1651 to 1653 that was not certain.

Tracing God's will through signs ("mercies") proved harder in the complexities of peace than they had in the upheavals of war. To begin with, however, victory was not accompanied by a purge of the defeated. Only a small number of the nobility who had backed Charles II paid with their lives. The Act of Oblivion, in February 1652, rather ambiguously promised to put aside vengeance, while still leaving Parliament the power to seize the estates of Royalists who had committed acts of High Treason. In the same mould of ambiguous magnanimity an Act passed in September 1650 had repealed the most savage of the anti-Catholic legislation and removed the compulsion of attending a (Protestant Anglican) church on Sundays, while still banning the Mass.

More intriguingly, the proposed settlement might yet involve some accommodation with the defeated Stuart dynasty. In the same conversations regarding the Settlement of the Nation referred to earlier, Bulstrode Whitlocke asked the question of whether this should be, "an absolute Republic, or with any mixture of Monarchy"? He went on to suggest that the whole system of English laws were so interwoven with monarchy that to abandon it completely was difficult to contemplate. The army officers present were not impressed by this argument and Colonel Desborough asked, "why may not this, as well as other Nations, be governed in the way of a Republic?" Clearly, he had not seen one king executed (although he had avoided participation in the trial of Charles I) in order to see another raised in his place. Later he would oppose any possibility of Cromwell taking the crown. Colonel Whalley reminded those present that both of the late king's eldest sons were their enemies. Although one other present at the meeting mooted that the third son, Henry Duke of Gloucester, was both very young and in Parliamentary captivity – and might be of use. What is interesting is that Cromwell's view was apparently "that a Settlement with somewhat of Monarchical power in it would be very effectual".[8]

Nothing came of the vague mixed-settlement option that contained a "mixture of Monarchy". The Duke of Gloucester was eventually sent into exile. What this reminds us of, though, is that Cromwell, although a regicide, was not a committed republican. The wording of Cromwell's conclusion ("somewhat of Monarchical power in it") makes one wonder if he was already considering the political desirability of assuming this critical role himself. If so, the Old Testament examples of rule, as we have seen, would not have precluded this.

A GODLY MILITARY COUP?
DISSOLVING THE RUMP PARLIAMENT

Cromwell wanted the Rump Parliament to set a date for new elections and to establish a national church that allowed Independents and other acceptable Separatists the right to their own fellowships. This, the Rump failed to do. On one hand, it delayed setting a new election date and could not agree an acceptable new structure for the church or a method of paying for it except for the established tithes (so resented by Separatists who did not attend parish churches). It did, though, allow for some basic liberty of conscience in terms of religious beliefs; although restricted to Protestant Christians and excluding open Catholic activities. Episcopacy, so loathed by Puritans, was effectively suppressed and the Act of Uniformity of 1559 was repealed in September 1650, so granting toleration to the Independent churches and the moderate Separatist ones also. This was done on the insistence of the army which contained many members of both persuasions.

When the Rump continued to resist calls for a vote of dissolution to end its sitting, Cromwell acted, on 20 April 1653, to close it down. Accompanied by forty musketeers, he cleared the chamber, using increasingly intemperate language, had the Speaker pulled down from his place, and dissolved Parliament by force. This included the famous phrase, "You are no Parliament! I say you are no Parliament! I will put an end to your sitting."[9] It is alleged that Cromwell seized the mace, the symbol of Parliamentary power, and dismissed it as a mere "bauble".[10] It was to all intents and purposes a military coup.

It should, though, be remembered that the Rump, for all its lack of Puritan zeal, passed legislation designed to regulate people's moral behaviour. This included closing down theatres and requiring strict observance of Sunday in terms of acceptable behaviour and activities. It was under the Rump that the 1650 Adultery Act and Blasphemy Act were passed. Similarly, the 1652 Act of Oblivion not only exempted determined Royalists from pardon but also those guilty of "the Detestable and abominable vice of Buggery with Mankind or Beast" and those guilty of "the carnal ravishment of women". Clearly, the Rump took seriously its role as guardian of the nation's sexual morals and safety. It also instituted punishments for drunkenness and swearing in public. However, it failed to outlaw the use of face paint and the wearing of fashion patches and immodest dresses. These unsuccessful attempts to stamp out these latter practices revealed a typical puritanical anxiety concerning female fashion. It also made some small improvements to court procedures, such as ensuring that they should be conducted in English rather than in Latin, or in the medieval-originated legalese known as "Law French". However, it failed to reform the so-called Common Law; nor did it protect the property rights of poorer members of the rural community from enclosures. It was such failures that enraged the Diggers.

Once more, Cromwell read the signs of the times in the march of events and was clearly certain that his actions were right. The extreme nature of his language and his rigorous behaviour was typical: hesitation and halting steps and then precipitous action. But what would come next? For, if Cromwell was certain of what he did not want (the discredited Rump), he was less certain of what he did want.

THE PARLIAMENT OF SAINTS

The apparent answer was the "Barebone's" or "Nominated Parliament". This was the closest that the country would come to a republican theocracy. Made up of those nominated from the "gathered churches", it was envisaged as an assembly of saints which was set the crucial task of finding a settlement for the constitution and a religious settlement for the church.

At first, Cromwell's hopes appear to have been high. Addressing the opening of the Parliament, in July 1653, he declared: "Truly God hath called you to this Work by, I think, as wonderful Providences as ever passed upon the sons of men in so short a time." Reflecting on the convoluted path that had led to this point he revealingly concluded, "It's come, therefore, to you by the way of necessity; by the way of the wise Providence of God – through weak hands."[11] This was fairly typical of how Cromwell identified the revealing hand of Providence and the will of God. Believing in the rightness of his cause he inevitably read events and the direction they took as indicative of God's will. These were the "mercies" he had identified in the wars. And then once things reached a tipping point he acted, confident that he was in line with God's will. However, the complexities of peacetime politics were more difficult to read for God's will than the course of a battle; for the theocratic assembly was to prove a severe disappointment.

As we have seen (Chapter 9) the most radicalized members of the godly, the Fifth Monarchy Men, only constituted a minority of the assembly, but they were enough to panic the more moderate members with their demands for the abolition of tithes and prosecution of the Anglo-Dutch war. On 12 December 1653 these moderate members voted for dissolution. The experiment in a theocratic assembly had collapsed in less than six months. What next?

THE PROTECTORATE

After the collapse of the Nominated Parliament, a document known as the "Instrument of Government" was passed by the Council of State. By this, the executive power in the country was vested in a Lord Protector who ruled in collaboration with the Council of State. Not surprisingly, Cromwell was appointed Lord Protector for life. At last a constitution with, "somewhat of Monarchical power in it" had emerged; and that "Monarchical power" (though not a monarchy as such) was expressed in the person of the Lord Protector.

The wheel of Providence appeared to have turned yet again and Cromwell found himself in the position that he might have been envisaging as early as the winter of 1651, following the battle of Worcester. The Instrument of Government ensured that the Lord Protector needed a majority vote of the Council of State in major decisions, but he was still a very powerful figure and was paid an allowance of £100,000 a year. The Lord Protector was also compelled to summon triennial Parliaments to complete the legislative part of this new governmental structure. However, this did not start well, as the first "Protectorate Parliament" wished to limit the army's influence on the government and also aimed at reducing the powers of the Lord Protector. It was too republican in a state that was tending more toward something of monarchy. As a consequence, Cromwell soon dissolved this Parliament, in January 1655. It had only been sitting since September 1654. Finding the right answer to the question of godly rule was not proving easy.

There was a little more success in the area of church reform. So-called "triers" were authorized to assess the suitability of future parish ministers. This was designed to be part of a package which established a loosely regulated national church, but still ensured acceptable standards (as decided by the Protectorate government). At the same time "ejectors" were given the job of dismissing unsuitable ministers and schoolmasters.

An interesting example of Cromwell's tolerance of the right to private worship outside the Puritan church was his encouragement of Jews to return to England in 1657, having been expelled by Edward I in 1290. As well as wanting their economic expertise, he also hoped that by allowing Jews to return, they would convert to Christianity. This, he believed, would hasten the Second Coming of Christ. It was a combination of tolerance and millenarianism.

THE RULE OF THE MAJOR-GENERALS

Following the defeat of a Royalist uprising in the spring of 1655, Cromwell imposed a form of military government on England

and Wales. This was the rule of the major-generals. The context of this experiment was the disappointment with the first Protectorate Parliament, Royalist-inspired unrest, and difficulties faced in foreign policy initiatives in the West Indies. These prompted a refocusing of attention on the morals of the nation, since it was concluded that sinful behaviour was obstructing the development of a godly society and that the aforementioned setbacks were signs of God's disapproval. The rule of the major-generals constituted the most serious effort to date to impose radical godly values on the nation.

The major-generals began work in October 1655 and each had authority over one of twelve regions; and each was directly answerable to the Lord Protector. They were instructed to maintain public order: disarming Royalists, breaking up illegal assemblies, and hunting down thieves and highwaymen. They were empowered to raise a cavalry militia made up of Protectorate loyalists, funded by an income tax of 10 per cent which was paid by Royalists: the "decimation tax". Having now given up on a policy of reconciling Royalists, their movements were strictly monitored.

The major-generals also played a key part in a campaign designed to reform morals. They banned plays, horse-racing, bear-baiting, and cock-fighting. They took action against drunkenness, sexual misbehaviour, ale-houses with a reputation for trouble, swearing, and blasphemy. These unelected army officers worked alongside existing magistrates and sheriffs, but their energetic pursuit of godly conduct was resented as a military imposition. In order to establish the permanence of the system they attempted to manipulate elections to a new (and hopefully sympathetic) Parliament. In this they failed spectacularly.

During the first session of the Second Protectorate Parliament, which began in September 1656, MPs voted down a bill that would have made the decimation tax permanent. This took taxation firmly back into the traditional hands of Parliament and undermined the viability of the major-generals. Cromwell acquiesced in this. Modern opinions vary as to whether he withdrew support from this experiment (which was very much in line with his values) because it had proved unpopular and untenable or because he was taken by surprise at the degree of Parliamentary opposition. The former seems more likely. The wheel of Providence appeared to have turned yet again, and Cromwell shut down the experiment early in 1657. Recent study of it has drawn attention to both its dynamic, energetic, and efficient pursuit of the most ambitious godly reformation of the nation and its total failure to achieve sufficient financial backing, grassroots support, or lasting social change. Finally, the major-generals failed to manage elections to a Parliament they had recommended calling and were then abandoned by the Lord Protector whose cause they were zealots to pursue.[12]

CROMWELL AND CHRISTMAS

Cromwell is often described as the man who banned Christmas. The truth of the matter, however, is more complex. For while the celebration of Christmas continued to be proscribed following his accession as Protector, this had certainly not started under Cromwell.

The Scottish kirk attempted to abolish Christmas festivities in the 1560s. James VI and I restored the feast there in 1617, but it was banned in Scotland again in 1640. From 1641 this hard-line Puritan attitude was also evident in England. By 1645 the Oxford Royalist John Taylor could lament, in his *The Complaint of Christmas*, how traditional Christmas celebrations "are now extinct and put out of use… as if they had never been," and that "thus are the merry lords of misrule suppressed by the mad lords of bad rule at Westminster". Christmas had fallen foul of a Puritan-led campaign against both its perceived over-exuberant activities and its association with (they claimed) Catholic traditions. While clearly believing firmly in Christ's birth, they maintained that, since the feast had no biblical precedent, it should be banned. As early as 1643, Puritan-inclined tradespeople opened their shops as normal on Christmas Day and MPs sat in Parliament. Churches were kept shut. In 1644 the feast day was declared a fast. In January 1645 Parliament issued its *Directory for the Public Worship of God*, an alternative to the *Book of Common Prayer*, with no reference to Christmas as a church event. Thus, by Christmas 1645, Christmas officially ceased to exist in Parliamentary areas of the country. There is evidence that this was very unpopular and there were even pro-Christmas riots in East Anglia, in London, and in Canterbury in protest at the Parliamentary ordinance that celebration of Christmas was a punishable offence. With Parliamentary victory the – temporary – fate of Christmas was sealed; although in 1652 John Taylor's *The Vindication of Christmas* claimed that Devon farmers still celebrated it.

So, Cromwell cannot be held responsible for the anti-Christmas campaign but he certainly supported it, holding government meetings on 25 December. It was not until the Restoration of 1660 that Christmas was again restored. And there is plenty of evidence to show its return was greeted with widespread joy.[13]

SHOULD ONLY GOD BE KING? "TAKE 2"

In 1657, during the Second Protectorate Parliament, a group of MPs proposed that the crown be offered to Cromwell, to combine the Protectorate with the traditional form of government. Cromwell considered the offer but declined. He knew that he faced strong opposition from the republicans in the army and the most radical among the godly. Instead, he was reinstated as Lord Protector in a quasi-monarchical ceremony which saw him enthroned at Westminster Hall on King Edward's Chair. It looked like a coronation. Although not hereditary, Cromwell could now name his successor. His new powers were revealed in the Humble Petition and Advice, which replaced the Instrument of Government. His signature on official documents, after 1657, was the quasi-regal "Oliver P[rotector]".[14]

In finally abandoning thoughts of the crown he expressed his thinking in true Cromwellian style: "I will not seek to set up that which Providence hath destroyed, and laid in the dust; I would not build Jericho again!"[15]

THE DEATH OF THE LORD PROTECTOR

Cromwell died at Whitehall on 3 September 1658, aged fifty-nine. The date was the anniversary of his great victories at Dunbar and Worcester. He was buried at Westminster Abbey. For those of the godly who had held fast to the Protectorate it was difficult to interpret exactly what this meant in terms of the actions of Providence. Within two years it had become apparent that it was not a foreshadowing of future victories for the godly cause.

He was succeeded as Lord Protector by his son, Richard. Having no powerbase in either Parliament or the army he was forced to resign in May 1659. After an unsettled period, senior army leaders re-established the Long Parliament which eventually led to the recall of Charles II. The most extensive episode of godly rule had ended.

THE CONSEQUENCES OF THE RULE OF GOD AS ENVISAGED BY CROMWELL

Much of what Cromwell did in the 1650s can be seen as conventional providential Calvinism. Starting from the premise of the sovereignty of God, which should be reflected in human government and society, alongside the concept of God's will being providentially revealed through signs and circumstances (Cromwell and others tended to refer to these signposts of divine will as "mercies"), he shifted position in order to accommodate what he considered to be the revealed will of God. Given that there was no biblical blueprint for government this allowed him to be pragmatic, innovative, experimental, and flexible.

However, it also caused him to be inconsistent and arbitrary and this style of godly rule destabilized the system of government in Britain. If he could justify to himself that an action was in line with what he perceived to be the will of God, as revealed through circumstances or his saints, then Cromwell would do it. There was no governmental concept that it could be measured against. Taxes were levied without the consent of Parliament. Different executive structures were adopted and discarded. Parliaments were called on differing electoral or nomination principles and then dissolved. The source of power could oscillate between military and civilian forms of government because Cromwell could persuade himself that, since he had prayerfully chosen it, God willed it so, whatever others said. Those who offended the Protectorate could be imprisoned without trial. The rule of law was flexibly interpreted and the elites came to lack confidence in it as a safeguard of their liberty and property. Finally, there was no "Cromwell system" to be bequeathed to his successors other than a semi-monarchical Protectorate that had failed to establish well-rooted support. It is little wonder that it rapidly collapsed following his death.

While the Restoration of Charles II was regarded as the ultimate failure of godly rule by many of the saints, it came about precisely because nobody had definitively established what form godly rule should take. The most radical of the saints had been determined that the death of Charles I would usher in an era when God was King, but they failed to implement a coherent or consistent plan of what this meant in practice. The most radicalized had aspirations but few consistent programmes. Ultimately they looked to God himself to directly intervene to establish his rule. But whether this meant the visible and actual Second Coming of Christ, the prophetic insights of the saints, or the revelation of God's will through providential signs was never established. And in the latter two modes of understanding the will of God, there was much leeway for disagreement among the godly (let alone the rest of the population). Destabilizing conflict was inadvertently hardwired into the whole system. As a consequence, the fear of disorder and the (exaggerated) anxieties about the threat posed by the most radical of the godly left (be they Fifth Monarchists or Quakers) – coupled with resentment of military influence in the body politic – meant that the Protectorate imploded and, by 1660, Charles II was on the throne vacated by his executed father. What future was there for godly rule when the rule of the saints had so abruptly collapsed?

12

The End of the "Good Old Cause"

Following the resignation of Richard Cromwell in May 1659, the Rump Parliament was recalled.[1] There was much distrust between the civilian members of the Parliament and the army, despite them all officially being republicans. In order to bring the army under control the Rump sacked nine senior officers but this provoked an attempted military coup when Major-General Lambert drove out the MPs and set up a new government called the Committee of Safety.[2] It seemed a repeat of what Oliver Cromwell had done in 1653, but this time the show of force failed. When Parliament called for support it found help in a faction of the army unimpressed by Lambert's impetuous act. General George Monck was the commander-in-chief of the Parliamentary army in Scotland and he sided against Lambert and demanded the return of Parliament. His reason was simple: it was the only legally constituted government. In contrast, Lambert's actions represented illegitimate force. It had suited Oliver Cromwell (who no doubt would have cited circumstances dictated by Providence as a reason for precipitous action) but this style of rule was wearing thin and, furthermore, the sight of an unelected military committee sitting in Westminster as the de facto government was likely to destabilize the whole country.

THE END OF THE REPUBLIC OF THE GODLY

With the saints at each other's throats, preserving order and stability was taking a higher priority than preserving the godly republic. Monck marched on London in January 1660 in defence of Parliament.[3] But he was set on something more fundamental than simply reinstating the previous assembly. Instead, he turned the clock back to before the 1648 Pride's Purge when he demanded that those Presbyterian MPs of what had once been the "Peace party" were reinstated along with those expelled by Lambert. In February 1660 these long-absent members were readmitted. Now it was as if the previous ten years of constitutional upheaval had never happened; the Long Parliament was back in session.

Across the Channel, Charles II and his advisers were watching the governmental chaos unfolding in Britain. Seizing his chance, the exiled king secretly contacted Monck with a promise of stability if he was allowed to return as king. Monck responded favourably. Given that long ago, in 1651, there had been talk of whether a settlement had to be "an absolute Republic, or with any mixture of Monarchy", the actions of Monck were not as astonishing as they might seem at first glance.[4] There had originally been reflection on whether a suitably compliant monarchy might be acceptable and in 1660, with things beginning to fall apart, it was no longer out of the question. Clearly, for die-hard godly republicans of the Fifth Monarchist kind it was, but for the less ideologically determined of the saints it seemed a pragmatic solution to present problems. The issue was: how compliant would Charles II be?

As a result of these contacts with the exiled king, the Long Parliament dissolved itself in March 1660. Before it did so it called elections for what became known as the "Convention Parliament" that would resolve the crisis by negotiating with the king. In return, Charles offered an olive branch in the form of the Declaration of Breda, in April 1660.[5] This promised a pardon for crimes committed over the past ten years, protection of confiscated (Royalist) property purchased in that time period, religious toleration, payment of the army and the bringing of it into royal service. This was accepted by the Convention Parliament.

Charles was proclaimed the rightful king on 8 May 1660. Returning from exile, he arrived in London on 29 May 1660 and was crowned the following year on St George's Day, 23 April 1661. The experiment in a godly republic and the rule of the saints was over. For those who, in 1649, had considered that God was King in place of earthly monarchs, the blow was terrible.

One contemporary commentator said of the collapse of Lambert's military coup that, "the Lord has blasted them and spit in their faces."[6] To many of the godly, who had traced the hand of Providence through the events that had unfolded since the outbreak of the Scottish rebellion against King Charles I in 1637, it must have been hard to think of a reply. There is, however, much evidence to suggest general support for the Restoration across the country.

THE "TRIAL" AND "EXECUTION" OF OLIVER CROMWELL

On 30 January 1661, on the twelfth anniversary of the execution of Charles I at Whitehall in 1649, the body of Oliver Cromwell was exhumed from its grave in Westminster Abbey.[7] The body of Cromwell's daughter, who was buried with him, was allowed to remain in the abbey and was not subjected to the same treatment that was meted out to the corpse of her father.

Cromwell's body was put through the indignities of a – posthumous – "trial" for High Treason and "executed". His body was hanged in chains at Tyburn, in the manner of a common criminal and, afterwards, disposed of by burial in unconsecrated ground. Alongside Cromwell's body hung two other deceased once-leading Parliamentarians and regicides: John Bradshaw, President of the High Court of Justice for the trial of King Charles I, and Cromwell's son-in-law, Henry Ireton, who had been a general in the New Model Army. At sunset the bodies were taken down and their heads cut off and displayed on poles outside Westminster Hall. There they remained in an increasingly desiccated state until 1685. This, ironically, was the year of the failed Monmouth Rebellion (see below) which was in many ways the last uprising of the godly. In that year a storm brought down the pole holding Cromwell's head, which was found by a passing soldier who kept it hidden in his chimney. When he died it was bequeathed to his daughter. In 1710 the severed head appeared in a public show and was described as "The Monster's Head". After this, the head passed through a number of hands, until Josiah Henry Wilkinson bought it in 1814. It then remained in the ownership of his family until 1960.

Just to prove that conspiracy theories are not the invention of the twenty-first century, some people in the seventeenth century questioned whether the body exhibited in 1661 was actually that of Cromwell.[8] These rumours were reported by Samuel Pepys and other near contemporaries; and then others appeared in print in the eighteenth century and gained a wider audience in the nineteenth century. These doubts arose because it was alleged that between his death in September 1658 and the exhumation of his corpse in January 1661, Cromwell's body had been buried and reburied in several places to protect it from Royalists eager to be revenged on one they had failed to defeat during his life. The stories suggested that his bodily remains were buried elsewhere in London, or in Cambridgeshire, or in Northamptonshire, or in Yorkshire.[9] It continues to be questioned by some whether the body mutilated at Tyburn was in fact that of Oliver Cromwell. However, the vague and uncorroborated nature of the rumours suggests that they were nothing more than that.

Assuming these rumours are incorrect and the correct body *was* disinterred in 1661, the head from that body finally found a permanent resting place in 1960, when the Wilkinson family offered it to Cromwell's old Cambridge college. The head was finally buried under the floor of the antechapel in Sidney Sussex College. The exact position has not been publicly disclosed in order to better protect it after years of misuse, but today a plaque marks the approximate location of its burial. The plaque reads,

Near to
this place was buried
on 25 March 1960 the head of
OLIVER CROMWELL
Lord Protector of the Common-
Wealth of England, Scotland &
Ireland. Fellow Commoner
of this college 1616–7.

The actual copper-gilt death plate, buried with Cromwell's body in 1658, sold for £74,500 when auctioned at Sotheby's in

December 2014.[10] The plate had been removed from Cromwell's coffin in 1661 by James Norfolke, who was the Sergeant of the House of Commons, when the body was disinterred.

The Cromwell vault in Westminster Abbey was later used as a burial place for Charles II's illegitimate children. It is an irony that they share the vault with the daughter of Oliver Cromwell. In the abbey the site where Cromwell was once buried is now marked by a floor stone that reads, "THE BURIAL PLACE OF OLIVER CROMWELL 1658–1661". This area of the church is now designated as the Air Force Chapel.

THE FATE OF THE LIVING REGICIDES

In August 1660 the Act of Indemnity and Oblivion became law, thereby pardoning most supporters of the Commonwealth and Protectorate. However, some were exempted from this leniency. In fact about sixty were slated for capital punishment; but in the event, thirty-three of the surviving regicides were brought to trial. These included the men who had been directly involved in the trial and execution of Charles I.

In October 1660 a court was established in order to bring to trial the regicides who were held in custody. Ten of these were condemned to death for High Treason, and were publicly hanged, drawn, and quartered at Charing Cross or at Tyburn. The ten executed were: John Carew, Gregory Clement, Thomas Harrison, John Jones, Thomas Scot, Adrian Scrope (signatories to the King's death warrant); the preacher Hugh Peter (not directly involved in the trial and execution of Charles, but a vocal supporter of the regicide); Daniel Axtell and Francis Hacker (commanders of the guards at the king's trial and execution); and, finally, John Cook (the lawyer responsible for directing the prosecution of the king). Their estates were confiscated. In some cases, death sentences were commuted with a further nineteen of the regicides imprisoned for life. A further twenty republicans were forbidden from holding public office. The wheel had turned full circle since January 1649.

In addition to the above death toll, the Marquis of Argyll, who had led the Scottish Covenanters, was executed in 1661; Major-

General Lambert, who had attempted the military coup in 1659 and attempted to stop the Restoration was imprisoned for life; the leading Commonwealth politician, Sir Henry Vane, was executed in 1662; the leading republican, Sir Arthur Heselrige, died in prison before he could be brought to trial.

The Convention Parliament also declared that all the regicides who had died before the Restoration occurred should be posthumously attainted for High Treason. As a result, their property was confiscated by the crown. As with the treatment of Cromwell's body, vengeance attempted to reach beyond the grave.

A further twenty regicides fled from Britain and ended up in Europe or North America. Three of these were arrested by Sir George Downing, the English ambassador to the Netherlands, and returned to England where they were executed in April 1662. Two fled to the old godly exile place of Switzerland. There, John Lisle was murdered at Lausanne by a Royalist agent in 1664; however, Edmund Ludlow survived and eventually died at Vevey, in 1692. Strangely enough, the man most immediately responsible for the king's death – the executioner – was never identified and so escaped Restoration vengeance.[11]

It now remained to be seen what would be done with the legacy of a decade of republican godly rule and a previous decade of turbulence.

DEALING WITH THE LEGACY OF THE RULE OF THE SAINTS

Over the remaining months of 1660 the Convention Parliament worked on what has been called the "Restoration settlement", or at least its first phase. Its main aim was to turn the clock back to a point in 1641, when the Long Parliament had passed reforms designed to limit Charles' arbitrary use of royal power. This gave reason to think that erasing the most radical Acts of Parliament (and, of course, the Commonwealth and Protectorate) would not undo all that had been achieved in moderating royal power prior to the outbreak of hostilities. This meant that every law that had received royal assent by Charles I before the breakdown of peace was retained on the statute book. As a result of this, the controversial courts that he had established to bolster royal power but had been forced to abolish remained annulled, and Parliament still had the expectation of being called every three years. The upheaval had not been for nothing. However, every law passed during the Commonwealth and Protectorate was erased.

The New Model Army was disbanded and action taken to meet its arrears of pay. A poll tax was instituted to cover the cost but the sum raised by it was inadequate. So an additional tax was levied on property owners. Despite these problems, the money was eventually raised and the New Model Army was finally disbanded in January 1661. It was the end of an era. The army of saints which had won the Civil Wars, subdued Ireland, crushed the Presbyterian Scots, and intervened in civilian politics was no more. Its political legacy would be a lasting distrust of a large standing army and any interference of the military in politics.

The settlement also affected land, since any royal or church land confiscated and sold to new owners during the Commonwealth and Protectorate was to be restored to the original landowner. However, the Declaration of Breda had promised that the purchasers of these lands would be compensated for any loss. Leasing out the lands to the – now disappointed – purchasers at low rents fixed this in many cases. Many Royalists were less fortunate. If they had been forced to sell land to pay Parliamentary fines, then these land transactions did not revert to them. This disappointed many lesser Royalists, while many more influential ones used their connections to gain some measure of compensation.

Attitudes harden

The Convention Parliament finally came to an end in December 1660. It was then replaced by a new parliament, called by the new king himself. Elections for it were completed in April 1661, when it was clear that it was going to take a less conciliatory tone than the Convention Parliament. High Church Anglicans and Royalists felt that it had been too lenient and that they had lost out accordingly. In early 1661 the Fifth Monarchists Thomas Venner and Vavasor

Powell led an abortive uprising in London against Charles II. As a result, the elections were held against a background of anxiety about more uprisings by godly extremists. Alarm increased during the voting for the new parliament when the four London parliamentary seats were won by Presbyterians.

The new "Cavalier Parliament" comprised of high numbers of Royalists and Anglicans. It met in May 1661 and was not dissolved until January 1679. During these seventeen years it energetically targeted the cause of the godly and their ability to once more threaten the status quo.[12]

The first move – the Militia Act of 1661 – dealt with a matter that had triggered the Civil Wars, the matter of control of the armed forces. This law established the monarch as supreme commander of the army and the navy. The controversial courts that had enabled Charles I to rule personally without Parliament in the 1630s were not brought back but, on the other hand, the monarch's right to appoint government officials and run foreign policy was accepted. Years of anti-episcopalianism were reversed when the Bishops' Exclusion Act (of 1641) was repealed, allowing the Anglican bishops to return to the House of Lords, which had been restored by the Convention Parliament. Monarchical power was enhanced in 1664, with the adjustments made to the Triennial Act, which removed the *compulsion* on the monarch to call Parliament every three years.

THE RELIGIOUS SETTLEMENT

There was to be no compromise over the nature of the national church such that it would meet the demands of the Presbyterians. The Anglican and Royalist nature of the Cavalier Parliament saw to that. The writing was soon on the wall: bishops returned to the House of Lords; conformity was enforced regarding the doctrines of the Church of England; a chill wind was blowing toward Presbyterians and the gathered churches of the godly.

This was a severe blow to Presbyterians, who had been deeply unhappy with the church under Cromwell, had hoped to gain from the Restoration and the suppression of the sects and a return to national conformity. This was always going to be a long shot since Charles II was surrounded by supporters of the episcopalian Church of England. However, there were grounds for hope that a compromise might be reached since the Declaration of Breda, while promising the restoration of the Church of England, also promised religious toleration for those outside it. As if to emphasize this, Edward Reynolds, a leading Presbyterian, was made both Bishop of Norwich and chaplain to the king in 1660 (and he remained bishop until 1676). Perhaps at least the Presbyterian wing of the godly might be satisfied with the nature of the re-established national church?

In line with this possibility Charles II encouraged the idea that a revised *Book of Common Prayer* might be produced in such a way as to make it acceptable to Presbyterians. If so, it would draw a large number of the godly back into the Church of England. During April 1661 the Savoy Conference saw the bishops and the leaders of Presbyterianism, including New Model Army chaplain Richard Baxter (see Chapter 4), meet in discussion. There were twelve in each party and it seemed to promise a balanced outcome. However, the Presbyterian proposals for a reformed *Book of Common Prayer*, which had been compiled by Richard Baxter, were largely rejected by the bishops. The Cavalier Parliament brought about the final end of Presbyterian hopes.[13] The final religious settlement was enshrined in four Acts of Parliament that were known collectively as the Clarendon Code.

In May 1661, the Cavalier Parliament passed the Corporation Act. This barred from holding office in a city or corporation all who had not received communion in the Church of England over the past year. This ruled out every Separatist (not that this worried Presbyterians) but also everyone else who had attended alternative congregations (which did affect them). In addition, all officeholders had to swear the Oath of Allegiance (to the king), the Oath of Supremacy (royal headship of the church in England), and to accept the Doctrine of Passive Obedience (total obedience to the monarch). And they had to renounce the Covenant. The latter sealed the matter as far as Presbyterianism was concerned.

The Act of Uniformity of 1662 insisted that all ordained clergy must accept the doctrines and liturgy of the Church of England. Also, all had to be ordained by a bishop and this had to be done according to the rites of the Church of England. All clergy must renounce the Solemn League and Covenant and accept the revised *Book of Common Prayer* and all Anglican doctrines. This led to the ejection of hundreds of Presbyterian and other "Nonconformist" clergy from their positions on St Bartholomew's Day, 24 August 1662,[14] for refusing to comply with the Act of Uniformity. This date became known, among these "Nonconformists", as "Black Bartholomew's Day" and drew parallels with the St Bartholomew's Day massacre of 1572, when Protestants had been slaughtered in France. Eventually about two thousand ministers resigned from their positions in the Church of England. In this way the Puritan character of large parts of the national church (made up of the godly *within* the national church as distinct from the godly Separatists *outside* it) was ended. Following this momentous event in 1662, the term "Nonconformist" or "Dissenter" is generally used, instead of "Puritan", to describe those who would not accept the purged Church of England and instead operated outside of it.

Nevertheless, it should be remembered that the majority of the ministers who had served in the state church under Cromwell did conform to the *Book of Common Prayer* and accepted the Act of Uniformity. Ex-members of the state church of the Commonwealth and Protectorate who conformed in 1662 were called by the pejorative term of "Latitudinarians" by their contemporaries.[15] Indicating that these ministers failed to adhere to a strict conformity to a particular doctrine or standard, the term eventually was levelled at anyone who could tolerate variations in religious opinion; and so, by the nineteenth century, it was used negatively to describe those who were prepared to tolerate deviance from traditional Christian doctrines not just churchmanship. The fragmentation of the godly movement that had begun during the late 1640s and 1650s, when Independents fell out with Presbyterians, and Separatists increased their movements out of the national church altogether, was accelerated by the decision of the Latitudinarians.

There were various attempts from the side of the government and the bishops to establish a basis for "comprehension": a set of circumstances under which some Nonconformist ministers could return to the Church of England. These schemes for comprehension would have driven a wedge between Presbyterians and the Independents; but the discussions that took place between Latitudinarian figures in the national church and leaders, such as Baxter, outside it never bridged the gap between Nonconformists and the High Church party in the Church of England. As a result, comprehension proved impossible to achieve.

Despite being expelled from their churches in 1662, many of these Nonconformist clergy continued preaching to their followers; but now based in private homes and other available meeting places. At the time these Nonconformist meetings were called "conventicles". From these conventicles would eventually develop the Baptist, Congregationalist and Presbyterian church denominations in Britain. The Cavalier Parliament did all it could to inconvenience these Nonconforming ministers and disrupt their communities of believers. The Conventicle Act of 1664 threatened fines or imprisonment for those attending one of these independent prayer meetings or acts of worship.

In a similar way, the Five-Mile Act of 1665 prohibited Nonconformist ministers from living within five miles of any church they had held before the Act. There was an exception for those willing to swear an oath never to resist the king or challenge the government of the church or the state. In addition, they had to swear an oath of non-resistance to royal authority before they were allowed an appointment as a tutor or a schoolmaster.[16]

Interestingly, Charles II tried to reduce the harshest of these laws in order to soften their impact on Nonconformists and Catholics. This caused friction between him and those in Parliament eager to crush Nonconformity, including Catholicism.

A FAILED ATTEMPT AT TOLERATION

An interesting insight into Charles II's religious outlook can be found dating from 1670. In that year he signed the Secret Treaty of

Dover with Louis XIV of France.[17] By this he promised religious toleration for the Roman Catholics who continued to practise their faith in England. Then, in March 1672, he issued the Royal Declaration of Indulgence. This suspended the penal laws against the Nonconformists and also reduced restrictions on the *private practice* of Roman Catholicism. It was following this that many imprisoned Nonconformists (including the Baptist preacher, John Bunyan) were finally released from prison. Charles' motivation was twofold. He clearly wished to create a more inclusive society, but he was also increasingly sympathetic to Catholicism. This set him on a collision course with the most enthusiastic High Church Protestants in the Cavalier Parliament. They did not like the godly but were even less tolerant of Catholics. Indeed, the Nonconformist godly (released by his Indulgence) shared this horror of Catholicism. This would reveal itself in the Monmouth Rebellion of 1685 in which many of the godly would show their antagonism toward both Catholicism and High Church Anglicanism (enemies who were themselves mutual opponents).

Many in Parliament (although supporting monarchy) feared that Charles II was intending to restore Catholicism in England, and hostility forced Charles to withdraw the Declaration of Indulgence. The penal laws once more applied to Catholics. Building on this royal climbdown, Parliament passed the first Test Act in 1673, requiring every officeholder in England to reject the Catholic doctrine of transubstantiation (that the bread and wine of the Mass becomes the body and blood of Christ). This ensured no Catholics could hold public office in England, a situation that lasted until the late 1820s.

THE MONMOUTH REBELLION OF 1685

James Scott, the son of Lucy Walter, a mistress of King Charles II, was born in Rotterdam in 1649, during the time when the king had been in exile. Created Duke of Monmouth in 1662, he served for a time in the navy and then in the army, gaining experience in Continental wars. Charles II had no legitimate children, and so his heir was his brother, James, Duke of York. As a known Catholic, his prominence caused grave concern to Protestants. Consequently, Monmouth was acclaimed by many as the leader of the Protestant cause and a possible successor to the throne despite his illegitimacy. In 1680 he toured the Western counties in an event that resembled a royal "Progress" and which went down well in an area where Protestant-orientated clothworkers made up a sizeable proportion of the urban population in Somerset and south-eastern Devon.[18]

When, in February 1685, James II and VII succeeded Charles II as king of England, Monmouth, who was living in Holland, was persuaded to lead a "Protestant invasion" to topple the Catholic king. He landed at Lyme Regis in Dorset with only three small ships and eighty-two men. The poorly prepared invasion lacked money, weapons, and other supplies. Facing limited opposition at first, he entered Taunton on 18 June with supporters gathered from the towns of Chard and Ilminster. However, at Taunton he discovered that the town's corporation and the most prosperous of the townsfolk were reluctant to throw in their lot with him; although clothworkers (from an industry in recession) and poorer sections of the urban community joined him.[19] He was opposed by the Anglican clergy and the local gentry, which did not bode well for the future gathering of support elsewhere. At Taunton he was presented with a flag, made by a group of local schoolgirls from their petticoats, before being proclaimed king on 20 June.

After Taunton, Monmouth and his army marched north and, crossing the river Avon at Keynsham, finally decided against storming Bristol. Instead they marched to Bath, but there they were refused entry. Increasingly aimless, and without the promised support said to have been on its way from Wiltshire, they eventually turned south-westward again. Now, however, they were being shadowed by the royal army.

The ideology of many of Monmouth's supporters can be seen in the damage done to the Cathedral at Wells, where musket fire damaged the West Front of the building. In addition, they ripped lead from the roof with which to make bullets, they broke windows, and smashed the organ (which was often deemed offensive by the godly) and other furnishings. They were only prevented from desecrating the High Altar because their own commander of cavalry defended it with his sword drawn. As had been done by Parliamentary troops in the Civil Wars, they stabled their horses in the nave of the cathedral. It was déjà vu and looked as if the army of saints was again on the march; but this one lacked the equipment and the leadership necessary for victory.

Monmouth was finally defeated at the battle of Sedgemoor on 6 July. He escaped into Dorset where he hoped to find a ship at Poole to take him to France. It was not to be. A reward of £5,000 had been placed on his head and Monmouth was found hiding in a ditch. Taken to London, he pleaded for mercy, but was beheaded on Tower Hill on 15 July.

What happened next – the "Bloody Assize" – seared itself on West Country history and legend.[20] Mass executions took place throughout Somerset of between 150 and 230 prisoners. Their quartered remains were boiled in salted water, tarred, and nailed up as grim warnings to others. Many others were condemned to transportation and between 800 and 850 were sent to serve long sentences in the West Indies. Others implicated in the rebellion were fined heavily and had their land and property confiscated by royal authority. The families of the schoolgirls – those maids of Taunton who had presented Monmouth with his banner – had to pay a heavy fine to have the girls released from imprisonment.[21] The last great uprising of the godly in England had collapsed.

THE REVOLTS OF THE COVENANTERS

Scotland, like England, found its Presbyterian ministers reduced to preaching in conventicles. In 1666 (a prophetically marked year to some) a small force of poorly armed Covenanters was defeated at the battle of Rullion Green in the Pentland Hills. The government then used 6,000 Highland soldiers to subdue south-western Scotland.

Another rebellion broke out in 1679, but was eventually defeated at the battle of Bothwell Brig (where, ironically, the Duke of Monmouth had fought on the government side). In 1680 there was more Covenanter unrest and the government responded with field executions, the so-called "Killing Time".[22]

Most Covenanters welcomed the accession of the Protestant William III in 1688 and he allowed a Presbyterian-style settlement in the Church of Scotland. The Acts of Union (1707) between Scotland and England guaranteed the form of government of the Church of Scotland, although the eighteenth century saw splits occur within Scottish Presbyterianism over the administration of that church.

Things had come a long way since the revolt of the godly in 1637 against the royal imposition of the Prayer Book on Scotland. Much water had flowed under the bridge since then. Much blood had been spilt. And the politically influential days of the godly, and their competing concepts concerning the rule of God, appeared over.

13

A New Jerusalem in the New World?

For many readers in Britain their perception of the godly contribution to the history of North America will probably consist of a rather confusing kaleidoscope of Puritans, Pilgrim Fathers on the *Mayflower*, New England, the Salem witch hunt, Thanksgiving and turkey suppers, severely dressed men and women, killjoys, and maybe a glimpse of Pocahontas! In the US there will be a much clearer picture, but even there we might find some confusion about the relationship between these aspects of the past.

So, it may help to see the wood for the trees if at least we are strict with our terminology. Most of the early colonists in New England were what we can call "non-separating Puritans". This means that they did not wish to set up separate congregations distinct from the Church of England. However, as we shall see, they came from the Puritan and Independent wing of the national church and so they wished to enjoy a large degree of semi-autonomy within their individual church communities, while still maintaining allegiance to an overarching wider system. These we have labelled "Puritan" so far in this book. On the other hand, a fairly small minority of the New England colonists were what has been described as "separating Puritans"; these wished to establish congregations outside of any national church structure both in Britain and in North America. These were also briefly known as "Brownists", named from a sixteenth-century proponent of Separatism.[1] Indeed, in North America, "Brownism became a name for Separatists, especially those who had emigrated from Holland in the 1620s."[2] These are the groups that we have termed "Separatists" in this book. The Pilgrim Fathers were just such a Separatist group, and it was this particular group of settlers who established the Plymouth Colony in 1620.

Consequently, when one uses the term "Puritan" to describe these religious settlers in New England it is a fairly safe one to employ, since the vast majority did, indeed, come within the fairly strict definition that we (and many other historians) have used. On the other hand, the catch-all term that we have used – the "godly" and the "saints" – is an even more inclusive label since it encompasses both Independents and Separatists, and it is appropriate since all came under the broad umbrella of dissent from the official English Protestant church, and all participated in a distinctive puritanical mindset and worldview. As a result, we will continue to use the terms "Puritan", "Separatist", and "the godly"/"the saints", with the proviso that a number of the secondary sources we refer to will tend to use the term "Puritan" because it encompasses most of those religious settlers who colonized New England. For this reason, a number of those who study this period of North American history also use the terms "non-separating Puritans" and "separating Puritans" to differentiate between the majority and minority groups among the early colonists. If this is complex, at least we can remove Pocahontas from the equation. She interacted with the (non-godly) colonial settlement at Jamestown, Virginia (founded 1607) and died (and is buried) at Gravesend in Kent, in 1617, after travelling to Britain. She did, however, convert to Christianity in 1613–14 and changed her name to Rebecca.

THE EMIGRATION OF THE SEPARATIST "PILGRIM FATHERS"

British interest in the eastern seaboard of what is now the United States dated from the discovery of Newfoundland by John Cabot (sailing from the port of Bristol) in 1497. Since then British fishermen and those of other European nations had been exploring the waters of what was to become New England for over a century. This had given risen to claims on the land by the English crown, in competition with the Dutch and French.

The most famous early Protestant religious group to emigrate to North America was that later remembered as the "Pilgrim Fathers". These Separatists or Brownists arrived in 1620, and their landing at Plymouth Rock has been celebrated in art, song, and story, and is now an integral part of US mythology. They were, strictly speaking, not "Puritans"; but they *were* driven by the same desire for religious freedom and the aim of creating a community of the saints that motivated most of the godly in this period of British history.

Their settlement was one of the earliest successful colonies founded by the English on the North American continent (the commercial colony of Jamestown, Virginia, for example had been established earlier in 1607). Not all attempted colonies were successful, however; such as the Popham Colony on the coast of Maine, which failed in 1607–08. While these were part of a wider process of English colonization of the coastal regions of Virginia and New England, it is the godly colonies that concern us, such as the unrelated and smaller colony of godly settlers who had settled in Warrascoyack County in Virginia in 1618.

Those who sailed on the 1620 voyage were part of a Separatist congregation later led by William Bradford. Research has shown that about 40 per cent of those on board the *Mayflower* were from Bradford's community, "as twenty-eight out of the sixty-nine adults who sailed on the *Mayflower* appear to have been congregational members".[3] Originally from Scrooby, Nottinghamshire, they had faced persecution in England and following the imprisonment of several members of the congregation in 1607, the group emigrated to the Netherlands in 1609, where they settled first in Amsterdam and then in Leiden.

Although free to worship there, they were in exile in a foreign country and their young men were eligible for enlistment in the Dutch army. As well as this, they were not free from interference from England. For instance, an attempt was made to arrest one of their number, William Brewster, in 1618, due to his publication of critical comments relating to the English crown and the Anglican church. This prompted the community to seek a permanent home located further away.

In 1619 the group negotiated a land patent from the London Virginia Company, which allowed them to settle at the mouth of the Hudson River. Their emigration was to make use of two ships, the *Mayflower* and the *Speedwell*, and in July 1620 the group finally sailed from the Dutch port of Delfshaven. It consisted of the Nottinghamshire group plus others who had also decided that emigration to America offered the opportunity to enjoy religious freedom.

From the Netherlands they sailed to Southampton, from where a total of 120 passengers finally departed in August. Ninety sailed on the *Mayflower* and thirty left on the *Speedwell*. However, the *Speedwell* suffered serious leaks and the two ships were forced to dock at Dartmouth, Devon, for repairs. From there the two ships finally set sail on 23 August, but another major leak forced them to turn back to Plymouth where the *Speedwell* was declared unseaworthy. While some passengers gave up their attempt to emigrate, the rest joined the already overcrowded *Mayflower*. These serious delays had significant repercussions on the timing of the voyage and, consequently, the colonists had to spend the whole winter on board the *Mayflower*, anchored off Cape Cod.

After two months at sea, land was finally sighted on 9 November: Cape Cod. The colonists, expecting to disembark on the Hudson River further south, did not have a patent to settle this particular area, raising concerns among some passengers over the legality of disembarking at Cape Cod. In order to allay these anxieties, a leading group of those on board the *Mayflower* responded by drafting and ratifying what became the first governing document of the Plymouth Colony: the Mayflower Compact. The document is revealing as it was clearly modelled on the church covenants that Separatists used to form new congregations. The nature of the colony as one of the godly was clear.

The area eventually settled by the "Pilgrims" had been mapped in 1614 by Captain John Smith from Jamestown, and it was following this that the area had been named "New Plimoth" in 1616. The establishment of Plymouth Colony was made easier by the fact that Native American settlement along that area of coast had been devastated by diseases inadvertently brought by European settlers. This settlement was part of a pattern that drew large numbers of the disaffected godly, of various persuasions, toward the eastern coast of North America, and by 1640 the Puritan "Holy Commonwealth" was about thirty-five churches strong.

THE "PURITAN COLONIES" OF NEW ENGLAND

Despite the fame of the Pilgrim Fathers, most of the godly who emigrated to North America travelled there in the decade 1630–1640 (triggered by the personal rule of Charles I and mounting pressure on Puritans). They were "non-separating Puritans" of the Independent kind that would eventually come to prominence in the British Civil Wars. In what has become known as "the Great Migration", a similar number who emigrated across the Atlantic instead fled eastwards to the Netherlands to escape the conformist policies of Archbishop Laud and the High Church Arminian bishops of the Church of England. As we have seen, the Separatists of Plymouth Colony had themselves followed this exodus over a decade earlier, but like them, other exiles in the Netherlands had found that life there was not ideal. When the Thirty Years' War (1618–48) broke out in Europe, anxieties increased regarding the safety of Protestant communities. This, alongside attempts by the English crown to disrupt such communities during the 1630s, made the prospect of North America much more attractive. In this way, the North American colonies became deeply linked to the unfolding (and unravelling) situation in Britain leading to the Civil Wars.

As a direct consequence, "non-separating Puritans" played key roles in establishing the Massachusetts Bay Colony in 1629, the Connecticut Colony in 1636, and finally the New Haven Colony in 1638. These were not alone, since intra-colony conflicts in the rather claustrophobic context of radicalized godly communities led to offshoots. In this way the Colony of Rhode Island and that known as Providence Plantations were both instituted by settlers who had been expelled from the Massachusetts Bay Colony as a result of religious opinions deemed unacceptable by their fellow colonists. In addition, "non-separating Puritans" were also active in the settlement of New Hampshire before it became a crown colony in 1691.

In this movement of godly colonists perhaps the most important occurred in 1630 when John Winthrop led his "Winthrop Fleet" of eleven ships carrying 700 colonists. This movement was encouraged by the fact that the Plymouth Colony had survived its initial crises and now appeared to be a permanent fixture. This indicated that a godly New England really was possible. With royal power increasing in England, the fear that Catholicism might be restored by Charles I (an unlikely scenario but one that nonetheless troubled Puritans) and with the Protestant cause going badly in the Thirty Years' War there seemed no better time to found a "New Jerusalem" of scriptural holiness in the New World. This, alongside the hope of commercial gain, encouraged investors to sink money into the initial stages of funding the companies that lay behind settlement in the New World, such as the Company of Massachusetts Bay. The granting of a royal charter, in 1629 (by a monarch who seems not to have fully grasped the ideological potency of the colonies envisaged by founder members), secured their legal title to the land – the Native Americans, needless to say, being accorded no rights to their own territory.

The nature of the new colonies was made clear by Winthrop's manifesto, *A Model of Christian Charity*, which declared:

> *We are a Company professing ourselves fellow members of Christ, in which respect only, though we were absent from each other many miles, and had our employments as far distant, yet we ought to account our selves knit together by this bond of love, and live in the exercise of it.... We must be knit together in this work as one man.*[4]

Clearly, this was not going to be just another commercial venture, for as Winthrop explained to his companions on the sea voyage to the New World, their colony should be a "City upon a hill" (Matthew 5: 14–16). If ever God was to be truly recognized as King this looked like it really might be the place. The kind of theocracy later briefly explored by members of the 1653 Barebone's Parliament

190

looked like it really might be constructed in New England. For, in a context that was far from episcopal or royal control, a New Jerusalem really might be raised in the context of the New World.

The Great Migration effectively came to an end in 1642 when Charles I put a stop to emigration. Earlier, in 1634, he had attempted through the Privy Council to restrict it to those who conformed to the doctrines and churchmanship of the Church of England, but this had been impossible to enforce. It has been estimated that between 1629 and 1642 about 21,000 Puritans moved from England to New England, and of these about 13,000 moved to the Massachusetts Bay area. These predominantly family groups were in sharp contrast to the mostly single male emigrants who went to the Virginia settlements, further south, motivated by a desire for commercial advancement. Furthermore, in the 1650s, Virginia received more middle-class and Royalist settlers, who left England because of the reduction in their power and influence during the Commonwealth period. By way of contrast, what was happening further north was a spiritual experiment; a godly test tube within which holiness would be refined by the fires of adversity in a new and challenging land.

The early years were hard ones for colonists of all persuasions. For example, within five months of landing at Plymouth Rock about half of the original 102 colonists had died. In the US today the fourth Thursday in November still commemorates the Pilgrim Fathers' Thanksgiving for surviving their first winter in 1621, when things were close to disaster for their fledgling colony.

Life in the colonies where God was King

The godly settlers in New England lived distinctly different lives from other early settlers in America. Living in settlements in fenced villages rather than in dispersed homesteads, the fencing in of their communities became a key feature of their settlements as it marked God-given ownership: their "title to the land". It also contrasted with what they saw as the "laziness" of Native Americans who did not appear to be using the land since they did not use it in ways immediately recognizable to European farmer-colonists. In addition, the godly settlements were relatively self-sufficient and less integrated into wider trading networks than other settler communities. They were more socially homogeneous and deeply religious, which gave them a distinct ideological character. Overall, they were more organized, ordered and unified than any comparable colonial group in North America.[5] The historian Michael Zuckerman has called their tightly knit communities "a totalitarianism of true believers".[6] In such a model of society the congregation to which a person belonged was paramount for, in their view, "They had left a land of corrupt congregations in order to create pure ones.... If Puritans influenced colonial American culture, they did it mainly through their congregations."[7] Social control in such a community was maintained through, "fierce gossip, defamatory and often obscene billboards, and court suits. In one town, 20 per cent of the adults in each decade found themselves charged with an offense, usually a morals violation."[8] It was a conformity policed by mutual surveillance against all aspects of sinful deviance, frivolity, and covetousness. Since sin was seen as a pernicious spiritual contagion, it was to the benefit of all that it was rooted out. In this way, self-interest dictated that one policed one's neighbours. It brings to mind the comment that living in Calvin's Geneva was like being in a "house of glass". There was no room for secrets.

On top of this, their geographical isolation in the New World, away from their historical roots, and the contrast between their ordered little settlements and the vast unknown beyond their boundary fences, combined with the introversion of their ideology to produce a distinctively intense take on the familiar godly outlook which they had inherited from home:

> *Their sense that they were a new Chosen People of God destined to found a New Jerusalem – a New City of God in the midst of the wilderness – insured that American Puritanism would remain more severe (and, frequently, more intellectually subtle and rigorous) than that which they had left behind.*[9]

In such a world a person needed to discover their calling and role within a community which had a social cohesion and uniformity that was profound but also could be claustrophobic.[10] Here there was suspicion of the single and the masterless, for all needed to be brought under authority (family, husband, church). And church attendance and theological conformity was enforced by local magistrates to the extent that at least four Quakers were hanged for their beliefs. Clearly the definition of "the godly" would only stretch so far, but that too had been the Quaker experience in England in the 1650s and 1660s. On the other hand, literacy was high, as individuals were strongly encouraged to read the Bible; this, in time, fostered a personal sense of having the ability to discern God's will, which both strengthened the idea of an active and resilient citizenship and (controversially) *could* also prompt dangerous ideas which did not conform to the norm.

As strict Calvinists, membership of the local church consisted of those recognized as the regenerate minority. These had publicly confessed their experience of conversion; they had a personal spiritual story to tell. This excluded those without this experience and could, in time, undermine the very churches that instituted this concept of membership (see the "Halfway Covenant" below). Officially, the Cambridge Platform (1648) expressed the Puritan position on matters of church government: the local congregation was the highest tier of church authority, and civil magistrates had no power to intervene in church affairs other than to convene a church synod if a church community was considered to have seriously erred. In reality, however, a symbiotic semi-theocracy was established whereby ministers had immense political influence, but godly civil authorities (themselves church members) were also highly influential in church decisions. Indeed, this was always likely since, as the Cambridge Platform stated:

> *If any church, one or more, shall grow schismatical, rending itself from the communion of other churches, or shall walk incorrigibly or obstinately in any corrupt way of their own, contrary to the rule of the Word; in such case the magistrate is to put forth his coercive power, as the matter shall require.*[11]

The Massachusetts Puritans, therefore, generally favoured a Presbyterian-type of church government (but one that tended rather more toward Independent semi-autonomous congregations) while remaining in full communion with the Church of England. To them the Separatists, such as those in the Plymouth Colony, were "schismatics". Two early controversies offer us insights into *both* the challenge presented by Separatist tendencies *and* the tension between church authority structures and personal revelation.

In 1631 Roger Williams, a "separating Puritan" minister, arrived in Boston, where he refused an invitation to lead a local church because the congregation had not separated itself from the Church of England. The civil leaders at Boston then stopped him taking up a post at Salem due to his Separatist outlook. He also advocated the separation of church and state. Williams moved to the Plymouth Colony (of Separatists) but fell out with them and eventually took up the post at Salem in 1635, despite opposition from the civil authorities in Boston. Once in place he promulgated such views as: the Church of England was so sinful that membership of it constituted a sin; Charles I was no Christian, whatever the Massachusetts Bay charter declared; no oaths should be imposed by civil authorities, as this contravened Matthew 5:34–36. As a result, he was expelled from the colony and, in 1636, founded the colony of Providence Plantations, where freedom of religion was allowed.

A different kind of challenge to Puritan orthodoxy came in the form of Anne Hutchinson, who in 1634 moved, with her family, from Boston, Lincolnshire to Boston, Massachusetts Bay. They accompanied their minister John Cotton. There, a small group – a "conventicle" – met in Hutchinson's home on weekdays; although some objected to a woman occupying such a prominent role. She, like many of the godly was a Calvinist; indeed, in her case, she might be described as hyper-Calvinist. The real controversy started, though, when Hutchinson denounced other Puritan ministers in the colony as being too focused on works contributing to salvation in contrast with the "covenant of grace" that she felt was correctly taught by John Cotton. Hutchinson was accused of "antinomianism", the belief that God's elect do not have to conform to morality and are thereby freed from such constraints. It is now difficult to decide whether this was an accurate charge or not. However, when brought before the Massachusetts General Court, her claim that God had spoken directly to her through a revelation caused her to be condemned, since those judging her believed that God only revealed himself through the Bible. So, she had been attacked for the very practice of "prophesying" that had been the High Church charge against many among the godly. Life and condemnation was clearly complex. In 1638 she was banished and helped found a breakaway colony at what became Portsmouth, Rhode Island, and part of the Colony of Rhode Island and Providence Plantations.

She was not the only exile (voluntary or involuntary) from the semi-theocracy of Massachusetts Bay and a number of other colonies had their origins in those who sought to escape the theological restraints exercised within Massachusetts Bay. The irony, of course, is that Anne Hutchinson, the victim, was as intolerant of others of whom she disapproved as her detractors were of her. She was, therefore, a rather complex exponent of religious liberty. Yet today she has her statue in front of the Massachusetts State House. Although the statue was commissioned in 1920, it was not dedicated until 2005. This is an indication of her complex and controversial legacy and mythology. She eventually died in an Indian raid on a Dutch settlement in the Bronx, in 1643.[12]

The New England colonies were, as one might expect, decidedly patriarchal. Some preachers pronounced that the human soul had two parts: the immortal half was masculine, and the mortal part was feminine. The godly view of the role of women can be glimpsed in the form of personal names of women that can be found in the census returns for Massachusetts Bay. These include such revealing names as: Be-Fruitful, Comfort, Fear, Patience, Prudence – and Silence![13] Nevertheless, women played a key role both in sharing the work with men and in establishing the home and in bringing up godly children. This, therefore, enhanced the role of women even while sharply demarcating their sphere of influence. This complexity became particularly significant when a demographic trend was apparent by the mid-1660s which saw women assume the majority role within many churches in the colony. This was problematic as men were seen as the embodiment of political authority, and taxation was thus supporting church communities which were no longer gender-orientated in line with political and theological authority expectations. This was particularly problematic since women were denied the right to speak in church; a situation accelerated by the Anne Hutchinson controversy. This problem was accompanied by a perceived lack of piety and religious commitment among second-generation settlers who had been born to parents personally and spiritually committed enough to move there in the first place. One solution was the "Halfway Covenant" offered to the children of first-generation settlers who could not testify to a personal conversion experience that was deemed necessary for full membership of the church community. According to this arrangement those who accepted this status could have their children baptized in the church, but could not themselves accept communion or vote in the church assembly. It was hoped that, in this way, these "Halfway" members (which it was hoped would include more men) would eventually come to a personal experience of grace and a conversion experience through being engaged with the church community. This decision of 1662 did not go down well with older or more pious members, who felt it diluted the nature of the godly community.

The godly and the Native Americans

In the New World there were many things that were outside the colonists' previous experiences. Native Americans became the most obvious "other" to be contrasted with the Christian faith and outlook of the colonists. They were the "known unknowns" and the way in which they were viewed reveals a great deal about the godly outlook. The destruction brought by diseases, due to earlier interactions between Native Americans and French and English fishermen in the sixteenth century, had largely destroyed the native population of New England. Perhaps 90 per cent of the Wampanoag, Pequot, Nipmuck, and the Massachuset peoples (belonging to the Algonquin language group) died from European diseases.[14] This was interpreted as a sign of the favour of Providence, as John Winthrop expressed it in a letter written in 1634: "God hath hereby cleared our title to this place."[15] Although

196

he did recognize that this deprived the colonists of essential trade opportunities, there was no regret regarding the impact of smallpox nor any expression of compassion for its Native American victims. Another writer – John White of Dorchester who supported the settlements but never made it to America – commented on the providential "defoliation" which had left the eastern coastlands "void" and ready for English settlement.[16] With differing attitudes toward land use and land rights – the settlers were focused on inalienable possession of any land taken or traded by treaty – trouble was brewing. Native Americans did not consider that selling land meant granting exclusive, permanent ownership to the purchaser. The godly colonists believed in private property ownership, and so expected immediate and permanent vacation of any land purchased. Native population collapse encouraged the colonists' opinion that the land was not being properly used and could just be taken anyway, with or without treaty arrangements. So, Increase Mather in 1676 wrote of property rights over "the Heathen People amongst whom we live, and whose Land the Lord God of our Fathers has given to us for a rightful possession".[17]

The resulting warfare added to native population collapse and offered another glimpse into the mindset of the godly. With more references to Old Testament accounts of the conquest of Canaan than to the New Testament, they justified exterminatory wars in biblical terms. When, in 1636, war broke out between the New England settlers and the Pequots, the settlers exterminated the natives in a way that shocked their own native allies who were used to wars that minimized fatalities. Relating the destruction of a Pequot settlement on the Mystic River in 1637, Captain John Underhill wrote in *Newes From America*:

many were burnt in the Fort, both men, women, and children, others forced out, and came in troopes to the Indians, twentie, and thirtie at a time, which our souldiers received and entertained with the point of the sword; downe fell men, women, and children, those that scaped us, fell into the hands of the Indians, that were in the reere of us; it is reported by themselves, that there were about foure hundred soules in this Fort, and not above five of them escaped out of our hands.[18]

Underhill added:

> *sometimes the Scripture declareth women and children must perish*
> *with their parents.... We had sufficient light from the word of God*
> *for our proceedings.*[19]

Estimates of the dead range between 400 and 700 men, women, and children.

When Native Americans did convert, they were expected to sever all links with their culture and were grouped in European-style settlements referred to as "Praying towns". But this did not spare them. When further hostilities broke out in 1675 (King Philip's War) – when former Puritan native allies, such as the Wampanoags, in collaboration with other Algonquian tribes, collaborated to oppose the English – Christian natives were incarcerated on Deer Island in Boston harbour. Many died, and native relations with the colonists never recovered.

None of this was inevitable. In Pennsylvania the Quakers, under William Penn, did not indulge in intolerance or violence. More respect for Native American culture, treating Native Americans as equals, and respecting their land rights meant that Quakers and Native Americans lived together peacefully for over fifty years. Godly rule did not have to bring extermination of "the other".

The New England colonies after
the Restoration of 1660

Continued tensions in Britain after 1660 led to Protestants from Ireland emigrating to North America (the Scotch-Irish) and also emigration from Bermuda. It has been estimated that about ten thousand Bermudians of a godly persuasion emigrated before American Independence. Of the latter the majority went to colonies south of Virginia but some relocated to the Bahamas, to the colony of Eleuthera, which dated from 1648.

Back in New England, Puritan settlers in the Massachusetts Bay area outnumbered Plymouth's population by about ten to one and finally absorbed them in 1691. By then, however, the godly experiment in semi-theocratic government was over. As early as 1684 the crown annulled the Massachusetts Bay charter and, from 1686, the scattered colonies of New England were unified in the Dominion of New England, under royal authority. In 1689 power was briefly wrested back but, in 1691, King William III once again issued a charter unifying the colonies under royal authority (as the Province of Massachusetts Bay) and extended voting rights to non-Puritans. The godly semi-theocracy was effectively at an end; but by the following year part of its legacy would be shockingly revealed.

THE SALEM WITCH HUNT, 1692–93

Salem will forever be remembered for its infamous witchcraft trials of the 1690s. Nineteen "witches" were executed and hundreds more accused during the hysteria that engulfed this coastal colony. But why did the Salem witch hunt occur?

As New England towns became increasingly connected to the outside world, they became less cohesive and their inhabitants less deferential to their elites. Other changes were also having an impact on the godly. Since 1691, Massachusetts had returned to being a royal colony in which freedom of worship was granted to all Protestants and voting rights to all male property owners. Also, Baptists and Quakers from Rhode Island and Pennsylvania (where religious tolerance was practised) were beginning missionary activities in Massachusetts. There was rivalry with the wealthier community of Salem Town (present-day Salem) which was accused of worldliness and covetousness by the minister in Salem Village (present-day Danvers). The Puritan godly colony was on the defensive. In addition, there was economic disruption following a British war with France in the American colonies; during 1689–92 (King William's War), a smallpox epidemic had hit the area, and there was anxiety about neighbouring Native American tribes. These tensions all combined to provide some of the factors leading to the Salem witchcraft trials of 1692.[20]

The trials began in January 1692, when some young girls from Salem Village claimed to be possessed by the Devil (exhibiting fits and uncontrolled screaming). These were nine-year-old Elizabeth (Betty) Parris and eleven-year-old Abigail Williams. They were, respectively, the daughter and the niece of Rev. Samuel Parris, minister of Salem Village. They accused several local women of witchcraft: the Parris' Caribbean slave, named Tituba; and two other women, a vagrant named Sarah Good and the impoverished and elderly Sarah Osborne. Those initially accused fitted the description of poor, female, and vulnerable which characterized many accused of the crime in England in the 1640s. Other young girls began to show similar symptoms that today would undoubtedly be diagnosed as mass hysteria.

Good and Osborne maintained their innocence but Tituba "confessed" and, probably seeking to save herself by acting as an informer, named other witches. It was then that the situation exploded and began to go beyond "the usual suspects", when Martha Corey and Rebecca Nurse (well-regarded church and community members) and the four-year-old daughter of Sarah Good were accused of witchcraft. The accusations then drew in local citizens engaged in commercial enterprises; the kind of people earlier accused of worldliness and spiritual compromise. Names of "possible suspects" were suggested to the fitting girls.

Several accused "witches" followed Tituba and confessed to the court at Salem and named "accomplices". The local court was soon overwhelmed and, in May 1692, the royal governor of Massachusetts, William Phips, ordered the establishment of a special court to deal with these witchcraft cases. In June the first "witch" to die – Bridget Bishop – was hanged. She was soon followed by eighteen others, with 150 others accused as the phenomenon spiralled out of control. However, Governor Phips finally took a firm line and dissolved the special court in October. He then ordered that subsequent courts should disregard "spectral evidence" (testimony involving dreams and visions). In May 1693 Phips pardoned and released all those still held in prison on witchcraft charges. The hysteria was over.

One of the key features of the Salem witch hunt was the admissibility of so-called spectral evidence in a court of law. There was a precedent for this dangerous legal novelty. In 1673, Thomas

Cornell was accused of murdering his mother, Rebecca Cornell, in a house fire. Lacking any solid evidence to back up the accusation, Thomas was convicted when one of Rebecca's relatives claimed that the ghost of the murdered woman had implicated the boy. He was hanged. At Salem, the well-regarded Puritan minister, Cotton Mather, warned against the over-use of spectral evidence and was supported in this by his father, Increase Mather (the president of Harvard College) who, when insisting on the application of normal legal procedures, stated, "It were better that Ten Suspected Witches should escape than that one Innocent Person be Condemned."[21]

Finally, in January 1697, the Massachusetts General Court declared a day of fasting for the victims of the Salem witch hunt. Later, the trials were declared unlawful, and the leading judge, Samuel Sewall, apologized for his actions. Legislation cleared all those condemned and in 1711 compensation was paid to their heirs. Never again were any so-called witches executed in New England.

The Salem trials exemplified the dangers inherent in a community of the godly, where normal standards of legality were suspended in the face of high levels of mutual policing that combined with hunting out imagined "others" and the uncritical acceptance of claimed spiritual insight. It was a bitter and tragic end to an era when the saints in North America had felt that they were the ones who would ensure that God was King.

14

The Legacy of the Godly in Britain

W hen the godly experiment in theocracy collapsed, the groups involved eventually became the Baptist and Congregationalist (ex-Independent) churches that we find in Britain by the end of the seventeenth century. Many Independents, having finally severed ties with Anglicanism, had become Congregationalists. Some of the godly, however, remained *within* the "broad church" of the Church of England. There they would be recognized within the "Latitudinarian" and "Evangelical" strands. Presbyterians had a more influential profile in Scotland.

Relations between the Presbyterians and Independents/Congregationalists did not improve and, in the 1690s, non-cooperation became permanent. They were turning into the separate denominations that would continue into the twentieth century when, in 1972, English Presbyterians finally merged with English and Welsh Congregationalists, forming the United Reformed Church. This was over three hundred years since negotiations between these groups had broken down in the late 1640s.

Into the Eighteenth Century and Beyond

After 1662, the term "Nonconformist" described any English Christian who belonged to a non-Anglican church or, indeed, a non-Christian religion. Presbyterians, Congregationalists, and Separatists such as Baptists – and less-organized sects such as the Ranters and the like – were targeted as Nonconformists by the 1662 Act of Uniformity. Following this new law, other groups were added to this number, including the Quakers, and the non-Trinitarian Unitarian

Church, in the seventeenth century. These are often referred to by historians as "Old Dissenters". They were added to by the English Moravians and Methodists in the eighteenth century (although neither's founders – Nicholas von Zinzendorf, or the Wesley brothers – had intended to form a separate and distinct church). These are often referred to by historians as the "New Dissenters".

These all became labelled as "Nonconformists" (and later, "Dissenters") once they operated outside the Church of England. In addition, a breakaway Baptist New Connection was formed in 1770, which splintered the Baptists. The newly formed Methodist Church also experienced fragmentation in 1797, when the Methodist New Connection seceded from the Wesleyan Methodists; then the so-called Primitive Methodists (popular among the labouring classes) broke away in 1812. Later, in the 1830s, the Plymouth Brethren added to these groups; but the Plymouth Brethren itself split into Exclusive and Open Brethren in 1848. A common pattern emerged in which groups that split off from a previous group were themselves subject to the same fragmentary tendency. This was one of the legacies inherited from the DNA of the original godly fellowships.

DISCRIMINATION AND RESPONSES

Alongside the term "Nonconformist", that of "Dissenter" also came to be used after the Act of Toleration in 1689 relaxed discrimination a little – exempting Nonconformists who were prepared to take oaths of allegiance to the crown from being penalized for non-attendance at Church of England services. The former title then gave way to the latter and was then itself somewhat replaced from the nineteenth century onwards by the former label again. The terms are basically interchangeable and since Nonconformist was the one used first, that is the one we will use here, although the other term will appear in some of the evidence. The Toleration Act, which also allowed such people their own places of worship, revealed that the government had finally given up all hope of enforcing uniformity through the Church of England, and was now committed to managing division.

However, Nonconformists/Dissenters were still barred from holding any political offices and, for two hundred years, it was difficult for them to graduate from Oxford or Cambridge universities. Until the Oxford University Act of 1854, a religious test was imposed on those seeking admission. In response, some Nonconformists travelled to the universities of Leiden and Utrecht in the Netherlands or Glasgow and Edinburgh in Scotland, where they were allowed to study.

Discrimination against Nonconformists continued throughout the eighteenth century. For example, in 1711 the Occasional Conformity Act imposed fines on any person who, after taking communion at an Anglican church, was then found worshipping at a Nonconformist meeting. This targeted those who did this in order to escape legal difficulties but, otherwise, behaved as Nonconformists. In 1753 Hardwicke's Marriage Act stipulated that legal marriage could only take place in an Anglican church. After this, it was common for Nonconformists to be baptized in their own meeting place but married in their local parish church. It was not until 1837 that couples could be legally married in a Nonconformist church.

The 1779 Dissenters' Relief Act was one minor exception to this pattern of legal discrimination, removing the obligation on ministers to subscribe to the Thirty-Nine Articles of the Church of England – a demand of the Toleration Act. The Dissenters' Relief Act also allowed tutors and schoolmasters the right to teach without needing to be licensed (an obligation that had been used to restrict access to work). There were, however, few other comparable areas of progress for Nonconformists in the rest of the eighteenth century.

In the nineteenth century things began to improve from the perspective of Nonconformists. The University of London – founded in 1826 – was the first English university to admit students regardless of their religion. However, an acceptance of the Church of England's Thirty-Nine Articles of faith was still required for both matriculation and graduation at Oxford until 1854. A similar demand was made prior to graduation at Cambridge until 1856. Even after these dates the requirement continued for degrees in

Divinity (Theology). It was not until the University Tests Act of 1871 that Nonconformists, Roman Catholics, and non-Christians (principally Jews) could take up *fellowships* at the universities of Cambridge, Oxford, London, and Durham. Despite this, the old restrictions remained for anyone wishing to take up a Divinity (Theology) fellowship or professorship at Oxford or Cambridge until 1913.

It was in response to these educational restrictions that "Dissenting Academies" were formed in order to provide training for Nonconformist ministers. Between 1663 and 1688 over twenty were founded, and a further thirty had been founded by 1750. These offered a broader education than the very restricted traditional content available at Cambridge and Oxford.

Despite the longevity of these educational restrictions, others fell a little earlier. In 1812, both the Conventicle and Five Mile Acts were repealed. The next year Unitarians were granted full freedom of worship on the same terms as Trinitarians, by the Trinity Act (1813). In 1828 the Test and Corporation Acts were repealed, which gave Nonconformists the legal right to hold offices in local government. However, it was not until 1835, and the Municipal Reform Act, that most were able to take up such posts.

An Act that, in theory, was unconnected with religion but which increased the influence of the "Nonconformist voice" was the 1832 Reform Act. By extending the franchise to – mostly – middle-class urban voters it increased both the influence of this class of people and (correspondingly) the influence of Nonconformists in British politics, since they were well represented in this group. This was to be very significant because the Nonconformists had by no means withered away in the face of restrictions. The Compton Census estimated that at least 4 per cent of the population were Dissenters in 1676, with far higher proportions in some places.[1] A census of religious practice, carried out in 1851, revealed that Nonconformists, by that date, made up about 50 per cent of the people who attended Sunday services. Nowhere did they constitute less than 33 per cent of the worshipping population. In the industrial powerhouses of the Midlands and the North they often outnumbered Anglicans. In such towns the local government became dominated by Nonconformists. In Wales, Anglican "church" membership was dwarfed by the membership of the "chapels". As late as 1920 about 80 per cent of worshippers in Wales were Nonconformists.[2] For the first time since 1660, what has been termed the "Nonconformist Conscience" was about to have a real impact on British politics.

THE RETURN OF THE GODLY TO POLITICAL INFLUENCE: THE IMPACT OF THE "NONCONFORMIST CONSCIENCE"

While the late nineteenth and early twentieth centuries saw a surge in the influence of Nonconformism, this was not the start of the process. After a retreat from political activism in the later seventeenth century – following the shattering of hopes in 1660 and some forty years of failed activism by the more radicalized groups (Venner's Revolt, Covenanter uprisings, the Monmouth Rebellion) and legal restrictions on all Nonconformists/ Dissenters – the late eighteenth century saw something of a revival of political engagement.

The Quakers, for example, became very active within the movement for the emancipation of slaves. As a consequence, the state of Pennsylvania led the way as an anti-slavery state in North America and they continued to be active in the "Underground Railroad" there, assisting escaping slaves in the years 1850–60. Friends were similarly active in the United Kingdom, where they played a key role in the movement leading to the abolition of the slave trade. This dated back to 1657, when George Fox wrote to slave-owning Friends reminding them of the Quaker belief in the equality of all people. He followed this up by visiting Barbados and by urging better treatment of slaves. This culminated in 1676 with the publication of *Gospel Family-Order* outlining his anti-slavery views. From the 1720s this anti-slavery activism increased on both sides of the Atlantic until, in 1783, the London Society of Friends presented a petition to Parliament against the slave trade, which was signed by nearly 300 Quakers. They went on to set up a committee to oppose the slave trade. The movement gained in influence when it was joined by evangelical Anglicans (who enjoyed full political rights); but it had started as a Quaker initiative. This Quaker-inspired movement was responsible for ending the British slave trade in 1807, and eventually led to the abolition of slavery itself within the British Empire in 1838. In this they were more successful than American Quakers who both faced violent opposition from slave owners and were more divided over the stance they should take. The British and Foreign Anti-Slavery Society was founded in 1839, by Joseph Sturge, to continue campaigning to free the world from slavery, and continues today as the organization known as Anti-Slavery International.

In a similar display of Quaker activism that also took the campaigns into the nineteenth century, Elizabeth Fry (1780–1845) and her brother Joseph Gurney (1788–1847) campaigned for more humane treatment of prisoners in British prisons and also for the abolition of capital punishment. Elizabeth had a significant impact on improving conditions for female prisoners in Newgate Prison, London, and influenced Sir Robert Peel's prison reforms of the 1820s.

In a very different area of life, the chocolate-making enterprises of the Cadburys (at Bourneville, Birmingham) and the Rowntrees (in York) involved an enlightened concern for their workforce. Most famous of these were the 144 cottages built for workers at Bourneville, where, by 1915, infant mortality and death rates were half those of Birmingham as a whole.[3] Cadbury was the first industrial enterprise to grant workers a five-day working week and, on top of this, to provide workers with medical facilities, a canteen providing decent food, leisure activities and gardens which were shared by the community. Meanwhile, just north of York, Rowntree set up the model village of New Earswick in 1902 for families on low incomes. Here, education was provided for both children and adults (including adult schools). It was a member of this family – Seebohm Rowntree (1871–1954) – whose study, entitled *Poverty: a Study of Town Life* (1901), influenced the Liberal reforms of 1906–14; reforms themselves driven forward by Lloyd George, who came from a Welsh chapel family (his much revered uncle being a minister in the Church of Christ, a Nonconformist denomination, at Criccieth). This was a remarkable synthesis of Nonconformist economic, social, and political radicalism.

The Quaker chocolate makers were not the only Nonconformist industrialists to promote worker welfare. Another famous example was Titus Salt (1803–76), who constructed workers' houses, bathhouses, an adult institute, a hospital, almshouses, and churches to accompany his textile mill, opened at Saltaire in 1853. Salt, though not teetotal himself, forbade the opening of any "beer shops" in the village. He was a Congregationalist but also donated land on which a Wesleyan Methodist Chapel was constructed. Similarly, in Birmingham, the radical Liberal MP and famous reforming mayor Joseph Chamberlain (1836–1914) came from a Unitarian family. He supported elementary education and promoted a programme of urban renewal in Birmingham by which the city would be, "parked, paved, assized, marketed, gas and watered and improved".[4] Slums were cleared, municipal buildings constructed and parks established; all of which greatly improved the lives of working-class citizens of this major industrial city. He is also famous for promising agricultural labourers, in 1885, "three acres and a cow" (although his "Unauthorized Programme" was never enacted) and for splitting the two major political parties due to his opposition to Irish Home Rule (split the Liberals in 1886) and Tariff Reform as opposed to Free Trade (split the Conservative-Unionist Party in 1903), but that is another story.

It has been suggested that the "Nonconformist conscience" of the "Old Dissenters" focused more on religious freedom and equality, social justice, and opposition to discrimination, whereas the "New Dissenters" focused more on personal morality, including alcohol-temperance, Sabbath observance and sexual behaviour. This is, however, a generalization and the reality was more complex.

Up until the 1850s the "Old Dissenters" tended to generally support the Whig Party and then the Liberals; whereas the "New Dissenters" tended to support reformists among the Conservatives. By the later nineteenth century both groups tended to throw their weight behind the Liberal Party, although it must be noted that there were fierce disagreements with Gladstone's Liberal government over the Education Act of 1870 (Forster's Education Act) regarding the idea of public money going from local authority school boards to existing Church of England schools. This escalated into a disagreement over the role of religious instruction in state-sponsored schools. Religious teaching in new elementary "Board Schools" was to be non-denominational, or absent; and parents could withdraw their children from religious education in any school. This managed to anger both sides, who wanted religious instruction (they were shocked at its absence), *but* in line with their own outlook. Nonconformists were particularly angry as they had hoped to see Anglican schools abolished but these continued to prosper under this system. But, on the other hand, they opposed paying the local education rate so that it could support what they termed "godless Board Schools". William Gladstone, though a committed Christian and an Anglican, did not think that religion would be damaged by a secular education system. He thought it would spur churches to increase Sunday School provision and their own evangelical outreach.[5] The row contributed to Gladstone losing the 1874 general election and none of this helped meet the urgent need for educational provision for working-class children. After Gladstone's Education Act of 1870, church and chapel competed for control over local school boards.[6]

Despite this time of strained relations with the Liberals, the linkage remained and this was greatly enhanced by the activities of Welsh Nonconformists who produced a situation which made "Liberal nonconformity the overwhelming political force in Edwardian Wales".[7] Nonconformists enjoyed a wider influence nationally, constituting a key part of the Liberal Party before 1914,[8] and thereby exercising a significant political impact on issues such as education, temperance, and the franchise.

NONCONFORMISTS AND THE LABOUR MOVEMENT

Before the First World War, many members of the Labour movement (in trade unions and in the early Labour Party) came from within the ranks of Nonconformity. Methodists had been involved in very early "combinations" (unions), such as the agricultural trade unions of the Dorset "Tolpuddle Martyrs" in the 1830s, and that in Warwickshire under Joseph Arch in 1872. There is some evidence that Chartists (arguing for franchise reform prior to 1848) were inspired by the "Camp Meetings" of the Primitive Methodists. But, by the 1890s, it was Congregationalists and Unitarians who were more active in socialist organizations such as the Fabian Society. However, not all in these churches saw the urgency of what some considered a secular and economic (rather than spiritual) programme.

Morgan Phillips, then-general secretary of the Labour Party, commented in the 1950s that "Socialism in Britain owed more to Methodism than Marx".[9] This "chapel socialism" had a direct influence on Labour's commitment to constitutional rather than revolutionary politics. In this way the character of British Labour contrasted with the more Marxist-inspired Continental Labour movements such as in Germany.[10] It also helps explain the lack of anti-clericalism in the British Labour movement. This was a crucial contribution to this strand of British cultural history. For the Nonconformist input meant that such people would work for what they considered economic liberation, inspired by the nineteenth-century campaigns for civil and religious liberty, but without the heritage that separated church from worker-activists in a party such as the SPD in Germany. The earlier relationship with the Liberal Party also anchored them in a heritage of constitutional solutions to social and economic problems. For example, a document such as William Booth's *In darkest England, and the way out* was drafted by Frank Smith, who would later be elected as a Labour MP in the 1920s and 1930s. This was because the Salvation Army *and* the Labour Party had its roots entwined in the same milieu and the same commitment to actions designed to tackle social ills. This does not mean that all Nonconformists were sympathetic to socialism; but many were and many of these were involved in the Independent Labour Party (one of the constituent groups of what became the Labour Party after 1900).

NONCONFORMISTS AND PACIFISM
IN THE FIRST WORLD WAR

Nonconformists had a traditional distrust of militarism, and Quakers a commitment to actual pacifism. For example, in 1757 Quakers were allowed exemption from the militia; in the nineteenth century the radical MP John Bright (1811–89), of a Quaker family, was almost a lone voice in his condemnation of the Crimean War. Some Nonconformists were unhappy at the "military appearance" of Boys' Brigade units, to the extent that in 1910–11 the organization resisted War Office Plans for units to act as feeders for the Territorial Army (in contrast to the more militarized Anglican Church Lads' Brigade).[11] Nevertheless, the outbreak of the First World War divided the communities. The Boys' Brigade were soon supporting war-related activities and, in Wales, the wider case for supporting the war was persuasively made by Lloyd George, who stressed the righteousness of resisting German aggression in a biblical language that drew on his Welsh Nonconformist roots. Denzil Morgan, professor of Theology at the University of Wales Trinity Saint David, has commented on how Lloyd George managed to "manipulate his popularity as a religious figure in order to get the Welsh Nonconformists over to support the war".[12] His skills at deploying sympathetic Nonconformist preachers, such as Thomas Charles Williams of Menai Bridge, and John Williams, of Brynsiencyn, Anglesey (both Welsh Calvinistic Methodists), in a campaign to win over other Welsh Nonconformists has also been noted.[13] In this he was largely successful but not entirely. For it was around Nonconformist pacifists, such as the Aberystwyth poet T. Gwyn Jones, that the Welsh pacifist movement coalesced by the beginning of 1915. In Jones' view, "Jesus Christ is not a militaristic person. He is the Saviour of the world, he is the Prince of Peace. Therefore those who say they are Christians, followers of Christ must reject war totally."[14]

This outlook was reflected among Quakers more than any other group. It was Quakers who made up much of the membership of the Fellowship of Reconciliation (FOR), the group in which religious pacifists were the dominant influence. About 16,500 British men claimed Conscientious Objector status in the First World War. Of these, 350 (mostly Quakers) were granted unconditional exemptions from war service; some 3,300 were employed in work camps; 6,000 were sent into the army, where they experienced some harsh treatment (including thirty-four death sentences, none of which were, however, carried out) before compromises were reached, whereby most accepted some form of non-military service. Only 1,298 were absolutists, refusing all service.[15] This was eventually reduced to 985 (including the Quaker peace activist, Stephen Hobhouse).[16] Overall, though, these people's stand at a time of intense patriotism caused them to be "vilified to an appalling extent".[17]

In the Second World War more sensitive handling of the issue resulted in over 60,000 men and 1,000 women registering as Conscientious Objectors. Though from mixed backgrounds, many again were Quakers; 1,300 served in the Friends' Ambulance Unit. While treated more humanely than in the First World War, many still lost their jobs, were abused and ostracized, some were imprisoned.[18] Overall, there were more Quaker Conscientious Objectors in the Second World War than in the First.

AFTER THE FIRST WORLD WAR...
THE WEAKENING OF TIES

By 1914 the linkage of Nonconformity with Liberalism was weakening with the rise of the Labour Party, and by the late 1920s it was virtually dead. While, in Wales the disestablishment of the Church of Wales that was finally achieved in 1920, revealed the continuing influence of the Nonconformist community there, overall the First World War signalled "the eve of the death of Nonconformity as a political force".[19] This followed what was one of the most dramatic influences of Nonconformity on UK political decision-making, with the issuing of the Balfour Declaration of 1917 regarding a Jewish homeland in the Middle East. In this decision, a deep awareness of the Old Testament gained from chapel culture can be argued to have played a major part in the final declaration. In Lloyd George's 1916–17 war cabinet, seven out of ten came from a Nonconformist background.[20] However, it should also be noted that some nineteenth-century Evangelical Anglicans, such as Lord Shaftesbury, also promoted a Jewish return to the Holy Land.

However, in 1918, only eighty-eight Nonconformist MPs were elected and the old alliance between Nonconformity and the Liberal Party was broken (as the Liberals disintegrated) and as many Welsh chapel votes (especially within Methodism) shifted to the Labour Party. But the old chapel-based radicalism was in decline even there, alongside the decline of chapel attendance in the 1930s. This was a trend that accelerated after 1945 and especially from the 1960s onwards. Despite this, ten out of nineteen UK prime ministers of the twentieth century were raised in Nonconformist homes. This is an astonishing number and reveals the way in which Nonconformity continued to stimulate political activism, particularly (but not exclusively) on the centre-left of UK politics.

THE LEGACY OF THE "NONCONFORMIST CONSCIENCE" IN THE TWENTY-FIRST CENTURY

What is the influence of Nonconformity today? Since the 1960s the divide in Protestantism in the UK has become much more complex, with no simple binary split between Anglican/Nonconformist, due to the influence of the Charismatic movement (which has both supporters and detractors across the old denominational divide) and the emergence of New Churches that are not part of the historic mainstream (the Pentecostal movement's contribution to this predates the 1960s, going back to the early twentieth century in the US). Consequently, in the early twenty-first century there is no longer a recognizable block of believers that can be labelled "Nonconformists" in contradistinction to Anglicans and Catholics. This makes assessing the current impact of Nonconformity rather more difficult than in the past. Despite this, there is still a trend that can be identified. For example, Quakers have been noticeably involved in the establishment of several current campaign organizations, such as Amnesty International, Greenpeace, Oxfam, and Anti-Slavery International; although, of course, these movements have no religious affiliations and involve people of all faiths and of no faith.

So, overall, what legacy has puritanism left us in the complex world of the early twenty-first century? Well, within the churches there is a legacy: whenever a high view of the holiness of God is preached (with a corresponding emphasis on the sinful nature of humanity); when the Bible is elevated as the basis for beliefs; when the idea of salvation leading to a lifetime pursuit of holiness is emphasized; when there is a high view of the role of the community of the church; and when there is a belief that society should be brought into line with biblical principles.[21] But much of this would not be *explicitly* attributed to the legacy of the Puritan godly, who remain a "tainted brand" in the UK. This is less so in the US, where a number of church leaders and theologians are more willing to explicitly make connections with their Puritan heritage. However, this should not be allowed to obscure the legacy of the seventeenth-century godly (by way of their distant Nonconformist descendants) in political radicalism, social action, freedom of religious expression, and anti-militarism.

15

The Legacy of the Godly in North America

P erhaps the only generalization that can be made about the United States of America, is that no generalization adequately sums it up! This means that it is not a straightforward task to identify the Puritan legacy in such a complex and multicultural community. This is made all the more so because after the Puritan era America received waves of other immigrants from across Europe and the globe. Therefore, to identify one particular, if precocious, group of immigrants as ones that have made a significant lasting impact on the cultural DNA of the US may seem as unlikely as it is presumptuous.

Furthermore, it raises a key question: just because a modern cultural feature resembles an aspect of a past culture, does that mean it is a lineal descendant of it? After all, there can be more than one cause of a modern cultural characteristic, given the complexity and variety of human societies past and present. Or to put it another way: Puritans of the past were and are not the only people to be ideologically certain of being in God's favour, intolerant and self-policing, hardworking and upright, morally proactive in pursuit of "holiness", or identifying the "righteous self" in sharp contrast to the "sinful other". So, if we find echoes of any of these features in a modern society it does not necessarily mean we have located a strand of Puritan DNA in the double-helix of a modern community.

However, there can be formative periods of a nation's history which make such a contribution to what we might call "the national myth" that they are co-opted and adopted by later peoples who wish to become identified with the "national character". In which case, since the Puritan era lay at the beginning of the American self-definition, it may not be unreasonable to search for a legacy that is still active. Then, if we find something rather reminiscent of an earlier mindset (from a time of national myth-making) we may indeed have discovered a legacy or at least an echo of it. It was in such a way that the historian Perry Miller (though an atheist) identified the study of the Puritans as a way of exploring and explaining something of "the innermost propulsion of the United States".[1]

NORTH AMERICAN PURITANISM IN
A CHANGING WORLD

As we saw, in the case of Salem in 1692, the godly semi-theocracies of New England were facing disconcerting changes before the end of the seventeenth century. Within a century of their original foundation, their residents were becoming involved in export trading networks, the entry standards for church membership (the "Halfway Covenants") were being lowered, citizens petitioned for divorce, some moved to other settlements, and they were forced to accept a greater degree of religious diversity as increased royal control broke down the monopoly on power enjoyed by the godly.[2] In such a changing environment it became increasingly difficult to police standards of behaviour that had once been taken for granted. By the late 1700s, the godly churches became, as one historian has demonstrated, more open "centers of worship that could maintain a measure of peacefulness simply because the discontented could leave and join, or form, another group [church] whenever they pleased".[3] These were becoming "Congregationalist" churches in a manner reflecting the changes that also occurred in England; individual groups and denominations in a complex and diverse society, rather than a controlling monolithic theocratic community. Today the US continues to have a huge number and diversity of denominations that is rooted in this splintering of the godly community.

Now that New England was firmly under English royal control again, cities like Boston became noticeably more cosmopolitan. It is conventional to end the "Puritan period" in England in the late seventeenth century and in North America in the 1730s. By the 1730s, three main sects can be discerned among the Puritan communities. The term "Old Lights" was used to identify the many Congregationalist churches in New England who restricted their strict Calvinism in attempts to win new members. On the other hand, those fellowships who adhered to the older Calvinist traditions became known as "Old Calvinists". Then, in the 1730s and 1740s there occurred the first of a number of religious revivals. Known as the "Great Awakening", its leaders included the American Jonathan Edwards, and the English minister George Whitefield. Edwards' theology included a postmillennialist emphasis on Christ's return, after revivalist preaching had transformed the World order. Followers of this more outward-looking – evangelical – Calvinism became known as "New Lights". This meant that the Puritan legacy gained a new buoyancy and influence. This had a number of cultural effects. First, the Puritan sermon's denunciation of current sin and focus on future transformation (sometimes termed a "jeremiad" after the Old Testament prophet, Jeremiah) became firmly part of the literary and rhetorical character of North America. Second, the Puritan emphasis on sin and salvation, and a personal and individual calling married to a sense of national destiny, became firmly entrenched along with a tradition of revivalist preaching. This complex combination of moral self-confidence (once conversion was assured), individual energetic dynamism and entrepreneurialism, colonial pride, ambition, and competitiveness "would be eventually identified by others as the spirit of what foreigners called 'Yankees'".[4] It is not difficult to discern this as a significant feature of what one might loosely call the "American national character" in the twenty-first century.

When the British Parliament passed the Boston Port Act in 1774 (a response to the Boston Tea Party) – to force the town to compensate the royal treasury and East India Company for losses incurred due to rebellious colonists – several local ministers announced a traditional Puritan fast day and then preached against the British crown as a tool of "Satan" which had unleashed King George, "the great Whore of Babylon", to ride her "great red dragon" upon America.[5] We will be familiar with the language, taken as it was from the lexicon of millenarianism that had furnished earlier saints with prophetic denunciations of those of whom they disapproved. The episode demonstrates the longevity of a Puritan mindset and language that can still be discerned in some evangelical churches in North America (and in the UK) today although the targets now would be different.[6]

What is important to remember is that, whereas in England the Restoration of 1660 shut the godly out of political power for almost two centuries (causing them to develop into a Nonconformity more geared to economic activity and social action than political influence), in North America, though facing competing influences and loss of dominance, the heirs of the Puritans were at no point shut out of political power. They continued to be political "insiders", rather than Nonconformist "outsiders".

THE PURITAN HERITAGE AND "MANIFEST DESTINY"

In the turmoil of the War of Independence, American patriotism co-opted the Puritan concept of a peculiar destiny for the colonists of North America. The same outlook (and the genre of the jeremiad) was apparent in preaching during the Civil War in the 1860s. It has been argued that so influential is this Puritan-derived outlook and literary form, "in every war in which the United States has been involved, sermons and speeches about America's manifest destiny and sacred errand and heritage have been central to the discourses of the war."[7]

The westward movement of settlers and the accompanying destruction of Native American societies in the nineteenth century was accompanied by just such a doctrine of "Manifest Destiny" that owed much to both the individualistic self-confidence and the sense of community purpose that was inherited from the Puritan national myth. This belief that the expansion of the United States from coast to coast was inevitable and justified was first articulated in this particular phrase by John L. O'Sullivan in an article on the annexation of Texas, which was published in the *United States Magazine and Democratic Review* (July–August 1845).

218

We should recall that two centuries earlier almost exactly the same language had been used by godly settlers in New England to justify their destruction of Native American tribes. It created a concept of white, Protestant, non-native superiority and the right to exploit the resources of the continent. America offered a continuous promise to be fulfilled by those who were deemed worthy inheritors of this role. Much of this Puritan myth of confident superiority has entered the DNA of the United States.

The Puritan heritage and capitalist entrepreneurialism

A rugged individualism is often identified as a feature of the modern American character. This, when accompanied by an ethic of hard work and self-discipline, has been identified as a peculiarly Puritan contribution to North America. In the nineteenth century the German sociologist Max Weber argued in *The Protestant Ethic and the Spirit of Capitalism* that this emphasis on working hard as part of the earthly calling of the godly contributed to the development of market-driven capitalism. Weber has not been without his critics, some of whom point to the beginnings of what he described as a "Protestant ethic" actually being discernible in fourteenth-century Italy; or pointing out that the sixteenth-century commercial prosperity of Antwerp was based, not on a Protestant core, but on a cosmopolitan mixture of foreign merchants and traders working in cooperation with the city's financiers. Moreover, Weber's hypothesis, it has been argued, does not explain the industrial expansion of nineteenth-century Catholic Belgium or the relative economic underdevelopment of Calvinist Geneva or Scotland.

Nevertheless, even if not all modern sociologists and historians are convinced by Weber's link between Calvinism and capitalism, there does remain a particularly Puritan characteristic that emphasized hard work, denial of personal pleasure, and connection of success with Providence that is difficult to deny.

The work of Sacvan Bercovitch (1933–2014) in the field of "American Studies" has been influential in identifying within North American Puritanism far-reaching tendencies to sever ties with their origins as they sought a "Promised Land" in North America.[8] While his work has also attracted criticism, his arguments concerning "American exceptionalism" and the role of dissent in the service of a continual rediscovery of a fundamental American character, derived from the nation's Puritan roots, have been taken on board by a number of other academics.[9] As Bercovitch has argued – and other academics have agreed – a significant feature of this Puritan-originated American ideology was (and is) that "seeking spiritual salvation functions well with the spirit of capitalism", alongside "an unconscious recognition of the ways that the spiritual calling and the material calling, as they called them, could yield earthly and heavenly rewards at the same time".[10]

It is therefore not difficult to see the influence of this in modern American emphases on the virtues of enterprise, opposition to governmental regulation, long working hours, short holidays, and commitment to the workplace. So much so that a report in 2013 drew attention to the fact that at that time the US was the only advanced economy where employees had no right to paid holiday time and that almost 25 per cent of US workers had no paid holidays. This situation was particularly acute for low-paid workers, part-time workers, and for employees of small businesses.[11] This work ethic is allied to a belief that hard work brings success and that government should not interfere in this area. While these are secular features of modern capitalism in the US, it is not difficult to discern its Puritan cultural origins, and experimental psychology reinforces the idea that "Protestant work values have not become fully secular in American culture and continue to be linked to religious ideas."[12] This focus on work as a moral calling, to the exclusion of the demands of family, has been described as "Protestant Relational Ideology" and its highest incidence occurs among those with a religious culture rooted in a Calvinist work ethic.[13]

THE PURITAN HERITAGE AND RESILIENT BUT RESISTANT CITIZENS

While New England of the godly was authoritarian, it was also, paradoxically, one that drew large numbers of its citizens into active engagement with decision-making.[14] In addition, Puritan theology rested on the idea of covenants. The key one was that between God and man, but the concept of the "gathered church" also included that between people to take part in a shared enterprise that was not controlled by government. Central to those covenants was the principle of free choice. The historian Perry Miller put it this way: "The individual voluntarily promised to obey civil and scriptural law... [but] meaningful obedience could only grow out of voluntary consent, never out of coercion."[15] In the churches of the godly, choice – in the form of a conversion experience – replaced birth as the entry point into the church. This had implications for the way concepts of citizenship evolved in the later US, for it was not a long step to translate such a concept into the secular field of politics. Individual citizens' rights, political involvement and a fierce political individualism could all trace roots to the original concept of the Puritan contract. It created "a culture that stressed individual self-reliance, voluntary association, and resisting authority and hierarchy" which was buttressed by the original religious ideology of choice and contract. This outlasted Puritanism and now follows "more the preaching than the practices of the early Pilgrims and Puritans".[16]

It also had implications for creating an educated citizenry, for the search for religious truth through study of the Bible was a prompt to an American concept of educated citizens capable of taking part in the electoral process. Yet this also accompanied an emphasis on personal beliefs, freedom of expression and opposition to perceived "censorship" which in modern times can sometimes produce a political dialogue that is extremely combative.

All of this means that when twenty-first-century populist politicians and those often described as the Christian Religious Right attack the Washington elite or upholders of liberal secularism and central government generally, and call for national "transformation" (however that is phrased or envisaged), they are, arguably, tapping into both an individual-contract culture that resists central authority, while also evoking (consciously or unconsciously) what has elsewhere been described as the "puritan rituals of national repentance, reawakening, and renewal".[17]

On the subject of a resilient and independent citizenry, it has controversially been suggested that a commitment to a belief system that stressed personal sinfulness and moral weakness and guilt – that could only be countered by self-discipline, hard work, and austerity – encouraged a form of individualism that is tightly focused on personal salvation "that precludes much interest in, or sympathy for, others and their weaknesses". This, it has been suggested, encourages a tendency to moral judgment of others, alongside an intense sense of personal righteousness once one is convinced that one is part of an ideology and community that has the correct outlook. Such an attitude can reveal itself in matters as diverse as an intolerance of those who do not respond to health promotion strategies and also a belief in "economic punishment" (by way of higher medical bills and health insurance premiums) for those deemed to be suffering "self-inflicted" ills, particularly if these conditions "evoke certain moral objections, especially if pleasure is involved".[18]

On the other hand, it should also be remembered that the US has one of the highest rates of charitable giving as a percentage of GDP. However, sharing this accolade in 2016 with Myanmar and Australia (who have very different cultural histories), means that identifying the cause of this generosity is not easily done.[19]

THE PURITAN HERITAGE AND THE HIGH-PROFILE NATURE OF US CHRISTIANITY

As long ago as the 1950s, Clinton Rossiter, an American historian and political scientist at Cornell University from 1947 to 1970, wrote that,

> It must never be forgotten, especially in an age of upheaval and disillusionment, that American democracy rests squarely on the assumption of a pious, honest, self-disciplined, moral people.... If democracy has flourished in these states as strongly as anywhere in the world, it is because we are drawing still upon the moral vigor of Puritanism.[20]

This interpretation reminds us that one of the lasting impacts of Puritanism is on a sense of America having a moral character that it needs to return to. This may be mythical, in that the particular features of the past that are stressed are not necessarily historical, but this, nevertheless, plays a major part in American public debate and politics. In this it must be noted that the US has not experienced the degree of secularization of public conversation that has occurred in most other economically advanced Western societies.

This is particularly intriguing when one remembers that the US is a nation with no national church, has formal freedom of religion, and has an explicit commitment to the separation of church and state. In 1802, Thomas Jefferson spoke of "a wall of separation between Church & State".[21] This principle is contained in the 1791 First Amendment to the Constitution of the United States. In a similar way, Article Six of the US Constitution also specifies that "no religious test shall ever be required as a qualification to any office or public trust under the United States."[22] Jefferson's words echo those of the early American Puritan, the Baptist Roger Williams, who in 1644 wrote of a "hedge or wall of separation between the garden of the church and the wilderness of the world".[23] Yet few nations "do God" as openly as the US. In sharp contrast to many UK politicians who, in the words of Alastair Campbell in 2003, "don't do God",[24] even the most unlikely of US presidential candidates find a "God-moment" in order to appeal to a crucial constituency (usually the Christian Religious Right) no matter how unfamiliar the candidates may seem on religious terrain.

Given the fact that Catholics, Protestants, Jews, and Muslims all have high profiles in US political conversation it is nevertheless true that one particularly highly influential segment of the Christian community stands out. And these are Protestant evangelicals, who due to their usual political orientation are often referred to as the "evangelical Christian Religious Right". It has been argued that the Religious Right presents a conflicting view of America, being inclined *both* to stress the exceptionalism of the US having "'sacralized' many aspects of American culture (for example, its political and economic systems)", while they also "lament the loss of 'Christian America' largely because of the nation's permissive attitude toward sexual openness, homosexuality, and abortion."[25] Alongside these three particular areas of personal morality, one might also cite a very American antipathy to central government and gun control. Support for the State of Israel is also very high through what is sometimes termed "Christian Zionism".[26] American roots of aspects of this particular form of dispensationalist millenarianism can be traced as far back as the New England Puritan, Cotton Mather (died: 1728). Finally, opposition to policies relating to combating climate change is also often apparent.

The particular strand of Christian outlook in question can also show itself to be antagonistic to certain scientific ideas. The extent to which the teaching of Creationism within education is discussed in the US stands in stark contrast to the position in the UK educational system, and this adherence to a particular form of Christian fundamentalism is very recognisable in the cultural complexity of the US.

It is reasonable to conclude that, for all the complexity of this mixture of outlooks, much of it owes something at least to the mindset of confident adherence to biblical literalism inherited ultimately from the godly of New England, even though this might now be more geographically evidenced in the "Bible Belt". When one sieves out particularly twenty-first-century moral, social, and economic issues, one is left with ones that the godly of Massachusetts would have recognized in the 1680s: biblical literalism; strict personal sexual morality; and opposition to government interference. Even the opposition to gun control and climate change legislation can be seen as outworkings of the latter concern. And climate change denial can be linked to a traditional millenarianism that reduces the importance of such global threats compared with an emphasis on the apocalyptic role of God in bringing this present world order to its ultimate close (in contrast, human attempts to "save the planet" may be presented as irrelevant or doomed to failure). Belief in the imminent return of Christ is as much a feature of current US Protestant evangelicalism[27] as it was among the Puritans of New England and Britain in the seventeenth century. While the nature of "Christian Zionism" and its associated dispensationalism involves as much immersion in

224

the prophecies of the Old Testament as once occurred among the Fifth Monarchy Men and their North American equivalents.

This legacy of Puritanism reflects something of the cultural complications of the Religious Right in the US. The Puritans opposed the dictatorial powers of a national church structure (even when loosely remaining adherents to it). But at the same time they sought to impose a semi-theocratic view of society on the community. The same complicated (and seemingly contradictory) relationship exists today, holding to the strict separation of church and state, while "Reclaiming America as a 'Christian nation' in its origins and pointing to America's mission and destiny as a 'City upon a hill' [has] provided a bedrock of belief on which to base the moral and political agenda of the Christian Right."[28] This is not new; Ronald Reagan, for example, famously borrowed that very phrase, from the speech that John Winthrop gave aboard the ship taking some of the first Puritan settlers to the New World, when articulating his vision for the US in 1980 and again in 1989. President John F. Kennedy had done this earlier, which is particularly ironic given the way Puritans regarded Catholics.

STILL PURITAN IN THE TWENTY-FIRST CENTURY?

The Puritans remain a controversial and divisive part of US cultural history. On one hand, liberal critics of the Religious Right have sought to denigrate it by linking it to the most negative aspects of the Puritan past, and the more conservative decisions of the Federal Communications Commission and court appointees have been similarly labelled.[29] For these critics, Puritanism is a toxic brand. On the other hand, those seeking to defend "traditional Christian values" or "American exceptionalism" would see the Puritans as honourable antecedents. Others have traced the nature of modern US patriotism back to the Puritan belief in a providential "errand".[30] Still others have noted their contribution to both "progressive" as well as "conservative" causes and ideologies intent on national transformation.[31]

It is not always straightforward to draw a direct line between the moral and cultural values of seventeenth-century New England

and the complex multicultural nation that is the United States in the twenty-first century. Nevertheless, some characteristics seem too comparable to ignore. When the French political commentator Alexis de Tocqueville visited the US in 1831 he noted its religious devotion, individualism, and work ethic. That these are still such defining characteristics today indicates something of the exceptionalism of the US (when compared to other economically developed nations) and, as de Tocqueville himself noted, "are all traceable in part to the founding Puritan-Protestant communities of the United States".[32] The characteristics of a high level of religiosity, moral absolutism, biblical fundamentalism, individualism, and a highly developed work ethic do not draw their inspiration only from a seventeenth-century base – but this clearly played a major part in developing such a distinctive culture. So rooted have these norms become that, while they are understandably most pronounced among committed Protestant evangelical Christians, experimental psychology (as well as casual observation) reveals their prevalence far beyond this core group. It is a remarkable paradox that the Religious Right can still play such a major part in delivering US presidential success in a society where church and state are so firmly separated, but it is a paradox that is only fully explainable by reference to its roots in the Puritan heritage of the separated but highly influential godly. For one of the distinct features of that early period was a community in which, while there were distinct spheres of influence allocated to church and state, there remained strong church influence over that state. At the same time, the Puritan model of representative government and Christian engagement with public life existed alongside intolerance toward those of different religious persuasions.[33] These paradoxes, it might be suggested, can still be observed today. It is remarkable that the modern US republic is still so influenced by a time in its history when God was King.

Notes

INTRODUCTION

1. Whittock, M., "'The Sword Drawne': Christian Dissent and Politics 1649–1666, Particularly in the Fields of Millenarianism and Antinomianism", unpublished undergraduate dissertation, University of Bristol, 1980.

2. Whittock M. and E. Whittock, *Christ: The First 2000 Years*, Oxford: Lion Hudson, 2016.

3. "Manifest Destiny" was the belief that the expansion of the United States from coast to coast (at the expense of Native Americans and war with Mexico) was inevitable and justified.

4. 1 Samuel 15:3 in the 1599 edition of the *Geneva Bible*, used by the godly, reads: "Now therefore go, and smite Amalek, and destroy ye all that pertaineth unto them, and have no compassion on them, but slay both man and woman, both infant and suckling, both ox, and sheep, both camel, and ass." *Geneva Bible, 1599 Edition* (with modernized spelling), Dallas, GA: Tolle Lege Press, 2006; https://www.biblegateway.com (accessed August–November 2016). The Amalekites were a people who had mistreated the Israelites after the Exodus from Egypt under Moses and, as a result, the Old Testament stated that they were condemned by God and were to be utterly destroyed by the later king of Israel, Saul.

5. Matthew 5:7.

6. Consequently, when the Bible is quoted in this book it will be from the *Geneva Bible*, in the version referenced above in note 4, in order to give an insight into the mental and verbal world of the people being discussed, rather than from a modern translation which would be my normal practice.

1. ROOTS OF RADICALIZATION

1. Quoted in Capp, B. S., *The Fifth Monarchy Men*, London: Faber and Faber, 1972, p. 51.

2. *Plaine Scottish, or Newes from Scotland* (date unknown), p.7, quoted in Capp, B. S. *The Fifth Monarchy Men*, p. 52.

3. All too often we call them "The English Civil Wars" but this is a misnomer. First, the wars spanned the entire British Isles and affected England, Scotland, Ireland, and Wales. For this reason the conflict is occasionally known as "The Wars of the Three Kingdoms". Second, there were a number of different wars that coalesced in this violent period of upheaval. They truly were "The British Civil Wars".

4. The term "Antichrist" is found in the New Testament five times, in the letters known as: 1 John and 2 John. It appears once in plural form and four times in the singular. As the embodiment of evil opposition to Christ and Christianity the term, as first used in these New Testament passages, gives the impression of both a particular End Time opponent of Christ, and any serious opponents (plural) of Christ and Christian beliefs. Consequently, in Christian usage the term also came to be applied to other representations of evil who are described in prophecy, in the Old Testament Book of Daniel and in the New Testament in Revelation, although the term "Antichrist" is not, of course, used in the Jewish Old Testament; nor again in the Christian New Testament. These other opponents of God are described as: "the fourth beast" with ten horns from which a boastful little horn would rise up (Daniel 7:7–8); "the beast" (Revelation 13:1–17) clearly based on the earlier prophecy in Daniel; and the "false prophet" (Revelation 16:13–14). The Apostle Paul also spoke of a similar End Time figure, the "man of sin" and the "wicked [lawless] man" (2 Thessalonians 2:1–4 & 2 Thessalonians 2:7–10). In later Christian usage all these figures have been described as the Antichrist and brought under this one term. The commentary in the *Geneva Bible* does this with regard to the "man of sin" and the "wicked [lawless] man" and, when commenting on this figure and that in Revelation, explicitly identifies Antichrist as the Roman Catholic Church and the pope in particular. It may be noted that Jesus warned of "false Christs and false prophets" (Matthew 24:24 & Mark 13:22) or *pseudochrists* in the original Greek, but these gospel examples are in the plural and seem to be a warning against more general opposition.

5. https://en.oxforddictionaries.com/definition/theocracy (accessed December 2016).

6. Quoted in Fraser, A., *Cromwell: Our Chief of Men*, London: Granada, 1973, p. 424.

7. The brotherly relationship with Fear-God is partly conjectural, as the parish register for Charwelton parish, Northamptonshire, is incomplete for that period but the circumstantial evidence points that way.

8. The 1899 work of Hamo Thornycroft, which depicts Oliver Cromwell in Civil Wars buff coat with drawn sword, as Lord Protector of the Commonwealth of England, Scotland, and Ireland.

9. Bartlett, T., *Ireland: A History*, Cambridge: Cambridge University Press, 2010, p. 127, gives a good overview of the debate concerning the casualty figures, ranging from a high of 600,000 out of a population of 1.5 million (or 40 per cent), to figures of between 20 to 40 per cent of the population, put forward by more conservative historians. A number of these focus on the whole period of the Irish Rebellion, 1641–53, and include deaths caused by both sides.

10. Notestein, W., "A History of Witchcraft in England from 1558 to 1718", *American Historical Association*, 1911; (reissued) New York: Russell & Russell, 1965, p. 195.

11. Hill, C. and E. Dell (eds), *The Good Old Cause: The English Revolution of 1640–1660*, 2nd edition, New York: A.M.Kelly, 1969, Part 13: 160.

12. *The Oxford Dictionary of Quotations*, Oxford: Oxford University Press, 3rd edition, 1979, p. 400.

13. Probably co-written with Thomas More, who was later executed for his Catholicism in 1535. The Catholic title was rescinded by the pope in 1530 but re-granted by Parliament in 1544 as defender of the Church of England's faith.

14. It was under Edward VI, not Henry VIII, that it became illegal to bless candles in church, place ash crosses on foreheads on Ash Wednesday, give out palm crosses on Palm Sunday, process at Pentecost, build models of Easter tombs, ring the bells for the dead at All Souls (1548) or feast in celebration of St George (1552), among other purges of Catholic traditions.

15. Fraser, A., *Cromwell: Our Chief of Men*, p. 674.

16. Hill, C., "Providence and Oliver Cromwell", in I. Roots (ed.), *Cromwell: A Profile*, London and Basingstoke: Macmillan, 1973, p. 193.

2. "THE WORLD TURNED UPSIDE DOWN!"

1. Acts 17:6, in the 1611 *Authorized* – or *King James* – *Version* of the Bible.

2. Hill, C., *The World Turned Upside Down: Radical Ideas During the English Revolution*, London: Maurice Temple Smith, 1972.

3. Being King James VI in Scotland but the first of that name in England and in Ireland.

4. There was disquiet over a woman, even a queen, being the leader of the church and so the word "governor" was more acceptable than "head".

5. The Roman Catholic doctrine that Christ is physically present in the bread and wine, and summed up in the Catholic belief in Transubstantiation.

6. Gardiner, J. and N. Wenborn (eds), *The History Today Companion to British History*, London: Collins & Brown, 1995, p. 282.

7. Bender, M. E., "The Sixteenth-Century Anabaptists in Literature", in G. F. Hershberger (ed.), *The Recovery of the Anabaptist Vision: A Sixtieth Anniversary Tribute to Harold S. Bender,* Scottdale PA: Herald Press, 1957, p. 278.

8. See Sellars, I., "Edwardians, Anabaptists and the problem of Baptist origins", *Baptist Quarterly* 29, 1981, pp. 97–112.

9. Whittock, M. J., "Baptist Roots: The Use of Models in Tracing Baptist Origins", *Evangelical Quarterly*, Vol.LVII/No. 4, October, 1985, pp. 317–326.

10. Payne, E. A., "Who were the Baptists?", *Baptist Quarterly* 16, 1968, pp. 339ff.

11. At about the time that this label started to be applied in England, the Dutch followers of Jacob Arminius were condemned at the ultra-Calvinist Synod of Dort (1618–19). This made "Arminian" a useful and potent negative label which English Calvinists could then apply to their opponents in the Church of England.

12. "Roundhead" referred to the short haircuts associated with some among the godly and also among London apprentices and became used as a negative term from 1641, after upheaval in Westminster over the Bishops' Exclusion Bill. The godly/Parliamentarians hated it and it was a punishable offence in the New Model Army to call a fellow soldier a "Roundhead". Many leading godly/parliamentarians, such as Cromwell himself, actually had long hair. In contrast, "Cavalier" referred to Spanish *Caballeros* (horsemen) who oppressed Dutch Protestants during the reign of Elizabeth I. In contrast to the term "Roundhead", the "Cavaliers" embraced the term.

13. An unpopular tax levied on coastal towns and, during Charles I's reign, it gained added unpopularity since it was bypassing the tax-raising authority of Parliament. Charles spent most of it on his navy, but his navy in large part still took the side of Parliament in the Civil Wars.

14. Customs revenues collected by Charles I, despite only having had the right to do so granted by Parliament (in 1625) for one year only. He continued to do so until Parliament took back control over the right to levy them in 1641.

15. http://bcw-project.org/military/trained-bands (accessed September 2016).

3. NORTH OF THE BORDER: A VERY SCOTTISH GODLY RULE

1. Wales had effectively been brought under the English crown after the death of the last native Prince of Wales, Llewellyn II, in 1282 and, constitutionally, this was formalized in the Acts of Union (termed the 'Acts of Incorporation') under Henry VIII in 1536 and 1543. Consequently, Wales was already united with England before the arrangements with Scotland occurred in 1603 and then 1707 (which still left Scotland as a distinct kingdom). In contrast, Ireland was formally designated a kingdom in 1541–42, and this stipulated that the king of England was to be king of Ireland too. This means that in the historical context of this book we should refer to three kingdoms: England, Ireland, Scotland (Wales is not separately referred to since, constitutionally, it came under England).

2. A term popularized in the nineteenth century by Sir Walter Scott.

3. She travelled to France in 1548 to be brought up with him and eventually married him in 1558.

4. He was king of France from 1559 to 1560, ruling as Francis II. He was also king consort of Scotland as a result of his marriage to Mary (Queen of Scots), from 1558 until his death in 1560.

5. In fact the pamphlet was so controversial, even in the unequal gender politics and society of the sixteenth century, that Knox published it anonymously and only admitted to its authorship a year later. Elizabeth I was so annoyed that she refused him a passport to travel via England when he eventually returned to Scotland.

6. Carrington, C. E. and J. Hampden Jackson, *A History of England*, Cambridge: Cambridge University Press, 1932, p. 346.

7. Croft, P., *King James*, Basingstoke and New York: Palgrave Macmillan, 2004, p. 163, p. 165.

8. Carpenter, S., "Scottish drama until 1650", in I. Brown (ed.), *The Edinburgh Companion to Scottish Drama*, Edinburgh: Edinburgh University Press, 2011, p. 20.

9. http://www.scottishreformationsociety.org/the-magdalen-chapel/ (accessed September 2016).

10. Thomas, A., "The Renaissance", in T. M. Devine and J. Wormald (eds), *The Oxford Handbook of Modern Scottish History*, Oxford: Oxford University Press, 2012, pp. 198–199.

11. In 1611 the Kirk adopted the *Authorized – King James – Version of the Bible* and the first Scots version was printed in Scotland in 1633. However, the *Geneva Bible* continued to be employed well into the seventeenth century, as it was among many of the godly in England and North America.

12. Houston, R. A., *Scottish Literacy and the Scottish Identity: Illiteracy and Society in Scotland and Northern England, 1600–1800*, Cambridge: Cambridge University Press, 2002, pp. 63-68.

13. Not as bizarre as it sounds as there existed a strange habit of cross-dressing rioters in British lower-class traditions. An engraving from 1812, purporting to show Ned Ludd the mythical leader of attacks on textile machinery, depicts him in a spotted blue frock. In the Rebecca Riots, between 1839 and 1843 in South and Mid Wales, some rioters dressed as women in their attacks on toll gates.

14. A very accessible overview of the Bishops' Wars can be found at http://www. scotland. org.uk/scotland-in-the-seventeenth-century/the-bishops-wars-of-1639 (accessed September 2016).

4. A GODLY WAR?

1. The earlier Parliament being remembered as the "Short Parliament", because it had only met for three weeks during the spring of 1640.

2. Todd, M., *The Culture of Protestantism in Early Modern Scotland*, New Haven, CT and London: Yale University Press, 2002, p. 361.

3. Todd, M., *The Culture of Protestantism in Early Modern Scotland*, p. 361.

4. Abbott, W. C., *Writings and Speeches of Oliver Cromwell*, 4 Vols, Cambridge, MA: Harvard University Press, 1937–47, Vol. I, p. 294.

5. As clearly revealed in his negotiations with Parliament between 15 September 1648 and 27 November 1648, at Newport, Isle of Wight.

6. Vicars, J., *God in the Mount*, in *Englands Parliamentary Chronicle*, 1646, p. 273. For this book in its entirety see http://quod.lib.umich.edu/e/eebo/A95892.0001.001?view=toc

7. Bruce, J., *The Quarrel between the Earl of Manchester and Oliver Cromwell*, London: Camden Society, 1875, p. 72.

8. Baxter, R., *Reliquiae Baxterianae*, 1696, Vol. I, p. 57. For this book in its entirety see http://www.digitalpuritan.net/Digital%20Puritan%20Resources/Baxter,%20Richard/Reliquiae%20Baxterianae.pdf

9. In 1645, after the Battle of Naseby, Baxter visited the Parliamentary army and was shocked by what he saw as heretical ideas about the relationship of man to Christ, soldiers mocking Presbyterians as "priest-biters" and Westminster divines as "dry-vines", and support for republicanism and regicide. Fraser, A., *Cromwell Our Chief of Men*, St Albans: Granada, 1975, p. 165.

10. Hutchinson, L., *Memoirs of the Life of Colonel Hutchinson, Governor of Nottingham Castle and Town, c.1664–71*, London: Longman, Hurst, Rees, and Orme 1808, p. 184.

11. In May 1643.
12. In a letter to Sir William Spring (September 1643), found in Ratcliffe, S. (ed.), *Concise Oxford Dictionary of Quotations*, Oxford: Oxford University Press, 2011, p. 113.
13. Abbott, W. C., *Writings and Speeches of Oliver Cromwell*, Vol. I, p. 262.
14. The officers – Lieutenant William Packer and Lieutenant-Colonel Henry Warner – had been disciplined by Manchester's major-general, Lawrence Crawford. Warner, as a Baptist, had refused to sign the Presbyterian Covenant.
15. Abbott, W. C., *Writings and Speeches of Oliver Cromwell*, Vol. II p. 287.
16. Abbott, W. C., *Writings and Speeches of Oliver Cromwell* Vol. I, p. 339.
17. Abbott, W. C., *Writings and Speeches of Oliver Cromwell*, Vol. I, p. 360.
18. Abbott, W. C., *Writings and Speeches of Oliver Cromwell*, Vol. I, p. 364.
19. Bruce, J., *The Quarrel between the Earl of Manchester and Oliver Cromwell*, p. 72.
20. Clarendon, E., *The History of the Rebellion and Civil Wars in England*, 6 Vols, W. Dunn Macray (ed.), Oxford: Oxford University Press, 1888, Vol. IV p. 305
21. *Theauro John*, 1652.
22. Judges 3:12–30.
23. Judges 5:24–27.
24. Burnet, T. (ed.), *Bishop Burnet's History of His Own Time*, 4 Vols, London: for J. Nunn, R. Priestley and M. Priestley, 1818, Vol. I, p. 71, p. 78.
25. For a detailed account of this fascinating episode see Fraser, A., *Cromwell Our Chief of Men*, St Albans: Granada, 1975, p. 277.
26. Abbott, W. C., *Writings and Speeches of Oliver Cromwell*, Vol. II p. 189.

5. Hunting Down the Enemies of God

1. Carlton, C., *Going to the Wars*, London: Routledge, 1992, pp. 199–203; Hudson, G. L., *British Military and Naval Medicine, 1600–1830*, Amsterdam, NY: Rodopi, 2007, p. 123.
2. Hudson, G. L., *British Military and Naval Medicine, 1600–1830*, p. 123.
3. http://www.nationalarchives.gov.uk/education/civilwar/g4/key/ (accessed October 2016).
4. See http://www.catholiceducation.org/en/controversy/common-misconceptions/who-burned-the-witches.html (accessed October 2016).
5. Notestein, W., *A History of Witchcraft In England from 1558 to 1718*, American Historical Association, 1911, reissued New York: Russell & Russell, 1965, p. 195.
6. Russell, J. B., *A History of Witchcraft*, London: Thames & Hudson, 1981, pp. 97–98.
7. For an overview see Sharpe, J., *Instruments of Darkness: Witchcraft in Early Modern England*, Philadelphia, PA: University of Pennsylvania Press, 1996.
8. Trevor-Roper, H., *The European Witch-craze of the Sixteenth and Seventeenth Centuries*, Harmondsworth: Penguin, 1969.
9. Although the *Geneva Bible* translated Acts 8:9 and Galatians 5:19–20 as involving the sin of "witchcraft", there were no other New Testament uses of the word in this translation.
10. Kors, A. C. and E. Peters, *Witchcraft in Europe, 400–1700: a Documentary History*, Philadelphia, PA: University of Pennsylvania Press, 2nd revised edition, 2001, pp. 72–77.
11. See http://www.catholiceducation.org/en/controversy/common-misconceptions/who-burned-the-witches.html (accessed October 2016).
12. For an overview of some of the recent historical debate see Briggs, R., *Witches and Neighbours: The Social and Cultural Context of European Witchcraft*, Harmondsworth: Penguin, 1998.
13. Except where "petty treason" was also involved: betrayal of a superior. Then, a convicted woman was burned.

14. For an accessible overview see http://www.lancastercastle.com/the-pendle-witches (accessed October 2016).

15. Young, J. R., "The Covenanters and the Scottish Parliament, 1639–51: the rule of the godly and the 'second Scottish Reformation'", in E. Boran and C. Gribben (eds), *Enforcing Reformation in Ireland and Scotland, 1550–1700*, Aldershot: Ashgate, 2006, pp. 149–50.

16. The 1563 Scottish Act (with its 1649 extension) and the 1604 English Act were both finally repealed by the Witchcraft Act of 1736. This included penalties for the *pretence* of witchcraft.

17. Scarre, G. and J. Callow, *Witchcraft and Magic in Sixteenth and Seventeenth-Century Europe*, Basingstoke: Palgrave, 2nd edition, 2001, p. 28.

18. See Levack, B. P., *The Witch-Hunt in Early Modern Europe*, London: Longman, 3rd edition, 2006, p. 202.

19. Levack, B. P., *The Witch-Hunt in Early Modern Europe*, p. 219.

20. Sharpe, J., "The Lancaster witches in historical context", in R. Poole, *The Lancashire Witches: Histories and Stories*, Manchester: Manchester University Press, 2002, p. 3.

21. Davies, S. F., *The Discovery of Witches and Witchcraft: The Writings of the Witchfinders*, Brighton: Puckrel Publishing, 2007, Introduction, p. xi.

22. Levack, B. P., *The Witch-Hunt in Early Modern Europe*, p. 221.

23. Sharpe, J., "The devil in East Anglia", in J. Barry, M. Hester and G. Roberts (eds), *Witchcraft in Early Modern Europe: Studies in Culture and Belief*, Cambridge: Cambridge University Press, 1998, p. 238.

24. Scarre, G. and J. Callow, *Witchcraft and Magic in Sixteenth and Seventeenth-Century Europe*, pp. 26–28.

25. Levack, B. P., *The Witch-Hunt in Early Modern Europe*, p. 219.

26. Sharpe, J., "The devil in East Anglia", p. 241.

27. For this view see Macfarlane, A., *Witchcraft in Tudor and Stuart England*, London: Routledge, 2nd edition, 1999, p. 139; and also: K. Thomas, "The relevance of social anthropology to the historical study of English witchcraft", in M. Douglas (ed.), *Witchcraft Confessions and Accusations*, London: Routledge, 1970, p. 50.

28. Sharpe, J., "The devil in East Anglia", pp. 240–254.

29. See Elmer, P., *Witchcraft, Witch-Hunting, and Politics in Early Modern England*, Oxford: Oxford University Press, 2016, for the case against a connection, and the review by J. Pearson making a case for an evidence-link between prosecutions and Puritans in *The Seventeenth Century*, 2016, Vol. 31, No. 3.

30. Sharpe, J., "The devil in East Anglia", p. 250.

6. The "Rule of the Saints" in Ireland

1. Martin, F. X. and F. J. Byrne, *Early Modern Ireland, 1534–1691*, Oxford: Oxford University Press, 1976, p. xxxix.

2. Martin, F. X. and F. J. Byrne, *Early Modern Ireland, 1534–1691*, p. xl.

3. For example, the province of Munster was heavily colonized by English settlers during the 1580s.

4. For an overview of the different groups see Martin, F. X. and F. J. Byrne, *Early Modern Ireland, 1534–1691*, pp. xlii-xliii.

5. Also known as the Statute of Drogheda, and dating from 1494.

6. Connolly, S. J., *Divided Kingdom: Ireland 1630–1800*, Oxford: Oxford University Press, 2008, p. 92.

7. Connolly, S. J., *Divided Kingdom: Ireland 1630–1800*, p. 92.

8. Whitelocke, B., *Memorials of the English affairs from the beginning of the reign of Charles the*

First to the happy restoration of King Charles the Second, 4 Vols, Oxford: Oxford University Press,1853, Vol. III, p. 92.

9. Fraser, A., *Cromwell Our Chief of Men*, St Albans: Granada, 1975, p. 327.

10. "A Declaration of both Houses of Parliament concerning the affairs of Ireland", 1641, in *Cromwellian Settlement of Ireland, 1641–1650: Four Rare Puritan Tracts Concerning the Affairs of Ireland*, Dublin: Clery & Co, 1879, 'Arguments to promote the work', p. 3.

11. Connolly, S. J., *Divided Kingdom: Ireland 1630*–1800, p. 94.

12. Rankin, D., *Between Spenser and Swift: English Writing in Seventeenth-Century Ireland*, Cambridge: Cambridge University Press, 2005, p. 52.

13. Connolly, S. J., *Divided Kingdom: Ireland 1630*–1800, p. 94.

14. Reilly, T., *Cromwell, An Honourable Enemy*, London: Phoenix Press, 1999, p. 71.

15. Lenihan, P., *Conquest and Resistance: War in Seventeenth-Century Ireland*, Leiden, Boston, Köln: Brill, 2001, p. 263.

16. See Burke, J., "The New Model Army and the Problems of Siege Warfare 1648–51", *Irish Historical Studies* 27, (1990), pp. 1–29; he suggests the figure of 1000 dead civilians (p. 14).

17. Connolly, S. J., *Divided Kingdom: Ireland 1630–1800*, p. 94.

18. Ó Siochrú, M., *God's Executioner, Oliver Cromwell and the Conquest of Ireland*, London: Faber & Faber, 2008, p. 95.

19. Bartlett, T., *Ireland: A History*, Cambridge: Cambridge University Press, 2010, p. 127.

20. *State Papers, Irish Series*, Charles II. Vol. 307, No. 65, Public Records Office.

21. Quoted in: Martinich, A., *Hobbes: A Biography*, Cambridge: Cambridge University Press, 1999, p. 204.

22. Fraser, A., *Cromwell Our Chief of Men*, p. 345.

23. Quoted in Russell, Rev. M., *Life of Oliver Cromwell*, Vol. I, Edinburgh: Constable, 1829, p. 28.

24. Abbott, W. C., *Writings and Speeches of Oliver Cromwell*, 4 Vols, Cambridge MA: Harvard University Press, 1937–47, Vol. II, pp. 196–205.

25. Martin, F. X. and F. J. Byrne, *Early Modern Ireland, 1534–1691*, p. xliv.

26. For a very accessible overview see http://www.clarelibrary.ie/eolas/coclare/ history/ cromwell_settlement.htm (accessed October 2016).

27. Kenyon, J. and J. Ohlmyer (eds) *The Civil Wars, A Military History of England, Scotland and Ireland, 1638–1660*, Oxford: Oxford University Press, 1998, pp. 277–278.

28. Sturdy, D. J., *Fractured Europe 1600–1721*, Oxford: Blackwell, 2002, p. 2.

29. Kenyon, J. and J. Ohlmyer (eds) *The Civil Wars, A Military History of England, Scotland and Ireland, 1638–1660*, pp. 277–278.

30. Bartlett, T., *Ireland: A History*, p. 127; for a figure of 33 per cent see https://www. ncas. rutgers.edu/center-study-genocide-conflict-resolution-and-human-rights/16th-17th-century-plantation-ireland (accessed October 2016).

31. Professor Kevin Whelan, Michael Smurfit Director of the Keough-Notre Dame Centre, Dublin, in *The Irish Times*, 8 May 1999, http://www.irishtimes.com/news/cleaning-up-cromwell-1.182691 (accessed October 2016).

7. SOCIAL AND POLITICAL JUSTICE FOR THE COMMON MAN? THE LEVELLERS

1. http://www.burfordchurch.org/Groups/265118/The_Levellers.aspx (accessed October 2016).

2. Kean, H., "Tolpuddle, Burston, and Levellers: the making of radical and national heritages at English labour movement festivals", in L. Smith, P. Shackel and G. Campbell (eds), *Heritage, Labour, and the Working Classes*, London: Routledge, 2011, p. 278.

3. The Diggers, as we shall see, referred to themselves as "True Levellers".

4. For an accessible overview of the Levellers see http://bcw-project.org/church-and-state/sects-and-factions/levellers (accessed October 2016).

5. Quoted in Knoppers, L. (ed.), *The Oxford Handbook of Literature and the English Revolution*, Oxford: Oxford University Press, 2012, p. 281.

6. Quoted in Bradstock, A., *Radical Religion in Cromwell's England*, London: I.B. Tauris, 2011, p. 28; and final quote from: Patrides, C. A. and R. B. Waddington, *The Age of Milton: Backgrounds to Seventeenth-century Literature*, Manchester: Manchester University Press, 1980, p. 49.

7. Richardson, R. C., *Freedom and the English Revolution: Essays in History and Literature*, Manchester: Manchester University Press, 1986, pp. 83–84.

8. Hill, C., *The World Turned Upside Down: Radical Ideas During the English Revolution*, London: Penguin, 1991 (originally published by Maurice Temple Smith, 1972), p. 114.

9. Bradstock, A., *Radical Religion in Cromwell's England*, p. 28.

10. Marotti, A. F., "The Intolerability of English Catholicism", in R. D. Sell and A. W. Johnson (eds), *Writing and Religion in England, 1558–1689: Studies in Community-Making and Cultural Memory*, Farnham: Ashgate Publishing, 2013, p. 63.

11. Brackney, W. H., *Historical Dictionary of Radical Christianity*, Lanham, MD and Plymouth: Scarecrow Books, 2012, p. 67.

12. Overton, for example, published a pamphlet in 1644 (*Mans Mortalitie*) arguing that the human soul died with the body but was raised to life at the general resurrection of the dead on Christ's return. This was a theological position rejected by the contemporary Christian mainstream and which divides modern Christians. Overton was not alone in his belief, and a number of Anabaptists held it and John Milton adhered to a form of it.

13. Haller W. and G. Davies (eds), *The Leveller Tracts 1647–1653*, New York: Columbia University Press, 1944, p. 374.

14. Quoted in Key, N. and R. O. Bucholz (eds), *Sources and Debates in English History, 1485–1714*, Chichester: John Wiley & Sons, 2009, p. 189.

15. The *Representation of the People Act 1918* widened UK suffrage by abolishing almost all property qualifications for men and also by giving the vote to women over 30 who met minimum property qualifications.

16. Quoted in Bradstock, A., *Radical Religion in Cromwell's England*, p. 34.

17. He had been killed by Royalists in Doncaster, in October 1648, during a failed kidnap attempt, while engaged in the siege of Pontefract Castle.

18. Those of Ireton, Reynolds, Harrison, and Skippon.

19. Kean, H., "Tolpuddle, Burston, and Levellers", p. 278. Until the 1970s this was the only inscription there to commemorate what occurred. A copy of this graffito can be seen at: http://www.victoriacountyhistory.ac.uk/ explore/items/burford-and-levellers (accessed October 2016).

20. http://www.victoriacountyhistory.ac.uk/explore/items/burford-and-levellers (accessed October 2016).

21. Kean, H., "Tolpuddle, Burston, and Levellers", p. 278.

8. A VERY ENGLISH KIND OF COMMUNISM: THE DIGGERS

1. http://www.stgeorgeshillgolfclub.co.uk/ (accessed October 2016).

2. http://www.stgeorgesra.com/home/ (accessed October 2016).

3. Gerrard Winstanley's first Digger manifesto, in April 1649, was entitled *The True Levellers Standard Advanced*. The term had earlier been used, in 1647, by Lawrence Clarkson who was later a Ranter.

4. Chalklin, C., *The Rise of the English Town, 1650–1850*, Cambridge: Cambridge University Press, 2001, p. 5

5. It is appropriate to use the term "Commonwealth" to describe the whole of the period 1649 to 1660. However, it should be noted that some historians only use the term to cover the years leading up to Cromwell's formal taking of the office of Lord Protector in 1653. They would then call the period from 1653 until the end of the rule of Richard Cromwell (Oliver's son), in May 1659, the "Protectorate" rather than the "Commonwealth". Oliver, just to confuse things, was titled, "Lord Protector of the Commonwealth of England, Scotland and Ireland".

6. Quoted in: Kelsey, S., *Inventing a Republic: The Political Culture of the English Commonwealth, 1649–1653*, Manchester: Manchester University Press, 1997, p. 224.

7. Hill, C. (ed.), *Winstanley 'The Law of Freedom' and Other Writings*, Cambridge: Cambridge University Press, digitally printed 2006 (originally published in Pelican Books, 1973), Introduction, p. 30.

8. Tate, W. E., *The English Village Community and the Enclosure Movements*, London: Gollancz, 1967, pp. 122–125.

9. Yerby, G., *The English Revolution and the Roots of Environmental Change: The Changing Concept of the Land in Early Modern England*, London: Routledge, 2015, p. 251.

10. See Manwaring, K., *Northamtonshire Folk Tales*, Stroud: History Press, 2013, Chapter 24.

11. For an overview of the comparison between the two groups see J. Gurney, *Brave community: The Digger Movement in the English Revolution*, Manchester: Manchester University Press, 2007.

12. Yerby, G., *The English Revolution and the Roots of Environmental Change*, p. 252.

13. Quoted in Yerby, G., *The English Revolution and the Roots of Environmental Change*, p. 252.

14. Quoted in Yerby, G., *The English Revolution and the Roots of Environmental Change*, p. 252.

15. Quoted in Bradstock, A., *Radical Religion in Cromwell's England*, London: I.B. Tauris, 2011, p. 52.

16. Quoted in Bradstock, A., *Radical Religion in Cromwell's England*, p. 53.

17. Referring to the Christian belief in Jesus Christ being born "in the flesh" as a man.

18. Referring to the Christian belief in the "End Time", particularly the Second Coming of Christ and the end of the current fallen world order through the creation of a "New heaven and earth".

19. Quoted in Hill, C., *The World Turned Upside Down: Radical Ideas During the English Revolution*, London: Penguin Books, 1991 (originally published by Maurice Temple Smith, 1972), p. 129.

20. More formally called *A Declaration to the Powers of England*.

21. Quoted in Hill, C., *The World Turned Upside Down*, p. 130.

22. Hill, C., *The World Turned Upside Down*, p. 130.

23. Quoted in http://quod.lib.umich.edu/e/eebo/A66687.0001.001/1:3?rgn=div1;view=fulltext (accessed October 2016)

24. Sabine, G. H. (ed.), *The Works of Gerrard Winstanley*, Ithaca, NY: Cornell University Press, 1941, p. 269.

25. Hill, C., *The World Turned Upside Down*, p. 129; also A. Bradstock, *Radical Religion in Cromwell's England*, p. 53.

26. Hill, C., *The World Turned Upside Down*, p. 128.

27. Thomas, K. V., "Another Digger Broadside", *Past and Present* No. 42, (1969) pp. 57–68.

28. The idea that the Bible account and history generally are divided into discernible periods ("dispensations") marked at beginning and end by events of great religious importance and, together, driving history forward to a point predetermined by God.

9. "God's People Must Be a Bloody People!" The Fifth Monarchy Men

1. This quote from the Fifth Monarchy Men pamphlets, now held in the British Library, London, is from Whittock, M., "'The Sword Drawne': Christian Dissent and Politics 1649–1666, Particularly in the Fields of Millenarianism and Antinomianism", unpublished undergraduate dissertation, University of Bristol, 1980.

2. The Medes and Persians.

3. Some said: Assyria, Babylon, Greece, and Rome. But the fourth was generally agreed as representing Rome by the seventeenth century.

4. 1 John 2:18 (both singular and plural form used) and 1 John 2:22, 1 John 4:2–3, 2 John 1:7 (all singular). Jesus also warned against "false christs" (plural) in Matthew 24:24 and Mark 13:22.

5. He is certainly identified as "Antichrist" in the commentary found in the *Geneva Bible*.

6. See Revelation 13:1–18, Revelation 16:13–14, Revelation 19:19–20, Revelation 20:10.

7. Those believing that prophecies refer to events after the time of their writing are subscribers to "Historicism". "Preterism" interprets prophecies of the Bible, especially the Books of Daniel and Revelation, as events which have already happened in the past. "Idealism" interprets the book of Revelation as non-literal allegory and is a common viewpoint among many modern Christian scholars. "Futurism" interprets the Book of Revelation and the Book of Daniel as foretelling future events literally and is associated with "Dispensationalism", which interprets history as divided by God into defined periods or ages and which will culminate in the millennial reign of Christ on earth, which will end with God's judgment on a final rebellion and is an outlook which has become deeply rooted in many evangelical churches in the US, UK, and globally. There are many variants within this latter school of interpretation.

8. For an overview see Capp, B. S., *The Fifth Monarchy Men*, London: Faber and Faber, 1972, Chapter 2, "The Origins and Rise of Millenarianism to 1649".

9. Archbishop Arnulf of Reims accused Pope John XV of being the Antichrist in 991; Cardinal Benno (died 1098) accused Pope Gregory VII; Eberhard II von Truchsees, Prince-Archbishop of Salzburg, denounced Pope Gregory IX, in 1241.

10. For example, its commentary on Antichrist in 2 Thessalonians 2:3–4; and its commentary on Revelation 13:1, and Revelation 13:11–12, 15–18.

11. Capp, B. S., *The Fifth Monarchy Men*, pp. 38–39.

12. William Bridges in *Babylon's Downfall*, 1641, quoted in: Capp, B. S., *The Fifth Monarchy Men*, p. 39.

13. Citing the correlation of days with years in the Old Testament book of Numbers 14:34 (where forty years in the wilderness were matched by forty days investigating the Promised Land).

14. Whittock, M., "'The Sword Drawne': Christian Dissent and Politics 1649–1666".

15. Quoted in: Capp, B. S., *The Fifth Monarchy Men*, p. 54.

16. Quoted in Fraser, A., *Cromwell: Our Chief of Men*, London: Granada, 1973, p. 424.

17. Bradstock, A., *Radical Religion in Cromwell's England*, London: I.B. Tauris, 2011, p. 122.

18. The Calvinist-leaning Fifth Monarchists opposed the Dutch for tolerating Arminianism and as trade rivals. The latter point arose from the outlook of clothworkers and artisans, from whom Fifth Monarchists drew much support.

19. Quoted in Woolrych, A., "Political theory and political practice", in C. A. Patrides and R. B. Waddington (eds), *The Age of Milton: Backgrounds to Seventeenth-century Literature*, Manchester: Manchester University Press, 1980, p. 56.

20. Quoted in Firth, C. H, *Cromwell's Army*, London: Methuen, 1921 (3rd edition), p. 338.

21. Quoted in: Capp, B. S., *The Fifth Monarchy Men*, p. 65.
22. Some believed that Christ would appear and reign; others that he would appear and then leave the rule to the saints (premillennialism); others that the saints would rule until Christ appeared after 1,000 years; yet others thought the saints would rule until perfection had been achieved and only then would Christ appear (postmillennialism).
23. Firth, C. H., *Cromwell's Army*, p. 338.
24. Quoted in: Capp, B. S., *The Fifth Monarchy Men*, p. 133.
25. Fritze, R. H. and W.B. Robison (eds), *Historical Dictionary of Stuart England, 1603–1689*, Westport, CT: Greenwood Publishing Group, 1996, p. 193.
26. Quoted in Forsyth, N., *John Milton: A Biography*, Oxford: Lion Hudson, 2008, p. 148.
27. Greaves, R. L., *Glimpses of Glory: John Bunyan and English Dissent*, Stanford, CA: Stanford University Press, 2002, p. 138.
28. Schonhorn, M., *Defoe's Politics: Parliament, Power, Kingship and 'Robinson Crusoe'*, Cambridge: Cambridge University Press, 1991, p. 18.
29. Fritze, R. H. and W.B. Robison (eds), *Historical Dictionary of Stuart England, 1603–1689*, p. 193.

10. Not Very Quiet Quakers!

1. Davis, J. C., *Fear, Myth and History: The Ranters and The Historians*, Cambridge: Cambridge University Press, 1986.
2. Friedman, J., *Blasphemy, Immorality and Anarchy: The Ranters and the English Revolution*, Athens, OH: Ohio University Press, 1987, p. 74.
3. Bradstock, A., *Radical Religion in Cromwell's England*, London: I.B. Tauris, 2011, pp. 76–77.
4. Quoted in Bradstock, A., *Radical Religion in Cromwell's England*, p. 81.
5. Quoted in Cohn, N., *The Pursuit of the Millennium*, St Albans: Paladin, 1970, p. 324.
6. *British History Online*, Institute of Historical Research, http://www.british-history.ac.uk/no-series/acts-ordinances-interregnum/pp387-389 (accessed November 2016).
7. *British History Online*, Institute of Historical Research, http://www.british-history.ac.uk/no-series/acts-ordinances-interregnum/pp387-389 (accessed November 2016).
8. *British History Online*, Institute of Historical Research, http://www.british-history.ac.uk/no-series/acts-ordinances-interregnum/pp409-412 (Accessed November 2016.)
9. Quoted in Bradstock, A., *Radical Religion in Cromwell's England*, pp. 88–89.
10. McGregor, J. F., "Seekers and Ranters", in J. F. McGregor and B. Reay (eds), *Radical Religion in the English Revolution*, Oxford: Oxford University Press, 1984, p. 137.
11. Quoted in Bradstock, A., *Radical Religion in Cromwell's England*, p. 96.
12. Whittock, M., "'The Sword Drawne': Christian Dissent and Politics 1649–1666, Particularly in the Fields of Millenarianism and Antinomianism", unpublished undergraduate dissertation, University of Bristol, 1980.
13. Both can be seen, along with other re-used woodcuts, at https://mercuriuspoliticus.wordpress.com/2010/11/06/recycled-woodcuts-part-2/ (accessed December 2016).
14. Whittock, M., "'The Sword Drawne': Christian Dissent and Politics 1649–1666".
15. Bradstock, A., *Radical Religion in Cromwell's England*, p. 95.

11. Cromwell and the Rule of God

1. Carlyle, T. and S. C. Lomas (eds), *The Letters and Speeches of Oliver Cromwell, with elucidations by Thomas Carlyle*, London: Methuen, 1904 edition, Vol. III, p. 362.
2. Morrill, J., *The Nature of the English Revolution*, Routledge electronic book text, 2014

(original 1992), Chapter 1, "The Nature of the English Revolution", section X. Originally written for the Sino-British Historical Symposium in Nanjing, May 1987.

3. For an overview of the biblical roots of puritanical politics, the interaction between politics and the belief in God's Providence, and the key features of Cromwell's attempt to secure godly reformation see Worden, B., *God's Instruments: Political Conduct In The England Of Oliver Cromwell*, Oxford: Oxford University Press, 2012.

4. Describing a meeting that Cromwell called for a number of MPs and army officers at the house of the Speaker of the House of Commons. A event dated by a contemporary as occurring in December 1651 but now difficult to date with certainty.

5. Carlyle, T. (ed.), *The Letters and Speeches of Oliver Cromwell*, London: Chapman and Hall, 1845, Vol. II, p. 164.

6. Quoted in Smith, T., *Select Memoirs of the English and Scottish Divines*, C. M. McMahon and T. B. McMahon (eds), Coconut Creek, FL: Puritan Publications, 2012, p. 411.

7. Abbott, W. C., *Writings and Speeches of Oliver Cromwell*, 4 Vols, Cambridge, MA: Harvard University Press, 1937–47, Vol. II, p. 503.

8. Carlyle, T. (ed.), *The Letters and Speeches of Oliver Cromwell*, Vol. II, pp. 164–166.

9. Quoted in Lockyer, R., *Tudor and Stuart Britain: 1485–1714*, London: Routledge, 2014, p. 364.

10. Abbott, W. C., *Writings and Speeches of Oliver Cromwell*, Vol. II, pp. 642–643.

11. Carlyle, T. (ed.), *The Letters and Speeches of Oliver Cromwell*, London: Chapman and Hall, 1897, Vol. III, p. 58.

12. See Durston C., *Cromwell's Major-Generals: Godly Government During the English Revolution*, Manchester: Manchester University Press, 2001.

13. For an accessible overview of the fate of Christmas under the Puritans see http:// www.historyextra.com/ feature/no-christmas-under-cromwell-puritan-assault-christmas-during-1640s-and-1650s (accessed November 2016).

14. An example of this style of Protectorate signature can be seen in Cambridge University, *University Archives, Lett.13 A*, http://www.lib.cam.ac.uk/exhibitions/Cromwell/cromwell. kiosk.htm (accessed November 2016).

15. Carlyle, T. (ed.), *The Letters and Speeches of Oliver Cromwell*, Vol. II, p. 532.

12. THE END OF THE "GOOD OLD CAUSE"

1. For more information on Richard Cromwell see Peacey, J., Chapter 10, "'Fit for Public Services': The Upbringing of Richard Cromwell", in P. Little (ed.), *Oliver Cromwell: New Perspectives*, London: Palgrave Macmillan, 2008.

2. Farr, D., *John Lambert, Parliamentary Soldier and Cromwellian Major-General, 1619–1684*, Woodbridge: Boydell Press, 2003, p. 197.

3. For thoughts on why Lambert failed see Farr, D., *John Lambert*, p. 213.

4. Mayers, R. E, *1659: The Crisis of the Commonwealth*, Woodbridge: Boydell Press, 2004, pp. 256–257, explores reasons for Monck's success.

5. The entire declaration can be found in: Kekewich, M. L., *Princes and Peoples: France and the British Isles, 1620–1714: An Anthology of Primary Sources*, Manchester: Manchester University Press, 1994, pp. 60–62.

6. Charles Fleetwood, quoted in Woolrych, A., *Britain in Revolution: 1625–1660*, Oxford: Oxford University Press, 2002, p. 755.

7. Knoppers, L. L., *Constructing Cromwell: Ceremony, Portrait, and Print 1645–1661*, Cambridge: Cambridge University Press, 2000, p. 184, gives a detailed description from contemporary accounts, including the payment of 6d per person to see the corpse.

8. MacMains, H. F., *The Death of Oliver Cromwell*, Lexington, KY, University Press of

Kentucky, 2015, p. 171, discusses the possibility that the real corpse might have been sold by James Norfolke, who oversaw the exhumation.

9. Gaunt, P., *Oliver Cromwell (Historical Association Studies)*, Oxford: Blackwell, 1996, p. 4

10. *Ely Standard*, 23 December 2014. http://www.elystandard.co.uk/news/historic_ death_ plate buried_with_oliver_cromwell_fetches_more_than_70_000_at auction_1_ 3895811 (accessed November 2016).

11. For a detailed examination of the regicides see Spencer, C., *Killers of the King: The Men Who Dared to Execute Charles I*, London: A&C Black, 2014; Peacey, J., *The Regicides and the Execution of Charles I*, Basingstoke: Palgrave, 2001.

12. See Seaward, P., *The Cavalier Parliament and the Reconstruction of the Old Regime, 1661–1667*, Cambridge: Cambridge University Press, 2003.

13. Keeble, N. H., *The Restoration: England in the 1660s*, Oxford: Blackwell, 2002, p. 85.

14. Sell, A. P. F (ed.), *The Great Ejectment of 1662: Its Antecedents, Aftermath, and Ecumenical Significance*, Eugene, OR: Wipf and Stock, 2012.

15. Griffin, M. I. J., *Latitudinarianism in the Seventeenth-Century Church of England*, Leiden: Brill, 1992.

16. An accessible overview of the punitive actions of the Cavalier Parliament can be found in Bucholz, R. and N. Key, *Early Modern England 1485–1714*, Oxford: Wiley-Blackwell, 2009, p. 281.

17. Kent Clark, J., *Whig's Progress*, Cranberry, NJ, Fairleigh Dickinson University Press, 2004, p. 52.

18. See Keay, A., *The Last Royal Rebel: The Life and Death of James, Duke of Monmouth*, London: Bloomsbury, 2016.

19. Earle, P., *Monmouth's Rebels: The Road to Sedgemoor 1685*, London: Weidenfeld and Nicolson, 1977, provides a detailed assessment of the kinds of men who followed Monmouth, including many of the godly.

20. See Sawers, G., *The Monmouth Rebellion and the Bloody Assizes*, Reading: Two Rivers Press; 2nd revised edition, 2007.

21. http://www1.somerset.gov.uk/archives/ASH/Bloodyassize.htm (accessed November 2016).

22. Childs Kohn, G., *Dictionary of Wars*, London: Routledge, 2013, p. 130.

13. A NEW JERUSALEM IN THE NEW WORLD?

1. As in the pamphlet entitled: *The Humble Petition of the Brownists* of 1641.

2. Brackney, W. H., *Historical Dictionary of Radical Christianity*, Lanham, MD, Plymouth: Scarecrow Books, 2012, p. 67.

3. http://www.histarch.illinois.edu/plymouth/Maysource.html (accessed November 2016).

4. Morison, S. E. (ed.), *Winthrop Papers, Volume II: 1623–1630*, Boston: Massachusetts Historical Society, 1931.

5. See Fischer, C. S., *Made in America, A Social History of American Culture and Character*, Chicago: University of Chicago Press, 2010, Chapter 4, "Groups".

6. Quoted by Fischer, C., professor of sociology, Berkeley, University of California, "Pilgrims, Puritans, and the ideology that is their American legacy", 24 November, 2010, in http://blogs.berkeley.edu/2010/11/24/ pilgrims-puritans-and-their-american-legacy/ (accessed November 2016).

7. Brooks Holifield, E., "Peace, Conflict, and Ritual in Puritan Congregations", *The Journal of Interdisciplinary History*, Vol. 23, No. 3, Religion and History (Winter, 1993), p. 551.

8. Fischer, C., "Pilgrims, Puritans, and the ideology that is their American legacy".

9. Cody, D., Associate Professor of English, Hartwick College, "Puritanism in New England", in http://www.victorianweb.org/religion/puritan2.html (accessed November 2016).

10. See Greene, J. P., *Pursuits of Happiness: The Social Development of Early Modern British Colonies and the Formation of American Culture*, Chapel Hill, NC: University of North Carolina Press, 1988.

11. Cambridge Platform, Chapter 9, article 17, in Backus, I., *Church History of New England from 1620 to* 1804, Philadelphia, PA: American Baptist Publ. Society, 1844, p. 70.

12. For an interesting and accessible examination of her importance see LaPlante, E., "A heretic's overdue honor", *The Boston Globe*, 7 September 2005: http://archive.boston.com /news/globe/editorial_opinion/ oped/articles/2005/09/07/a_heretics_overdue_honor/ (accessed November 2016).

13. http://www.ushistory.org/us/3d.asp (accessed November 2016).

14. http://www.womenhistoryblog.com/2007/10/native-americans-and-massachusetts-bay.html (accessed November 2016).

15. Quoted in Armstrong, C., *Writing North America in the Seventeenth Century: English Representations in Print and Manuscript*, Aldershot: Ashgate Publishing, 2007, p. 67.

16. Armstrong, C., *Writing North America in the Seventeenth Century*, p. 68.

17. http://www.womenhistoryblog.com/2007/10/native-americans-and-massachusetts-bay.html

18. Quoted in Blaisdell, B., *Essential Documents of American History, Volume I: From Colonial Times to the Civil War, Volume 1*, Mineola, NY: Courier Dover Publications, 2016, p. 19.

19. Quoted in Wise, S. M., *An American Trilogy: Death, Slavery, and Dominion on the Banks of the Cape*, Philadelphia, PA: Da Capo Press, 2009, p. 33.

20. Fischer, C., "Pilgrims, Puritans, and the ideology that is their American legacy".

21. Goodheart, L. B., *The Solemn Sentence of Death: Capital Punishment in Connecticut*, Amherst & Boston, MA, University of Massachusetts Press, 2011, p. 36.

14. THE LEGACY OF THE GODLY IN BRITAIN

1. http://www.victoriacountyhistory.ac.uk/explore /themes/religious-life-and-buildings/ nonconformity (accessed November 2016).

2. Green, S. J. D., *The Passing of Protestant England: Secularisation and Social Change, c.1920–1960*, Cambridge: Cambridge University Press, 2011, p. 41.

3. http://www.quakersintheworld.org/quakers-in-action/263 (accessed November 2016).

4. Kelly, R. N. and J. Cantrell, *Modern British Statesmen, 1867–1945*, Manchester: Manchester University Press, 1997, p. 83.

5. Payne, E. A., "The Religious Education Dilemma", *The Baptist Quarterly* 23.8 (October 1970), p. 363.

6. Bebbington, D. W., *The Nonconformist Conscience (Routledge Library Editions: Political Science Volume 19)*, London: Routledge, 2014, pp. 130–131

7. Green, S. J. D., *The Passing of Protestant England*, p. 41.

8. Green, S. J. D., *The Passing of Protestant England*, pp. 41–42. Also see K. O. Morgan, *Wales in British Politics, 1868–1922*, Cardiff: University of Wales Press, 1980, 3rd edition, Chapter 6.

9. Worley, M., *The Foundations of the British Labour Party: Identities, Cultures and Perspectives, 1900–39*, Farnham: Ashgate Publishing, 2009, p. 131. Keir Hardie, for example, was a lay preacher before he was an MP.

10. See Smith, L., *Religion and the rise of Labour*, Keele: Keele University Press, 1993.

11. Springhall, J., "'Boys Be Steady': British organized youth and the First World War", *The Historian*, Number 131, Autumn 2016, pp. 28–32.

12. In Shipton, M., "The First World War, pacifism, and the cracks in Wales' Nonconformism movement", http://www.walesonline.co.uk/news/wales-news/first-world-war-pacifism-cracks-8362287, 30 December, 2014 (accessed November 2016).

13. Eirug, A., former head of news at BBC Wales and later chair of the Wales Advisory Committee of the British Council, in Shipton, M., "The First World War, pacifism, and the cracks in Wales' Nonconformism movement".

14. See Shipton, M., "The First World War, pacifism, and the cracks in Wales' Nonconformism movement".

15. For an accessible overview see Patterson, D. S., "Pacifism", http://encyclopedia.1914-1918-online.net/article/pacifism (accessed November 2016).

16. Ceadel, M., Professor of Politics, University of Oxford, and Fellow of New College, Oxford, in https://www.bl.uk/world-war-one/articles/pacifism (accessed November 2016).

17. Kramer, A., *Conscientious Objectors of the Second World War: Refusing to Fight*, Barnsley: Pen & Sword, 2013, p. 2.

18. Kramer, A., *Conscientious Objectors of the Second World War*, p. 3.

19. Hamilton, J., *God, Guns and Israel*, Stroud: The History Press, 2009, p. xvii.

20. See Hamilton, J., *God, Guns and Israel*, Prologue.

21. An interesting and thought-provoking contribution to discussion concerning the legacy of Puritanism in UK churches can be found in: Johnston, M., "The Future of Nonconformity", *Foundations*, Spring 2005, pp. 36–43.

15. The Legacy of the Godly in North America

1. Miller, P., *Errand Into The Wilderness*, Cambridge, MA: Harvard University Press, 1956, p. viii. For an overview of the Puritan legacy see J. Coffey, 'Puritan legacies', in J. Coffey, P. C. H. Lim (eds), *The Cambridge Companion to Puritanism*, Cambridge: Cambridge University Press, 2008, Chapter 19.

2. Fischer, C. S., *Made in America: A Social History of American Culture and Character*, Chicago: University of Chicago Press, 2010, p. 106.

3. Brooks Holifield, E., "Peace, Conflict, and Ritual in Puritan Congregations", *The Journal of Interdisciplinary History*, Vol. 23, No. 3, Religion and History (Winter, 1993), pp. 551–570.

4. Elliott, E., "The Legacy of Puritanism", *Divining America, TeacherServe®*, National Humanities Center, http://nationalhumanitiescenter.org/tserve/eighteen/ekeyinfo/legacy.htm (accessed November 2016).

5. Elliott, E., "The Legacy of Puritanism".

6. Modern-day targets, well evidenced in modern millenarian literature and online sources emanating from the US, and to a lesser extent the UK, include: the papacy (a historical target); the European Union (a modern target); a worldwide conspiracy of complex form involving liberalism, political elites of varied political persuasions, international finance and a supposed anti-Christian worldwide religion (a modern target).

7. Elliott, E., "The Legacy of Puritanism".

8. Bercovitch, S., *The Puritan Origins of the American Self*, New Haven, CT and London: Yale University Press, 1975.

9. See, for example, his *The Rites of Assent: Transformations in the Symbolic Construction of America*, New York and London: Routledge, 1993; *Cambridge History of American Literature*, 8 Vols, Cambridge: Cambridge University Press, 1986–2004.

10. Elliott, E., "The Legacy of Puritanism".

11. Ray, R., M. Sanes and J. Schmitt, "No-Vacation Nation Revisited", *Center for Economic and Policy Research*, May 2013. Available at http://cepr.net/publications/reports/no-vacation-nation-2013 (accessed November 2016).

12. Uhlmann, E. L and J. Sanchez-Burks, "The Implicit Legacy of American Protestantism", *Journal of Cross-Cultural Psychology*, March 2014, p. 8.

13. Uhlmann, E.L & J. Sanchez-Burks, "The Implicit Legacy of American Protestantism", p. 9.

14. For an examination of this apparent paradox see Hall, D. D., *A Reforming People: Puritanism and the Transformation of Public Life in New England*, New York: Alfred A. Knopf, 2011.

15. Quoted in Fischer, C. S., *Made in America:* p. 105.

16. Claude Fischer, professor of sociology, Berkeley, University of California, "Pilgrims, Puritans, and the ideology that is their American legacy", 24 November, 2010, in http://blogs.berkeley.edu/2010/11/24/ pilgrims-puritans-and-their-american-legacy/ (accessed November 2016).

17. Elliott, E., "The Legacy of Puritanism".

18. Kilwein, J. H., "No Pain, No Gain: A Puritan Legacy", *Health Education and Behaviour*, Vol. 16 number 1, March 1989, p. 9 (whole article, pp. 9–12).

19. *Charities Aid Foundation (CAF) World Giving Index 2016*, https://www.cafonline.org/about-us/publications/2016-publications/caf-world-giving-index-2016 (accessed January 2017).

20. Rossiter, C., *The First American Revolution*, New York: Harcourt, Brace, 1956, p. 94.

21. Jefferson, T., "Jefferson's Letter to the Danbury Baptists: The Final Letter, as Sent", *The Library of Congress Information Bulletin: June 1998*, Washington, DC: Library of Congress, June 1998.

22. https://www.law.cornell.edu/constitution/articlevi (assessed January 2017).

23. Dreisbach, D., *Thomas Jefferson and the Wall of Separation Between Church and State*, New York: New York University Press, 2003, p. 77.

24. Temple, M., *The 20 British Prime Ministers of the 20th Century: Blair*, London: Haus, 2006, p. 88. Alastair Campbell was the Director of Communications and Strategy (2000–2003), for Prime Minister Tony Blair.

25. From Professor Richard Kyle's review of *Religious Myths and Visions of America* and quoted in C. Buck, *God & Apple Pie: Religious Myths and Visions of America*, Kingston, NY: Educator's International Press, revised edition., 2015, p.72.

26. Buck, C., *God & Apple Pie: Religious Myths and Visions of America*, pp. 83–84.

27. Buck, C., *God & Apple Pie: Religious Myths and Visions of America*, pp. 82–83.

28. Buck, C., *God & Apple Pie: Religious Myths and Visions of America*, pp. 84–85.

29. Bremer, F. J., *Puritanism: A Very Short Introduction*, Oxford: Oxford University Press, 2009, pp. 108–109.

30. McKenna, G., *The Puritan Origins of American Patriotism*, New Haven, CT and London: Yale University Press, 2007.

31. Murphy, A. R., *Prodigal Nation: Moral Decline and Divine Punishment from New England to 9/11*, Oxford: Oxford University Press, 2009.

32. Uhlmann, E. L and J. Sanchez-Burks, "The Implicit Legacy of American Protestantism", p. 11.

33. Kurian, G. T. and M. A. Lamport (eds), *Encyclopedia of Christianity in the United States*, Vol. 5, Lanham, MD, Rowman & Littlefield, 2016, p. 1893.

About the author

Martyn Whittock graduated in Politics from Bristol University in 1980, where his degree special study was in radical Christian politics of the seventeenth century. He taught history for over thirty-four years and latterly was curriculum leader for Spiritual, Moral, Social and Cultural education at a Wiltshire secondary school. He has acted as an historical consultant to the National Trust and English Heritage. He is a Licensed Lay Minister, in the Church of England. He retired from teaching in July 2016 to devote more time to writing.

He is the author of forty-five books, including school history textbooks and adult history books. The latter include: *A Brief History Of Life in the Middle Ages* (2009), *A Brief History Of The Third Reich* (2011), *A Brief Guide To Celtic Myths and Legends* (2013), *The Viking Blitzkrieg 789-1098* (2013), *The Anglo-Saxon Avon Valley Frontier* (2014), *1066 and 1066: Why The Vikings Caused The Norman Conquest* (2016), *Norse Myths And Legends* (2017); the last four co-written with Hannah, his eldest daughter. *Christ: The First 2000 Years* (2016) was co-written with his youngest daughter, Esther, and also published by Lion Hudson. He is currently working on *The Story Of The Cross*, with Esther, and *The Vikings: From Pillagers To Pillars of Civilization*, with Hannah; both of these books with Lion Hudson.

Glossary

Anabaptists: believed only adult believers should be baptized, church members should elect their leaders and be involved in church decision-making. Became a pejorative term and more moderate adult baptizers preferred the term "Baptist".

antinomianism: the belief that God's elect do not have to conform to moral codes.

Arminianism: based on the theology of the Dutch theologian, Jacob Arminius, that God's grace restores free will to human beings who are therefore able to accept or reject God's offer of eternal life.

Barebone's Parliament: also called the "Nominated Parliament" or "Parliament of Saints", met from July to December 1653 and was made up of those nominated by **Independent** churches.

Calvinist: theology associated with the ideas of the French theologian John Calvin that all Christian beliefs had to be rooted in the Bible, and closely associated with the belief in **Predestination**. Theology espoused by both **Congregationalists/Independents** and **Presbyterians**.

Cavalier: term used to describe Royalists in the Civil Wars period. Meant as a pejorative (derived from the Spanish *Caballeros* – horsemen – who oppressed Dutch Protestants) but eventually embraced by those so called.

Commonwealth: term often used to describe the whole of the period 1649 to 1660. However, some historians only use the term to cover the years from 1649 up to Cromwell's formal taking of the office of Lord Protector in 1653.

245

Congregationalists: members of church fellowships outside of the established Church of England. Also called **Separatists** and **Independents**. Many Independents finally severed all ties with Anglicanism and became Congregationalists.

Covenanters: Scottish supporters of the "National Covenant" of 1638, which insisted on a **Presbyterian** system, and a Scottish church governed by the General Assembly of the kirk.

Diggers: agrarian communists, whose most famous leader was Gerard Winstanley. Also called "True **Levellers**".

Dispensationalism: interpretation of history as divided by God into defined periods which will culminate in the reign of Christ on earth (see **millenarianism**). Modern dispensationalism is often associated with a belief in distinct destinies for both the Church and Israel (Judaism generally and, since 1948, support for the State of Israel) and with the Rapture (the removal of Christians from the earth before a Great Tribulation that will precede Christ's return, to Jerusalem).

the **elect**: those chosen ("elected") by God to be saved. Often used in **Calvinist** theology to refer to "election" to eternal life, based solely on God's will, before a person is born.

End Times: term used to refer to events leading up to, and culminating in, the Second Coming of Christ.

Fifth Monarchists: radical group, active in the 1650s, believing in **millenarianism** and engaged in political agitation in support of the establishment of a theocracy.

the **godly**: term often used by **Puritans** to describe themselves. Also known as "the **saints**".

Independents: originally Church of England fellowships, but believing in local congregational control of churches, free from any wider church hierarchy; although at first some would accept a loose association with like-minded churches. Many eventually became **Congregationalists** and **Separatists**. It also came to be used to describe those who believed that only a military victory would resolve the conflict with the king.

Levellers: political radicals, mostly active 1647–49, demanding religious toleration, easier access to the law for ordinary people, an extended franchise, individual rights guaranteed by a written constitution, and government answerable to the people. They did not like the term.

Long Parliament: the parliament sitting 1640–60 (but interrupted by various political upheavals and constitutional experiments).

Lord Protector: title used by Oliver Cromwell after 1653 (and later by Richard Cromwell).

Lutherans: followers of the German Protestant leader, Martin Luther, whose actions started the Reformation after 1517.

millenarianism: belief in the "millennium", the thousand-year reign of Christ on earth with his saints, after his Second Coming and prior to the Last Judgment and the final transformation of the created order. There are variants within this belief with some believing in Christ's return at the start of the millennium ("premillennialism") and some at the end ("postmillennialism").

New Model Army: reformed parliamentary army, after 1645, which eventually defeated the Royalists.

Nonconformists: those clergy who would not accept the Act of Uniformity of 1662 and were expelled from the Church of

England. Came to be used of all Christian congregations outside the Church of England. Also called "Dissenters".

Predestination: the belief that salvation is not based on any merit shown by a person (who is saved only by God's undeserved love or "grace") and neither is it based on God foreseeing that the person to be saved would come to faith. In short, it owes nothing to the person whatsoever. Often associated with **Calvinist** theology.

Presbyterian: form of church organization in which pastors and a council of lay elders constituted church government and a strict control was exercised over church members, their beliefs, and behaviour. Presbyterian theology emphasized Calvinist beliefs and the authority of the Bible. Inspired by the church system in Geneva, it eventually became the national church system in Scotland.

Protectorate: the period from 1653 until the end of the rule of Richard Cromwell (Oliver's son), in May 1659.

Protestant: member of one of the Christian churches that originally broke away from Roman Catholicism in the sixteenth century. Later fragmented into a large number of denominations.

Providence: the power of God, directing human affairs and the created order generally.

Puritan: those demanding a stricter, more "reformed", **Protestantism** within the Church of England. They themselves preferred the labels "the godly" or "the saints" (although these terms came to be applied to those both *within* and *outside* the national church).

Quaker: members of the "Religious Society of Friends". The term "Quaker" began as a pejorative term. Started by George Fox after 1647.

Ranters: a group promoting **antinomianism** after 1649. An umbrella term, used by contemporaries to describe a mixed group of self-styled prophets, preachers, and rebels against both contemporary morality and the social hierarchy.

Reformation: The sixteenth-century events in which **Protestants** broke away from the Roman Catholic Church.

Restoration: the return of the monarchy, under Charles II, in 1660.

Roundhead: pejorative term for Parliamentarians in the Civil Wars period (derived from the short haircuts associated with *some* among the godly and also among London apprentices). Those so described hated the term.

Rump Parliament: a remnant of the "Long Parliament" sitting between "Pride's Purge" of 1648 and its dissolution by Oliver Cromwell in 1653.

the **saints**: term often used by **Puritans** to describe themselves. Also known as "the **godly**".

Separatists: members of church fellowships outside of the established Church of England. Also called **Congregationalists**.

Short Parliament: sat for less than a month in 1640.

transubstantiation: the Roman Catholic belief that, in the Mass, the bread and wine become the body and blood of Christ.

Lightning Source UK Ltd.
Milton Keynes UK
UKHW04n1931071018
330121UK00002B/34/P

9 780745 980416